9.95

82-166

Volume 5
Sage Yearbooks in WOMEN'S POLICY STUDIES

WOMEN AND HOUSEHOLD LABOR

Edited by

SARAH FENSTERMAKER BERK

SAGE Publications   Beverly Hills / London

For information address:

SAGE PUBLICATIONS, INC.
275 South Beverly Drive
Beverly Hills, California 90212

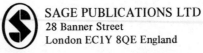

SAGE PUBLICATIONS LTD
28 Banner Street
London EC1Y 8QE England

Printed in the United States of America

Library of Congress Cataloging in Publication Data
Main entry under title:

Women and household labor.

   (Sage yearbooks in women's policy studies ; v. 5)
    1. Housewives--Addresses, essays, lectures.
2. Home economics--Addresses, essays, lectures.
3. Women--Social conditions--Addresses, essays,
lectures. I. Berk, Sarah Fenstermaker. II. Series.
HD6073.H84W65   331.4'81'64   79-23003
ISBN 0-8039-1211-0
ISBN 0-8039-1212-9 pbk.

FIRST PRINTING

CONTENTS

Prologue

REFLECTIONS ON
THE STUDY OF HOUSEHOLD LABOR

ANN OAKLEY

In Charlotte Perkins Gilman's utopian novel *Herland* (first published in 1979), three men representing the higher echelons of early twentieth-century American society (a playboy, a doctor, and a sociologist) chance, during a scientific expedition, on an all-female culture where for two thousand years women have given birth to daughters unaided by men. The three men are shattered by, and indeed ultimately unable to grasp, the fact that for the citizens of Herland civilization itself is a female concept. The problem is not only one of crediting women with the achievement of creating a truly civilized society (no wars, poverty, illness, crime, or dogs; population and economic resources neatly balanced; government by cooperation and mutual goodwill). Basically the issue is one of how people, and men especially, are able to break out of and move beyond that system of thought whose conceptual content and structure presupposes the necessity and desirability of pro-masculine gender differentiation.

This is the reason why many so-called utopias are not so for women, and why feminist utopias are not merely fictional but outside the limits of conventional fiction as a genre, which can only question the status quo with the status quo's own terminology and assumptions. And it is the reason why women in the 1970s are writing more science fiction. It offers them the opportunity to dispute the current conditions of gender and to envisage what a society with really liberated women might be like (see Hacker, 1977).

The study of housework is like the exercise of writing feminist science fiction: It constitutes an attempt to reverse the accepted order of concepts

7

and values. The task has to be set in its historical context. Capitalist society is pervaded by two historically new divisions: between work and the family, and between the family and personal life (Zaretsky, 1976). The "solution" of women becoming managers of the family and of personal life was facilitated in the late eighteenth and nineteenth centuries by the collective weight of specific circumstances: the absence of effective fertility control and a safe technology for the artificial feeding of infants; the constriction of employment opportunities with the move toward capital-intensive industry; a masculine hegemony in positions of public power (government, administration, the Church, and the legal, medical, and academic professions); and the creation of childhood as a legally protected and distinct state. These circumstances suggested a construction of women as private, nonproductive, domesticated, expressive, and nurturant. Cultural convenience was called natural necessity, and such a typification of women became institutionalized as the division of labor by gender, as the "position of women."

Central to the position of women today is the interpretation of female labor as an inferior version of male labor. In relation to male labor, female labor is characterized as unproductive, marginal, trivial, temporary, intermittent, dispensable, less valuable, less skilled, and less physically demanding. These stereotypes apply both to female household labor and to women's labor in paid occupations. Thus, it is normative to regard the employment work of women as an activity interrupted by domesticity and to view housework as an intermittent (and interruptable) rather than continuous activity; to reinforce the poverty (in relation to the male norm) of women's monetary rewards for paid work by the total lack of remuneration attached to housework; to see both housework and women's paid work as marginal contributions to the national economy. It is a definition which endows women with the status of a labor reserve to be drawn on during periods of national need (such as wartime) and dispensed with during periods of economic recession. As employed women are legally "protected" from the requirement of certain sorts of physically demanding work, so housework is categorized as essentially undemanding of the houseworker's physical energy. Since housework is preindustrial in nature it must be less skilled, as is women's other work. Most fundamental of all, since only those who are economically productive do "real" work, housework is not real work at all: In its unreality it is either not-work or an intrinsically trivial work activity.

Any academic study of household labor must challenge at least the last of these assumptions by saying that housework is important enough to be studied. Many of those who have researched and discussed household labor in recent years have challenged much more of the stereotype than this and have exposed other important dimensions of what could be termed the "official morality" of housework. The importance of doing this, and of going beyond it to research and make accessible the process of household labor, can hardly be overstated. In the first place, it is simply amazing that an activity which consumes a large proportion of the daily energy of 85% of the adult female population as housewives and of a majority of the total population in one form or another should have been ignored so completely for so long.[1] But, second, it is obvious that any understanding of the social position of women cannot proceed without a revelation of their role as houseworkers. Since stereotypes of housework apply to women's paid work as well, they, in an important sense, portray the attributed psychology of women in a capitalist society (see Miller, 1977). There is, in fact, no clear demarcation between production and the other structures of women's oppression (Mitchell, 1966), because the social construction of femininity mediates and pervades them all.

In talking about gender differentiation it is important to make a distinction between two types of differentiation: those identified by Rogers (1978) as "behavioral" and "ideological." The first refers to the performance by the two sexes of different social roles; the second refers to the perceptions males and females have of themselves. Differentiation by gender does not amount to discrimination against women except where behavioral and ideological differentiation are out of step, so that women's own view of themselves and their sphere in society undergoes a basic revision. From perceiving their own interests and activities as valued and valuable, as capable of conferring status and promoting self-esteem, women move to an altogether different valuation, in which their image of themselves is derived from masculine ideology and becomes crucially self-derogating. Rogers suggests that this disturbance of balance between the two systems of differentiation is what happens when industrialization intrudes into the domestic and social relations of the sexes. The resulting transformation of female values is connected with shifts in the distribution of power between men and women.

Changes in the valuation of household labor are at the core of this transformation. In the gender ideology of capitalist society the masculine stereotype of "women's work" has a prominent place, a highly significant fact which was not noted by academics discussing household work until the early 1970s. Sociology, in particular, demonstrated an uncritical adherence to the masculine stereotype of women and their work, dividing its subject areas and conceptual schemes so that women were relegated to the "expressive" area of family relations, and men, in the generic and misleading sense of Man, constituted the subjects of the main and important part of sociological work (Millman and Kanter, 1975). Functionalism, a dominant sociological paradigm, adopted the Victorian domestic mythology and said that what women did in the home was preeminently to manage personal relations, to symbolize the sanctity of order and domestic retreat in the harshly competitive world of capitalist business and industry. This was a good thing for women because it was a biological imperative, for men because it freed them of this burdensome responsibility, and for society because it provided a fully serviced and mobile work force (Beecher, 1978). From the 1950s until the early 1970s housework was only studied in empirical sociology as a component in female kinship, under the rubric of the euphemistic title the "division of labor" (a prefeminist or even antifeminist conception, as Glazer-Malbin [1976] notes), or as the projection of a "social problem" concern with the rising trend in the employment of married women. Most studies of the family proceeded with a taken-for-granted view that the documentation of family life amounted to a description of the entire field of women's lives. Elizabeth Bott's (1957) germinal work, *Family and Social Network,* which initiated a subsequently much relied-on distinction between "joint" and "segregated" conjugal role-relationships, illustrates the hidden relevance of the established stereotype. Describing two ways in which the couples in her sample organized their roles, Bott called these "joint" and "segregated," even though joint-role couples divided their responsibilities so that housework was hers and earning the money was his. Furthermore, because housework was "her" responsibility, Bott did not consider it important to spell out its character as a work activity—this despite the fact that her hypothesis about the relationship between family roles and the connectedness of families' social networks was a fertile ground for the investigation of the collective social definition of norms of housework behavior.

Community studies in the 1950s and 1960s did more than any other category of sociological work to represent the reality of women's household labor, "the industrial sociology of the housewife" (Frankenberg, 1966: 232).[2] But even they did so, for the most part, in the context of a preoccupation with the conditions of male labor and family life, and imbued by a presumption that the labor of women is trivial and not worthy of serious documentation (see Frankenberg, 1966, for discussion). The dominant conception was one of housework as an aspect of the marital relationship, a view which of course precluded the articulation of housework from the houseworker's point of view, and prejudged the issue of the interaction between housework and marriage on the one hand, and between housework and other work on the other.

In 1974 I published a study (Oakley 1974a) which aimed to look at women's attitudes to housework in the same way as other workers' attitudes to their work had been examined by sociologists. I did not see the book as a study of women and the family, but as a study of women's work. The original conception in its working out required the writing of a companion volume which analyzed the historical evolution of the female-housewife, male-breadwinner formula and its validating ideology (Oakley 1974b). The project evolved out of my personal experience of the contradiction between the male ideology of housework (nonproductive, expressive, fulfilling, and so on) and its reality as lived by me, a middle-class mother of two young children in urban Britain in the late 1960s. I was shocked to discover that housework was time-consuming, exhausting, and (in the social setting in which I was doing it) deeply alienating. I had been led in the course of both my formal and informal education to think that it would be otherwise. Reading Gavron's (1966) *The Captive Wife,* the only remotely relevant study of which I knew, I discerned that other women, academic and otherwise, shared my disillusionment.[3] The emergence of women's liberation groups in my area of London in 1969-1970 enabled me to state the problem with greater clarity. It is of historical interest now that my request to register a thesis entitled "Work Attitudes and Work Satisfaction of Housewives" at the University of London in 1969 met with either frank disbelief or patronizing jocularity. The only person I could find who was willing to supervise such a work spent the next three years trying to convince me that women's sexual satisfaction and adjustment were at the heart of the problem. Similarly, I am now mildly amused, though I was at the time outraged, by the fact that two major British publishers turned down the book I produced on the grounds that everything that needed to be said about housework had already been said, and was I really serious in being serious about such a boring subject?

Since those days attitudes have changed somewhat (at least among publishers and thesis supervisors), and the study of household labor has expanded, especially in the last five years. One area of development has been the revision of the traditional Marxist approach to household work via its reinterpretation as a form of productive labor and of the family as a system of productive relations. Delphy (1976: 77) states the situation thus: "Marriage is the institution by which gratuitous work is exhorted from a particular category of the population, women-wives." Marxists disagree as to whether it is technically correct to term this labor "productive" (Benston, 1969; Dalla Costa, 1972; Secombe, 1974); at any rate what they are saying is that it is important, and that its importance and function are concealed by the mystification of the dominant ideology.

In the 1970s sociological studies of the family appear to have lapsed, and in their place has been a plethora of studies of particular aspects of marriage, reproduction, and the "division of labor." So far as this latter theme is concerned, there is now more recognition among sociologists of the distinction between *responsibility* for, and *participation* in ("helping" with), household tasks. The interaction between women's paid work and their unpaid domestic work has been seen without the obfuscation of "social problem" definitions. The importance of considering domestic work responsibilities in tandem with occupational and other opportunities in debates about sex equality is now receiving more than lip service and is indeed a major and persisting reason for studying women's household labor. Time-budget studies have proliferated and become more sophisticated, the evolution of domestic work over the life cycle is becoming a more prominent theme, and the relevance of socialization to domestic work-orientation is being more thoroughly explored. The effect of these contributions, many of which are represented in this volume, has been to explode myth, question stereotypes, and demonstrate how central domesticity remains as a defining feature of women's situation in the last quarter of the twentieth century.

Although the study of household labor has expanded in the last five years, it has not done so nearly as much as I hoped it would. There has, in my view, been too much emphasis on the theoretical role of housework in the Marxist schema, and too little in the way of empirical work exposing that much-needed corrective of established values, attitudes, perceptions, satisfactions, and work-styles of houseworkers themselves. Moreover, the extent to which the study of housework has been integrated with the main concerns of sociology (and other disciplines) has been disappointing. The growth of "women's studies" could in part be responsible for this, but I suspect both the spread of such courses and the failure of integration within disciplines stem from the same underlying cause: an ideological predisposition to segregate women. For these reasons, I particularly welcome the appearance of this volume, which I hope will encourage the habit of viewing household labor as a serious and central social and academic concern. There is no reason why those who research household labor should not, like science fiction writers, be able to effect a transformation of values; there is, however, every reason to suppose that we are, as yet, only at the beginning of this process.

NOTES

1. The 85% figure is taken from Hunt (1968). Hunt's definition of a housewife is "the person, other than a domestic servant, who is responsible for most of the

household duties (or for supervising a domestic servant who carries out these duties). She may be married or non-married and may or may not have a job in addition to her domestic duties" (Hunt, 1968: 5).

2. The U.S. counterpart of British community studies includes such works as Berger's *Working Class Suburb* (1960), Gans's *The Levittowners* (1967), and Komarovsky's classic *Blue-Collar Marriage* (1967). The concept of "community studies" emerged considerably earlier in America than it did in Britain (see Bell and Newby, 1971).

3. I should of course have read Friedan's *The Feminine Mystique* (1963) but I did not, in fact, come across this until later.

REFERENCES

BARKER, D. L. and S. ALLEN [eds.] (1976) Sexual Divisions and Society. London: Tavistock.

BEECHER, V. (1978) "Women and production: a critical analysis of some sociological theories of women's work," in A. Kuhn and A. Wolpe (eds.) Feminism and Materialism: Women and Modes of Production. London: Routledge & Kegan Paul.

BELL, C. and H. NEWBY (1971) Community Studies. London: Allen & Unwin.

BENSTON, M. (1969) "The political economy of women's liberation." Monthly Review 21, 4: 13-27.

BERGER, B. (1960) Working Class Suburb. Berkeley: University of California Press.

BOTT, E. (1957) Family and Social Network. London: Tavistock.

DALLA COSTA, M. (1972) "Women and the subversion of the community." Radical America 6 (January/February): 67-102.

DELPHY, C. (1976) "Continuities and discontinuities in marriage and divorce," in D. L. Barker and S. Allen (eds.) Sexual Divisions and Society. London: Tavistock.

FRANKENBERG, R. (1966) "In the production of their lives, men, sex and gender in British community studies," in D. L. Barker and S. Allen (eds.) Sexual Divisions and Society. London: Tavistock.

FRIEDAN, B. (1963) The Feminine Mystique. London: Gollancz.

GANS, H. (1967) The Levittowners. New York: Pantheon.

GAVRON, H. (1966) The Captive Wife. Harmondsworth: Penguin.

GILMAN, C. P. (1979) Herland. New York: Pantheon.

GLAZER-MALBIN, N. (1976) "Housework." Signs: Journal of Women in Culture and Society 1, 4: 905-922.

HACKER, M. (1977) "Introduction," in J. Russ (ed.) The Female Man. Boston: Gregg.

HUNT, A. (1968) A Survey of Women's Employment. London: Her Majesty's Stationery Office.

KOMAROVSKY, M. (1967) Blue-Collar Marriage. New York: Vintage.

KUHN, A. and A. WOLPE [eds.] (1978) Feminism and Materialism: Women and Modes of Production. London: Routledge & Kegan Paul.

MILLER, J. B. (1977) Toward a New Psychology of Women. Boston: Beacon.

MILLMAN, M. and R. M. KANTER [eds.] (1975) Another Voice: Feminist Perspectives on Social Life and Social Science. Garden City, NY: Doubleday.

MITCHELL, J. (1966) "Women: the longest revolution." New Left Review 40 (December): 11-37.

OAKLEY, A. (1974a) The Sociology of Housework. New York: Pantheon.
––– (1974b) Housewife. London: Allen Lane. (Published by Pantheon under the
    title Woman's Work)
ROGERS, S. C. (1978) "Woman's place: a critical review of anthropological theory."
    Comparative Studies in Society and History 20, 1: 123-162.
SECOMBE, W. (1974) "The housewife and her labour under capitalism." New Left
    Review 83 (January/February): 3-24.
ZARETSKY, E. (1976) Capitalism, the Family and Personal Life. London: Pluto.

INTRODUCTION

SARAH FENSTERMAKER BERK

It was the first time I had ever heard of women like me really coming together. My children were both under two years old. But I didn't go to the Women's Liberation Meeting—I couldn't get a *babysitter!* Later, I sat down and thought, there's something absurd about this.

—anonymous respondent (1977)

The previous four volumes of the SAGE YEARBOOKS IN WOMEN'S POLICY STUDIES addressed both the limits to and possibilities for the economic, familial, and social independence of women. This volume represents a continuation of these concerns, with a more detailed focus on women and household labor. It rests on the premise that the changing realities of work and family life for women cannot be fully understood or even adequately described without attention to this "invisible" labor and the social relations that surround it.

EDITOR'S NOTE: A number of friends and collegues provided aid and comfort during the period in which I served as editor of this volume. They helped make a notoriously painful process both efficient and satisfying. Richard Berk provided sound advice at critical moments and infectious enthusiasm for the project throughout. Vesle Stadstad Fenstermaker and Joan Manheimer were able to apply their experience and insights from literary pursuits to give moral support to this effort. I also thank Cheryl Goluch for her administrative and clerical skills, as well as for her ever-present good humor in preparing the manuscript. Finally, the contributors to this volume demonstrated that the relationship between editor and author can be a collaborative and not an antagonistic one. I am grateful to have shared this volume with them.

It is appropriate that Ann Oakley's reflections serve as a prologue to this collection. Prior to the publication of her now classic study of British housewives (Oakley, 1974), concern with women's household labor as *work* had seldom been explored empirically. Indeed, there were few studies of women's *market* work experiences, and those that did exist often transformed the work realities of women into a queer subtype of the male experience. Thus, it is little wonder that the productive activities of women engaged in household labor and child care would be ignored, dismissed, or denied as a legitimate social scientific pursuit.

As unpaid labor carried out in near isolation, household work does not share the formal characteristics of "real" work and thus has been systematically excluded from the purview of most traditional organizational research. As comparatively insensitive to the enormous growth of large-scale, high-technology production, household labor has escaped the scrutiny of social scientists who have been enamored by the more dramatic workings of advanced industrial society. Perhaps most surprising, as "woman's work," household labor has not even drawn significant attention from researchers who claim the family as their special preserve (for partial exceptions, see Lopata, 1971; Pleck, 1977). In fact, the labors of women, and household work in particular, have typically been consigned to the "folk" forums of "women's pages" and daytime talk shows. Yet, more than most, Ann Oakley's work did not so much force this world out of the "closet" as compel us to enter it with her. That is, rather than "fit" the work of women into existing theoretical or empirical frameworks, she began with women's direct experience and applied new sociological insights to it. It is this approach to women and household labor that informed my selection of the chapters to follow and which motivates my introductory remarks.

In her prologue, Oakley rightly points to important changes of attitude and research style connected to the study of women and household labor. Social scientists are turning to the organization of unpaid domestic labor, coupled with its implications for and responses to social change (e.g., Rowbotham, 1973; Himmelweit and Mohun, 1977; Gronau, 1977; Berk and Berk, 1978, 1979; Vanek, 1978). Numerous policy-related concerns have also surfaced in the context of how household labor contributes to the well-being of particular households (e.g., Becker, 1974) and the economy as a whole (e.g., Kreps and Leaper, 1976). Finally, some scholars have apparently recognized that besides structural and economic concerns, the production of household commodities and the general sustenance of families have important implications for the psychic welfare of the women who labor toward those ends (e.g., Berheide, 1976; Cannon, 1978). In short, the social science community has slowly begun to focus an array of its technical resources on the routine productive activities of women. Indeed, the process of editing this volume has convinced me that the number of people engaged in research on household labor may well be reaching the "critical mass" so necessary to the intellectual vitality of any research tradition.

However, it is also true that the problems Oakley notes in this emergent research area are far from solved. Prior to offering some brief remarks on the works collected in this volume, I will identify three disturbing tendencies in the extant research on women and household labor. All three are inextricably linked in a more general resistance to confront the world of women on its own terms.

First, even a glance over the literature on women and their work illustrates how many "damn good" reasons we have for exploring, either theoretically or empirically, the unpaid productive activities of women. We study such phenomena to better apprehend the psychological and social impact of increasing market employment for women, the alterations in family decision-making surrounding fertility, changes in family life-style, consumer behavior, the function of unpaid domestic labor for the generation of surplus value and cheap labor under capitalism, rising rates of divorce, child abuse, domestic violence, new demands for housing and transportation, and so on. Indeed, it would be difficult to exhaust the rationales for why household labor is worthy of study, partly because of its prior neglect, but also because it so shapes and orders the constraints, opportunities, and costs of everyday existence.

Yet (to use Oakley's term), it is this "social problem" orientation which reflects a genuine defensiveness on the part of those who are drawn, for whatever reason, to the study of women and household labor. We have yet to reach the point where, as in the study of "work and occupations" (i.e., men's work and men's occupations), research on household labor does not demand elaborate and apologetic justifications. In short, the study of women and their work is most frequently couched in terms that encourage the long-standing notion that such topics are trivial, irrelevant, or fundamentally derivative of men's experiences.

A second and related problem is one which, to varying degrees, plagues most of social science. But, given the historical neglect of empirical research on women, it is a special problem for those who wish to study household labor. Namely, we routinely make pronouncements on the meaning and implications of women's domestic labor while refusing to "soil our hands" with data. A close reading of the theory and research done in the past ten years suggests that too often conclusions are drawn about the nature, organization, and social-psychological impact of house-hold work, in the absence of direct empirical evidence. Oakley alludes to this problem by criticizing a preoccupation of Marxist scholars with the theoretical role of household labor to the exclusion of more empirically grounded assessments. However, I would argue further that the tendency to neglect the direct experiences of women and a real reluctance to search for evidence on how the social relations surrounding household labor materialize on a daily basis are shortcomings in almost all studies of women and their labors. In some cases, researchers seem strangely com-fortable with what is a fundamentally reified picture of the household and the work that goes on within it.

In fact, we have very little empirical evidence to justify confidence in the ways household labor has been categorized and conceptualized, let alone a clear picture of how women manage the imperatives of household work and child care. This reluctance to confront household labor in its own "back yard" coupled with the assumption that "everyone knows" about women and their work can distort our research, subvert our efforts to responsibly address policy questions, and relegate the best of intentions to empty academic debates and effete theoretical meanderings.

Without a firm empirical grounding on which to base their conclusions, researchers face a third and no less limiting temptation. The most com-pelling and distinctive qualities of women's domestic work lives are often defined away or simply overlooked because they do not "fit" the existing models and social scientific frameworks which seem to serve so well in explanations of other social phenomena. That is, the experience of women is systematically excluded even before inquiry begins. Below, Dorothy Smith (1977: 22) offers an example of how, when sociologists are wedded to existing perspectives, they may miss the very thing they wish to study:

> But women's existence cannot be comprehended within such frames. . . . Society has organized for women a different relation to the world. Attempts to apply a conceptual apparatus drawn uncritic-ally from the standard sociological frames in these areas, rest uneasily on the actual experience and situation of women as a means of analysis. . . . If we started with housework as a basis, the cate-gories of 'work' and 'leisure' would never emerge. And indeed, it is hard to imagine how making use of this conceptual framework it would be possible to make them observable. The social organization of the role of housewife, mother and wife does not conform to the divisions between being at work and not being at work. Even the concept of housework as work leaves what we do as mothers without a conceptual home.

Those who embark on investigations of the household's "invisible" labor are faced with the perplexing problem of having few conceptual resources on which to draw which adequately deal with the social relations under study. As Smith (1977: 29) notes:

> But the conceptual procedures developed in sociology serve to suspend the presence of an actor in her actions, what people are doing, what they experience, what is happening to them, becomes 'role', 'norm', 'system', 'behavior'. We have learned a method of thinking which does away with the presence of the subjects in the phenomena which only subjects can accomplish.

Briefly put, it is the interaction of women's household labor experiences as "women's work" and their household labor experiences as women's family life that defies routine conceptual categories. Consequently, if we are interested in charting some features of these relations as they directly influence women and the world outside the household, we must be open to an exploration of a *unique* work site, generating very special configurations of constraints, costs, and conflicts.

As the first of its kind, this collection raises a variety of questions posed by women's "private" labors for which old answers (and old questions) have proved inadequate. A glance over the contents listing of this book suggests that if the selections are anything, they are eclectic. Such eclecticism is appropriate for a research area that is only now overcoming the disabling effects of past neglect; it can only benefit from a wide variety of theoretical perspectives, methodological approaches, and the intellectual cross-fertilization of interdisciplinary exchange. Thus, the reader will find chapters representing sociology, economics, history, anthropology, and more applied policy concerns. Despite such wide-ranging treatments of the myriad questions raised by women and household labor, the selections are bound together by their common intent: to describe and analyze the heretofore unresearched world of women's work. Further, each chapter grants special importance to the variable context in which household labor occurs. Whether the particular research problems center on the impact of technology, the social meanings attributed to the role of housewife, the normative context in which members assess others' contributions, or the place which women have in a class analysis of household labor, all the selections view household work as a *situated* activity. Each in its own way, the chapters to follow convey the message that the household work activities of women cannot be fully apprehended without conscious recognition that they and the social relations which surround them are deeply embedded in the fabric of social life.

Any examination of historical research with women as central subjects connotes the same pattern found in the literature on current household labor patterns: Both have been neglected because both are perceived as substantively "insignificant." In the same way that work in modern society has been defined primarily by its visible links to paid market activities, so too has the history of women's domestic labor been lost to those political and economic events visible in extradomestic realms. In the same way that social science has typically neglected those household activities and contributions which are immediately relevant to everyday social life (but are "uninteresting"), so too have historians neglected the questions that connect to the everyday spheres inhabited primarily by women.

In her chapter, "An Enlarged Human Existence? Technology and Household Work in Nineteenth-Century America," Susan Strasser redresses the balance. She examines the critical difference between the *invention* of technology which might alter the everyday domestic lives of women and the *diffusion* of such technology to the typical household. Strasser provides extensive documentation for the fact that while the major appliances that could transform the content of household labor were invented prior to 1900, only very wealthy people in urban areas felt their impact. For the majority of nineteenth-century women, daily existence remained centered on the onerous chores of carrying water, making fires, the home production and preparation of foods, and the making of clothing. Strasser's work goes a long way toward counteracting the ahistorical and class-biased view that changes in the work lives of women are simply a function of technological invention. It resurrects the harsh realities of everyday domestic work and women's isolation that existed alongside the world of technological innovation and promise.

Yet, if the staggering array of twentieth-century technological advances have promised anything, it has been freedom from the drudgery of household labor. Popular belief (perhaps from those who do little housework) has it that the household worker of today is set free from her labors by machinery so sophisticated that all she need do is read operating instructions and push buttons. A number of researchers have provided evidence that while the content of household labor has been altered somewhat by so-called "labor-saving" devices, actual time spent on the job differs only slightly from that spent fifty years ago (e.g., Vanek, 1974). The chapter by John P. Robinson ("Housework Technology and Household Work Time") presents a comparison of time-use data from women in 1965 and 1975 to show that once the demographic and fertility differences in the two samples are taken into account, women in 1975 spent 22 fewer minutes per day in household and family care. More importantly, while this difference is statistically significant, Robinson argues that such a difference cannot be attributed to the increasing availability and diffusion of household technology. Declines in the time spent on household labor should continue as women's extrahousehold commitments increase. However, Robinson's work strongly suggests that the causal mechanisms behind these changes are far more complicated than simple shifts in the physical characteristics of the household work process.

Turning to a more elusive set of research questions, "Social Status of the Homemaker," by Christine Bose, explores the place of the occupational role of housewife in social mobility research. It has been argued that the study of occupational prestige provides a window on the complex process of social mobility and the social currency of the occupational reward structure. But Bose argues that after more than a generation of research, little is known about the occupational prestige attributed to the housewife role, or how the prestige accorded the housewife compares with the prestige of other occupations. To correct this flagrant neglect, Bose develops a single prestige score for the occupational role of housewife and compares it to other occupations (including the rough market "equivalents" of housewife).

Yet this chapter represents more than simply righting the wrongs of sociological neglect or an illustration that the overall prestige accorded the housewife role is higher than one might expect. Bose goes further to place her analysis in the broader context of women's work experiences to explain variation in prestige rankings. For example, she finds that prior employment experiences may lead women to attribute lower prestige to the role of housewife than do those who have not been employed. However, clear class differences emerge in the prestige rankings such that those raters who have held higher-status jobs rank the occupation of housewife more highly than those whose job options have been more limited. Thus, this research opens the door to an array of new questions on the links between the status accorded women in paid occupational roles and the status attached to their unpaid work activities. Together they form the unique context in which the social reward system for women operates. The chapter by Bose serves as an empirical introduction to the more extensive discussion and critical review by Myra Marx Ferree ("Satisfaction with Housework: The Social Context"). By attending to the central importance of the social context in which women's domestic labor is undertaken, Ferree reconceptualizes satisfaction with household labor and provides new insights into the class differences in satisfaction as reported in past research.

Ferree argues that studies of worker satisfaction with household labor have been modeled after worker satisfaction studies in paid occupational roles, but that such models have been applied with little concern for the historical shifts in the social meanings attributed to full-time domestic labor. In addition, scant attention has been paid to the social norms embedded within the role and which in part determine reported satisfaction with it. Ferree synthesizes and critically reviews a vast literature on satisfaction with household work and finds that three explanatory models dominate. When applied to a mixed set of findings that working-class women are more satisfied with household labor than are middle-class women, the three models emphasize different psychological and social characteristics of the workers themselves or, alternatively, the individual context in which the work is undertaken.

Through an illustrative examination of data on women's satisfaction with household labor, Ferree's analysis calls into serious question the assumption that class differences importantly determine variation in levels of satisfaction with housework. Her attention to the social context of household labor clarifies the complicated connection between traditional class effects and the "internal stratification process" of the household that shapes the ultimate satisfactions women derive from household work. Finally, Ferree explores the policy-relevant issues implied by the changing social context in which satisfaction with household labor resides. Changes in the meaning that household work carries as a full-time occupation, the increasing participation of women in the labor force, and the heightened aspirations of young women all suggest that the satisfactions which are currently identified with full-time attention to household labor may change markedly in the future.

With the chapter, "The New Home Economics: An Agenda for Sociological Research," a rather different breed of research is introduced. As discussed by Richard A. Berk, the New Home Economics has been developed over the past decade from neoclassical microeconomics as a hybrid of theory characterizing the behavior of consumers and the behavior of firms. The household is viewed as a "small factory" in which market goods and services are combined with the labor of household members to yield "household commodities." These household commodities, not the market goods and services, are the immediate sources of the household's well-being (i.e., utility).

Berk starts by arguing that, for good or evil, the New Home Economics will be with us for some time and that its derivative theoretical and empirical work has already had enormous impact on the study of household labor. In what is far more than an ecumenical gesture, Berk then turns to an exposition of the New Home Economics in order to make its tenets and conclusions accessible to noneconomists. In the process, he sets the stage for the second half of the chapter in which a number of sociological questions raised by the New Home Economics are addressed. He considers such issues as exploitation within households, and the nature of the value of household commodities, drawing heavily from Marxist views along the way. He also suggests some means by which insights from sociology and economics might be usefully combined. The idea of adding *normative* constraints to the formal maximization models of the New Home Economics is one particularly intriguing instance.

In the end, however, Berk argues that both the neoclassical and Marxist views on household labor suffer from the same infirmity: a failure to look closely at the routine activities undertaken within households. Until a cure is found, both traditions must be handled with care.

An important extension and application of the New Home Economics is represented in the chapter by Evelyn Lehrer and Marc Nerlove. "Women's Life-Cycle Time Allocation: An Econometric Analysis" focuses initially on the theoretical relationships between women's labor force participation, decisions to obtain schooling, and fertility over a substantial portion of the life cycle. Lehrer and Nerlove begin by arguing that at any moment in time these activities are related to one another and that focusing on any one in isolation will generate misleading conclusions. This underscores one important theme of the volume: Activities undertaken within households (in this case child rearing) are of inherent interest, but must also be addressed in the context of their critical effects on activities undertaken outside the household. Yet perhaps the major contribution of this chapter is its emphasis on changes in the relationships between education, fertility, and labor force participation over the life cycle, and the variation over time in both the direction of effects and the importance of exogenous causal factors. Lehrer and Nerlove suggest that in previous studies significant and dynamic life-cycle processes are at least neglected or, worse, are confounded within atemporal causal effects.

Lehrer and Nerlove proceeded by breaking the life cycle into five basic stages and estimating models for the endogenous variables of fertility and labor force participation over the last four stages. Readers with an interest in statistical matters will find the justifications for the use of reduced form equations, special estimation techniques for truncated endogenous variables, and cross-equation residual correlations particularly instructive. A large number of compelling findings also emerge with perhaps the most important conclusion being that, indeed, causal variables have different effects in different stages of the life cycle. For example, prior to the birth of the first child, the husband's income has no impact on the labor force participation of the wife. Yet later the impact is large and negative; households in which husbands earn more money are less likely to find wives employed. What is happening at home matters and cannot be ignored.

In the chapter by Linda Nelson, "Household Time: A Cross-Cultural Example," we seem to be transported rather far from the concerns of previous chapters. However, through an examination of daily activity patterns undertaken by Costa Rican homemakers, Nelson raises an important research problem for those interested in the measurement of household labor. She addressed herself to the meaning of time for household workers by distinguishing between "behavioral" and "ideational" activity patterns. That is, Nelson compares the observed patterns of activities to both the predicted and recalled activities from the housewives themselves. For example, she finds that the meaning of time devoted to activities varies for participants and does not always recapitulate the "clock-time" sequences observed by the researcher. Indeed, the ideational activity patterns of homemakers (i.e., recalled or predicted) reveal little repetition of tasks or recreation, few interruptions, and, in the case of child care, fewer activities than in fact are observed.

While clearly only a beginning, Nelson's research suggests nonetheless that we must broaden our notions about the measurement of human productivity with time as the metric. Perhaps the currency of time is different, depending upon where it is invested. The social context in which time is "spent" may alter both the meaning of the activity itself and the social significance of the investment. Again, the situated qualities of household labor demand both new questions and new answers.

The same underlying interest in the variable perceptions surrounding household labor activities is played out in the chapter "Contributions to Household Labor: Comparing Wives' and Husbands' Reports," by Anthony Shih and myself. We began by assuming that spousal discrepancies in reports of "who does what" in the household are more than a methodological annoyance; they could provide some insights into the multidimensional perceptions connected to domestic labor. We find that while overall there is a high level of agreement between spouses concerning the contribution of each to household work, the norms associated with sex-stereotyped tasks operate to systematically promote "underestimation" of each spouse's contribution by the other. In addition, the normative trappings of tasks interact with the gender of the contributor. For example, wives "underestimate" husbands' reported contributions to some tasks that stereotype the male role (e.g., cutting grass). Likewise, husbands "underestimate" wives' reported contributions to some stereo-typically "female" tasks (e.g., laundry). We conclude that the meaning of household labor contribution and the consensus (or lack of it) between members depends on much more than so-called "objective" information available to them. Yet far more research is indicated to determine how gender-specific norms operate to order spousal perception of contribution.

The power of norms and expectations as they are embedded in house-hold labor relations is also a theme in the chapter by Judith G. Wittner. "Domestic Labor as Work Discipline: The Struggle Over Housework in Foster Homes" takes a novel approach to understanding the "internal stratification process" of the household alluded to by Ferree. An em-pirical analysis of the experiences of children in state residential insti-tutions and in foster homes reveals a dual meaning and function of household labor as it applies to the young. Wittner finds that in institu-tions, domestic work requirements become just one more vehicle for the allocation of rewards and punishments toward the ultimate goal of con-trol. Thus, satisfactory performance in domestic work chores becomes a measure of overall obedience and discipline. In contrast, the placement of children in foster homes—domestic work sites—generates conflicts between foster mothers and their wards. There, household work chores represent less a measure of obedience and more useful activities in themselves. Indeed, the contribution of foster children to domestic labor is perceived by all parties as one appropriate payment for the caretaking services rendered.

Based on such evidence, Wittner extends her analysis to describe the inherent conflicts that can emerge when both foster children and their caretakers seek to establish and maintain control over both the expecta-tions connected to and the organization of domestic labor. Finally, Wittner argues convincingly that the likely interactions between state wards and their caretakers are particularly clear examples of the more general antagonistic relations built up between all dependent children and the women who care for them. They are, for all intents and purposes, bound in a political struggle over the control of their immediate work environments.

With Nona Glazer's chapter, "Everyone Needs Three Hands: Doing Unpaid and Paid Work," the more narrowly defined empirical questions of the previous selections are in part addressed through a broader theoretical treatment. Glazer's discussion is premised on a theme that underlies many of the chapters in this volume—namely, that the substance of women's lives is shaped by two worlds of work, the home and the labor market. Thus, to treat such realms as indendent or to imagine that the "public" has no connection to the "private" is to ultimately evade or distort the relation women have to the social world. Glazer argues that an understanding of the significance of women's domestic work can generate insights into their subordination in all societies, regardless of economic structure. Similarly, women's tenuous economic position in society can only be fully apprehended through attention to how women's position in the family orders their life chances and experiences over the life cycle.

By synthesizing past empirical and theoretical work, Glazer is able to paint a compelling picture of the ways in which women's attachment to the two worlds of work, ideologies that effectively exclude them from legitimating their own experience, and the organization of their domestic labors all combine to produce a set of special class-relevant characteristics. Glazer calls for an end to efforts designed to "fit" women into a class analysis on the same terms as men. An analysis of women's position in the social class structure must take account of women's unique class position by virtue of the marriage relation and the links between women's economic and ideological subordination as mediated by their subordination in the family.

The last chapter in the volume, "Household Work, Wage Work and Sexual Equality," by Joann Vanek, provides a review of significant empirical work to date on changing trends in the family and work roles of men and women. She begins by dispelling popular assumptions about the changes in women's work lives by citing evidence for the persistence of traditional attitudes about women's "appropriate" roles and the traditional ways in which household labor is organized and allocated. She presents the somewhat perplexing finding that despite the sharp rise in women's investment in and commitment to paid work roles, they and their husbands cling to interpretations that paid work for women and household labor for men constitute mere "assistance" and not primary responsibility. Her discussion highlights a conclusion that the harsh sex-segregation in the labor force is all too completely recapitulated (in reverse) in the household. Vanek explores the policy implications of this inequality for women and concludes that although many recent reforms are needed, they by no means speak to a more complete restructuring of paid and family work roles.

Vanek argues that without full employment, fair employment for women, and a recognition that the two worlds of work for women are interdependent, little will alter the reality of economic inequality. Further, the reorganization of family roles is indicated as more and more women take on full participation in the labor market. Vanek allows for the probability that husbands will not leap at the chance to alter their traditional contributions to household labor. Instead, Vanek anticipates a marked change in patterns of household consumption and greater use of market services for the production of household commodities. Finally, she points to possibilities in the expansion of child care services currently provided by the government, as well as a general upgrading of the economic status of housewives.

Vanek's work effectively returns us to the theme of the volume itself and its working premise: Productive policy directed to women must first address itself to the realities of women's domestic lives and second prove consistent with their direct experience of the social world, whether such experience departs from, contradicts, or complicates more traditional models of social change.

REFERENCES

BECKER, G. S. (1974) "A theory of marriage," pp. 229-344 in T. W. Schultz (ed.) Economics of the Family. Chicago: University of Chicago Press.

BERHEIDE, C. W. (1976) "An empirical consideration of the meaning of work and leisure: the case of household work." Ph.D. dissertation, Northwestern University.

BERK, R. A. and S. F. BERK (1978) "A simultaneous equation model for the division of household labor." Sociological Methods and Research 6(May): 431-468.

——— (1979) Labor and Leisure at Home: Content and Organization of the Household Day. Beverly Hills: Sage Publications.

CANNON, R. L. (1978) "The private sphere: how women feel about the work they do." M.A. thesis, University of California at Santa Barbara.

GRONAU, R. (1977) "Leisure, home production and work: the theory of the allocation of time revisited." J. of Pol. Economy 85: 1099-1124.

HIMMELWEIT, S. and S. MOHUN (1977) "Domestic labour and capital." Cambridge Journal of Economics 1: 15-31.

KREPS, J. M. and J. LEAPER (1976) "Home work, market work and the allocation of time," pp. 61-81 in J. M. Kreps (ed.) Women and the American Economy: A Look to the 1980's. Englewood Cliffs, NJ: Prentice-Hall.

LOPATA, H. Z. (1971) Occupation: Housewife. London: Oxford University Press.

OAKLEY, A. (1974) The Sociology of Housework. New York: Pantheon.

PLECK, J. H. (1977) "The work-family role system." Social Problems 24, 4: 417-427.

ROWBOTHAM, S. (1973) Women's Consciousness, Man's World. Harmondsworth: Penguin.

SMITH, D. E. (1977) "A sociology for women." Paper presented at the Women's Research Institute of Wisconsin, Inc.

VANEK, J. (1974) "Time spent in housework." Scientific American 231: 116-120.

——— (1978) "Housewives as workers," pp. 392-404 in A. H. Stromberg and S. Harkess (eds.) Women Working. Palo Alto: Mayfield.

AN ENLARGED HUMAN EXISTENCE?
TECHNOLOGY AND HOUSEHOLD WORK IN
NINETEENTH-CENTURY AMERICA

SUSAN M. STRASSER

Nineteenth-century Americans were awed by technological progress. Tourists and Washingtonians promenaded among the models at the Patent Office, one of the first government buildings erected in Washington, D.C. *Scientific American* printed the list of new patents every week from 1846 until after World War I. Large crowds flocked to technological exhibitions, beginning with the New York Crystal Palace in 1853, and highlighted by the 1876 Philadelphia Centennial and the 1892 World's Columbian Exposition in Chicago. In *The Progress of Invention in the Nineteenth Century*, published by *Scientific American* in 1900, Edward Byrn (1900: 465) expressed the contemporary feeling:

> Whatever the future centuries may bring in new and useful inventions, certain it is that the nineteenth century stands pre-eminent in the field of human achievement, so far excelling all other like periods as to establish on the pages of history an epoch as remarkable as it is unique. Never before has human conception so expressed itself in materialized embodiment, never has thought been so fruitfully wedded to the pregnant possibilities of matter, never has such an accretion of helpful instrumentalities and material resources been added to the world's wealth—not merely the miserly and inert wealth of gold and gems, but the wealth of an enlarged human existence.

AUTHOR'S NOTE: This chapter is excerpted from my dissertation, "Never Done: The Ideology and Technology of Household Work, 1850-1930" (SUNY, Stony Brook, 1977). Expansion of the ideas here may be found in *Never Done: A History of American Housework* (Pantheon, forthcoming).

Byrn might more accurately have confined his remarks to the men in the population, or (to use the phrase made current in the early part of the century) to the men's sphere. In the sphere of women—the household—invention did produce a higher standard of living and a wide range of technological possibilities by the end of the century. But the widespread diffusion of products and services which would change most housewives' routines was yet to come. Even in the cities, the household remained an arena of staggering work, still organized along precapitalist lines. In the absence of prepared foods, plumbing, and modern fuels, women shared little in "the wealth of an enlarged human existence."

INVENTION AND DIFFUSION

A variety of devices and services were invented and marketed before 1900 which were eventually to have substantial effects on household routine. But their diffusion has been exaggerated by popular writers, who have drawn their material from the upper classes and concentrated on invention, rather than diffusion. All of the major domestic appliances were invented—or at least their major operating principles were perfected—before 1900. The technological potential of the nineteenth-century house was fairly high; it could only be achieved, however, by wealthy people in urban areas. Indoor plumbing, electricity, and gas, the innovations which ended the necessity for making fires and carrying water, were luxuries.

Many authors of popular history obscure these class differences. Russell Lynes, for example, claims that "by the end of the 1830s the home refrigerator [by which he means ice box] sat solidly in the pantries or on the back porches of most houses." He cites Eliza Leslie, the author of a popular cookbook, who thought that everyone *should* have an ice box (Lynes, 1963: 123).[1] But prescription and description are two different things.

The first refrigerator patent had been issued in 1803, but mid-century writers by no means equated cold storage with refrigerators. Some recommended keeping meat in snow (Hale, 1844: 37; Randolph, 1824: 23). In 1869 Catharine Beecher, who had recommended manufactured refrigerators 23 years earlier, described a refrigerator in detail in *The American Woman's Home*; apparently some readers even that late might not know what they were (Beecher, 1848: 267; Beecher and Stowe, 1869: 376). Although natural ice harvesting, storage, and shipping was a substantial industry, per capita consumption of ice was low throughout the century, and the bulk of it was used for commercial food storage or to ice drinks, not for domestic refrigeration (Anderson, 1953: 7-10).[2] As late as 1925, the authors of a budget for workers' families in Portland, Oregon, omitted ice expenditures because "the climate of Portland makes it possible to dispense with ice though it is a convenience to be desired during a short season" (Reed College Bulletin, 1925: 12). Refrigeration may have been popular among the upper classes during the nineteenth centurry, but it is safe to say that the icebox by no means "sat solidly . . . in most houses" by 1830, as Lynes claims. This class bias is not isolated to twentieth-century historians; it pervades their nineteenth-century sources. Frances Trollope, author of one of the most important travel accounts of the nineteenth century, wrote in the late 1820s that ice "is in profuse abundance; I do not imagine that there is a house in [New York City] without the luxury of a piece of ice to cool the water, and harden the butter" (Trollope, 1960: 352).

Other writers obscure the difference between invention and diffusion. Siegfried Giedion, whose *Mechanization Takes Command* brought household technology to scholarly attention, is a prime example. Like more popular writers, he emphasizes the host of patents issued for apple parers, cherry stoners, egg beaters, meat grinders, and choppers, and illustrates his book with pictures, often from the patents themselves (Giedion, 1948: 554-555). Giedion gives the impression that every home—and surely every country home—had a mechanical apple parer, but Helen Campbell's comprehensive list of equipment for country houses, published in 1880, included only a (nonmechanical) tin apple corer. Campbell recommended only one mechanical device, the Dover egg beater. Catharine Beecher's earlier lists did not even include mechanical egg beaters, although three of the four which Giedion pictures were patented well before 1869, when she published *The American Woman's Home*. None of the patented contrivances with which twentieth-century writers love to delight us appears even in lists which were clearly ideals of the well-equipped kitchen.[3] Campbell maintained that she listed "in detail . . . every article required for a comfortably fitted-up kitchen" (Campbell, 1881: 51). Her list is not brief. It included a dozen popover cups as well as a dozen custard cups, five different sieves and wire baskets, a dozen muffin rings in addition to small cake tins and a muffin pan, and at least twelve different pots and saucepans exclusive of frying or baking pans—but none of Giedion's mechanical devices.

PRODUCTION TO CONSUMPTION

Some writers have stressed the removal of household tasks to the factory, the change from the productive household to one involved primarily in consumption. Clothing provides the primary nineteenth-century example of this transition. Step by step, the stages of this process moved out of the home and into the factory, affecting all classes to greater or lesser degrees. At the end of the century, however, the ready-made clothing "revolution" was only beginning.

The "family factory" was almost out of the textile business by mid-century. The classic source on household manufactures provides figures on household textile manufactures in New York State between 1825 and 1855.

> A decrease from 16,469,422 to 929,241 total yards and from 8.95 to 0.27 per capita yards is conclusive evidence that a great industrial revolution was going on. . . . The enormous decrease, both in total and in per capita yards, between 1825 and 1835 was largely the result of the passing of the family factory from the urban districts. . . . The all but total abandonment of the family factory even in the rural districts is demonstrated by what happened between 1845 and 1855. The great drop from 7,089,984 to 929,241 total yards demonstrates the fact that when the women decided to give up their time-honored home industry it did not take them long to do it [Tryon, 1917: 306-307].

The pattern was similar in the rest of the country. Not surprisingly, household manufactures died most slowly in the slave states and the far West, and there was some revival in the South during the Civil War. But "as a factor in the economic life and prosperity of the country as a whole"— and in the lives of most women—the system was "practically nil" by 1860 (Tryon, 1917: 376; see also Clark, 1928: 41).

Some ready-made clothing predated the invention of the sewing machine in 1846.[4] Although early clothing manufacturers prated about their fashionable garments, one writer claims that they "catered almost exclusively to slaves and sailors" (Clark, 1928: 759). This is probably an exaggeration with regard to the slaves, but an accurate representation of the status of early ready-made, which tended to fit poorly (on slaves' clothing, see Martin, 1940: 201-204). By the Civil War, men's clothing was frequently bought ready-made, but women's and children's clothes, and men's undergarments, were made at home. The wealthy continued to hire tailors and seamstresses. Men's clothing dominated the industry until the end of the century: The value of women's clothing classed as factory goods was less than one-third that of men's in 1890. After that the rise in women's ready-to-wear was spectacular. By 1914, the value of women's clothing was almost half a billion dollars, exceeding men's clothing by nearly $20 million (Clark, 1928: 759). Still, home sewing continued to be an important household task, producing children's clothes, underwear, sleepwear, and the like

The transition from home production to consumption of factory-made goods was even slower in food preparation. Prepared foods were available by the end of the century, but they were luxuries. In the country, of course, most food was grown or produced at home. Rebecca Burlend, a Yorkshire woman who settled in frontier Illinois in 1831, noted that storekeepers stocked food which they received in barter from established farmers and sold to newcomers. The Burlends, however, ate only what they could produce, except for coffee, "which we used very sparingly, for want of money" (Burlend, 1969: 72).

Even in cities, some home production was possible. Mrs. Trolloppe (1960: 62) commented on the keeping of cows in Cincinnati in the late 1820's.

> From the almost total want of pasturage near the city, it is difficult for a stranger to divine how milk is furnished for its supply, but we soon learnt that there are more ways than one of keeping a cow. A large proportion of the families in the town, particularly of the poorer class, have one. . . . These animals are fed morning and evening at the door of the house . . . while they eat, they are milked, and when the operation is completed the milk-pail and the meal-tub retreat into the dwelling, leaving the republican cow to walk away, to take her pleasure on the hills, or in the gutters.

Catharine Beecher and Harriet Beecher Stowe included chapters on gardening, fruit cultivation, and the care of domestic animals in a manual published for urban and suburban women in 1869. As late as 1890, except where land was completely nonexistent, city dwellers were producing food and raising livestock, poultry, and vegetable gardens (Smuts, 1971: 11). In short, poor people did what they could to get food cheaply. By 1900, the very poorest in the largest urban areas had no land, but for most of the century—and for most of the population even by the century's end—some home production was possible.

Even if purchased, food arrived in the kitchen unprepared. Meat, for those who ate it, was sometimes prepared by the butcher, but at additional expense. Chickens could be purchased "ready for table" at the Cincinnati market, but cost less alive, to be plucked and dressed at home (Trollope, 1960: 60; see also Devoe, 1867: 132-133). Larger animals were slaughtered before sale, but much of the meat eaten in the nineteenth century was never sold. Urban laborers' families slaughtered scavenger pigs which roamed the cities feeding on garbage; housewives battled the cart attendants sent to round them up in New York in 1830 (Cummings, 1940: 28). Even at the end of the century, pigs and goats could be seen in Manhattan as far south as 42nd Street (Smuts, 1971: 12). Wild game was important to the nineteenth-century diet. Sausage was prepared at home; ham and bacon were sold at the markets but not precooked or presliced. Although meat could be purchased in small quantities and cuts not very different from our plastic-wrapped varieties, probably few people outside the urban upper classes did so.

Other foods were purchased in bulk, full of impurities. Coffee was roasted and ground at home; spices had to be ground and sifted. Sugar (for those who could afford it; molasses was much more common) was in lump form and had to be pounded. The heavier flour then milled had to be sifted, for lightness and to separate out foreign matter. Many early cookbooks suggested that it be dried in an oven before use.[5] Raisins came with seeds, cocoa in shell form. Oatmeal required overnight soaking. Nuts had to be shelled. Beans and herbs had to be dried. Yeast was prepared at home, and had to be replenished constantly.

Food preservation tasks constituted some part of the housewife's routine, but probably not as much as we have been led to believe. Nineteenth-century cookbooks were never complete without directions for salting meat and making sugared preserves, but then neither are those of the twentieth century; these directions may have served only as reference for occasional use. Home canning of nonacid fruits and vegetables was impossible without the pressure cooker, the only method recommended in modern home canning (Rombauer and Becker, 1964: 748; Farmer, 1943: 753). In 1880, Campbell's manual for country housekeeping did not even mention the boiling water bath which modern cookbooks recommend for acid fruits and vegetables. She included no recipes for canned vegetables other than tomatoes and an okra-tomato mixture. Her method for sugared canned fruit, preserves, and jelly is familiar to modern preservers: sterilizing jars, filling them with hot sugared fruit, and screwing on the lids. But, she wrote, "most people consider it difficult," and "the directions generally given are so troublesome that one can not wonder it is not attempted oftener" (Campbell, 1881: 244-247). Apparently preserving was not as common as we tend to believe.

Some factory-prepared food was available in mid-century, but it was expensive. Hermetical sealing of glass jars was invented in France in 1810, and an American patent was issued on tin cans in 1825. Civil War military provisioning definitely spurred the industry: Output increased sixfold between 1860 and 1870. But the 1860 figure was only about five million cans of all types (Cummings, 1940: 69). Furthermore, the war's influence on the industry has been exaggerated—with evidence, for example, that "government purchases of California fruit were served at the officers' mess" (Cummings, 1940: 67; quoting Collins, 1924). It is unlikely that common soldiers saw much canned produce during the war, and even more unlikely that their families used canned goods in any quantity whatever for decades thereafter. For the most part, canned food was a luxury.[6]

Bread was the one prepared food common among urban working people in the middle of the century. It had long been available in cities; Boston, for example, had bakers in the 1630s (Friedmann, 1973: 168). The trade in baker's bread was never universal, and cookbooks and manuals warned against its expense and poor quality. But not everybody had ovens. Early in the century, most cooking was done in fireplaces, and, later, many poor people cooked on heating stoves. Even those with ovens brought bread in the summer, to economize on fuel and keep their kitchens cool. Crackers were commercialized on a large scale even earlier than bread, due to the ready market from ships and military provisioning, and the better storage and transport qualities. Philadelphia had nine bakeries producing only crackers in 1858 (Martin, 1940: 54).

At the end of the century, many new food products appeared on the market: pickles and preserves, baking powders, canned soups, condiments of all types. But in food, as in clothing, the change from home to factory production was by no means achieved during the nineteenth century. The widespread use of the new products depended upon the development of the distribution system—national marketing, national advertising, chain stores, national transportation—trends which were just beginning to appear.

TECHNOLOGICAL DEVELOPMENTS IN FIRE-RELATED TASKS

With so few prepared foods, and with the uncertain quality and high price of those which were available, cooking was a major task. It was made more so by the nature of the equipment. Pots and pans were made of only two materials—cast iron and tin—until 1874, when Jacob Vollrath produced the first enameled ware in Sheboygan, Wisconsin. By 1897, Sears was advertising a line of "gray enameled ware . . . formed from a *sheet of steel* enameled, inside and outside," costing about three times as much as their stamped tinware counterparts (Sears, 1968: 130-131). Enameled ware must have had wide appeal despite its extra cost. Sears offered 38 separate items, most in a variety of sizes, ranging from huge pots to basting spoons and funnels. Aluminum, introduced around the same time, was even more expensive. Sears' catalogue copy for aluminum cookware indicated the drawbacks of enamel ware as well as of the traditional materials:

There are several reasons why [aluminum] is so well fitted for kitchen utensils, among which are its lightness, its absolute purity (it is entirely free from all poisonous elements, no verdegris, or salts of tin), its remarkable heat-conducting and retaining properties. The fact that it will not rust, and that it will not corrode under the conditions usually met with in cooking; that there is no enamel to flake off, and that vinegar and fruit acids have no effect upon it, and last but not least, its beauty and its durability (being pure solid metal all the way through, it is practically everlasting), render it most desirable [Sears, 1968: 135].

The problems involved in caring for cooking utensils may not seem large to the reader who treasures a few cast iron skillets or carbon steel knives. But every pot and knife in the nineteenth-century household was subject to corrosion. Metals transmitted poisions and bad flavors to food, steel wool had yet to be invented, and the few extra minutes required for caring for the pots added up, along with all the other "extra few minutes" in the nineteenth-century housekeeping routine. No individual recipe can demonstrate the immense aggregate labor involved in cooking.

The one innovation which did lighten cooking—and the only technological advance over centuries-old conditions which achieved anything near universality—was the cast iron stove. Stove manufacture became a separate and extremely important branch of iron-founding between 1830 and 1860. Administrative centralization, improved transportation and distribution, and population growth "caused a great extension of their manufacture" (Clark, 1929: I, 503). But, again, modern writers have distorted the timing of stove diffusion. One historian claims that by 1850, "in the settled areas at least, the iron 'range' had replaced the great hearth" (Buehr, 1965: 30). Yet Beecher's equipment lists, published in the late 1840s for housekeepers "in the settled areas," included trivets and reflector ovens for use with open fires, as well as pots and pans without legs for use on stoves (Beecher, 1848: 260ff.). In 1852, Sarah Josepha Hale showed pots meant for stoves and discussed baking in an iron oven in her *Ladies' New Book of Cookery*. But roasting was done at the fire, and at least one recipe suggested "setting the pot in the chimney corner with the lid off" (Hale, 1852: 5, 28, 75, 331, 262, 71, 236). In 1869, Beecher discussed stoves and ranges as "the most common modes of cooking, *where open fires are relinquished*" (Beecher and Stowe, 1869: 69; italics added). But by the last decades of the century, stoves had supplanted fireplaces for most heating and cooking; few families relied solely on open fires.[7] Poorer families cooked on heating stoves or heated with cooking stoves. Wealthier people had both kinds; the wealthiest had cooking stoves and central heating.

By themselves, cast iron stoves failed to lighten housework substantially. They were considerably more efficient (in both fuel and time) than
were open fires. But small children had to be watched as vigilantly as ever.
And, since the stoves still relied on coal and wood, fire-building remained a
hot, dirty, and heavy part of housework. In a six-day experiment conducted in 1899 by Boston's School of Housekeeping, 5 hours and 26
minutes were spent on caring for a coal stove: sifting coal, laying and
tending the fire, emptying ashes, carrying coal, and blacking the stove to
guard against rust. This was compared to 10 minutes of fire-tending and
1½ hours of cleaning for a gas stove (Massachusetts Bureau of Statistics
of Labor, 1901: 11-12) Wood required more tending than coal; furthermore, the stove used in the experiment was an advanced model. The
experimental times, then, represent a minimum.

Tending heating and cooking devices fueled with coal and wood was
hard work. Even central furnaces required stoking. Coal and wood heat
produced sooty air and dirty surfaces. Spring housecleaning, the "household earthquake," was to disappear during the twentieth century thanks to
cleaner fuels for both heating and lighting; most of the ordeal consisted of
scouring surfaces covered with soot.[8] The devices which used the older
fuels were inflexible in comparison with modern appliances. Gas and
electric cooking stoves can be used one burner at a time; coal and wood
stoves were rarely used this way. A given fire could cook many dishes, heat
the kitchen, and heat water, so stoves were not "turned on." They were
used only when economical in terms of time, labor, and fuel.

Nor were lights simply "turned on." Candles were, of course, the
earliest popular light source. Although Beecher reprinted the candle-
making directions from her 1845 book in *The American Woman's Home*
(1869), she no longer considered them a major source of light. Campbell's
1880 guide for rural housekeeping gave no directions for making candles.
Following the Civil War, commercially made candles were so inexpensive
that few families would make them. More important, they were by then
widely supplanted by various kinds of lamps.

These lamps, consisting essentially of a base, a fuel font, and a burner
through which the wick was pulled, were made in many materials and used
a variety of fuels. The Argand burner, invented in 1783, was the first
major innovation in a long series of inventions for lamps and fuels which
continued until gas and electricity were firmly entrenched.[9] Kerosene,
invented in 1854 and cheapened after the discovery of petroleum in
Pennsylvania in 1859, was the most important new fuel. Ten years later, it
had superseded other lamp fuels "to such an extent . . . that it is scarcely
worthwhile to give any special directions in regard to them" (Beecher and

Stowe, 1869: 363). Lamps required considerable care, to keep them clean and to guard against explosion. Wicks had to be trimmed, and chimneys and shades were cleaned frequently to keep them bright. Fumes and soot made these tasks unpleasant.[10]

The new fuels, gas and electricity, were both used for illumination long before they made any impact on domestic heating or cooking. The first American luxury hotel, built in Boston in 1829, had gas lighting in the public rooms. By 1855, 297 companies sold gas, mostly for urban public lighting, but also for wealthy private customers (Martin, 1940: 149, 96-97). For most of the century, manufactured gas produced from coal provided unsteady, smelly light. "Water gas," introduced in 1873, was better, cheaper, and brighter. It rapidly supplanted coal gas, and by 1890 less than half of America's manufactured gas was of the older type.[11] Natural gas provided additional competition in places near gas fields by the end of the century.

By 1900, gas lighting was firmly established in some cities. At least two early twentieth-century studies of working people's houses in New York showed a majority with gas lighting (Chapin, 1909: 117; New York City Bureau of Standards, 1915: 36). But as late as 1914, most of the homes in a Chicago study were still lit with oil (Kennedy et al., 1914: 73). The rural situation was similarly uneven. Helen Campbell, writing in 1881 for country women, maintained that gas lighting "hardly requires mention, as the care of it is limited to seeing that it is not turned too high" (Campbell, 1881: 48). But sixteen years later, Sears offered no gas lighting fixtures. Apparently, Beecher and Stowe's assessment in 1869 remained true for most of the century: "Modern houses in cities, and even in large villages, are furnished with gas; where gas is not used, sperm-oil, kerosene or coal-oil, and candles are employed. . . . The economy of any source of light will depend . . . upon local circumstances" (Beecher and Stowe, 1869: 362).

Electricity was introduced late in the nineteenth century, but its common use properly belongs to a discussion of twentieth-century technology. The Edison Company, formed in New York in 1878, began production and distribution four years later. Edison's great achievement, one writer maintains, was not the invention of the light bulb, nor of any of the other parts of the system. "It was the conception of their total functioning together as a practicable kit for generating, controlling, measuring, distributing and utilizing power derived from a central generating station that is the great invention" (Banham, 1969: 60-61). By the century's end, 2500 private and 200 municipal electric light companies offered service in most cities, but it was definitely a luxury. New York

City, for example, had only 10,000 users in 1900, the majority non-domestic (Bacon, 1942: 216).

Both electricity and gas, then, were widely available by 1900, yet fire-building remained a major component of housework. Nineteenth-century patent records were full of inventions, but the precondition for wide dissemination of the new technology was a matter of large-scale economics and public policy, not individual choice. Gas and electricity were centrally controlled utilities, requiring large capitalization for their construction. No family would invest in appliances without having access to the fuels. A new improvement on an oil-burning lamp or a cast iron stove could spread rather readily; individual purchases depended on whether an appliance needed replacement and on the cost of a new device. The new fuels, on the other hand, required expensive installations.

TECHNOLOGICAL DEVELOPMENTS IN WATER-RELATED TASKS

Indoor plumbing was even more a matter of public policy. Like other household innovations, the technical processes were invented long before they gained currency. Industrial production of plumbing parts was necessary for their widespread use. As an architectural historian points out, "Plumbing . . . remain[ed] a luxury as long as it was a largely handicraft affair" (Fitch, 1966: 114). But diffusion was dependent as well upon the development of large systems of waterworks and sewage. The real impetus for the industrialization of plumbing and for the creation of municipal systems derived from pressing public health concerns.

Cities could ill afford to slight sewerage and waterworks, and even country people found that improper drainage ultimately poisoned their water supplies. Philadelphia pioneered modern public waterworks in 'the United States after massive yellow fever epidemics throughout the 1790s. Other cities followed suit, and by the Civil War 136 cities had some kind of public water. This meant, probably, that all towns larger than 10,000 provided water to their inhabitants. But many of these systems were rudimentary, providing no purification, serving a minimum of subscribers, or consisting of tank wagons which hauled water from a town well to fill private barrels. The number of waterworks increased considerably during the latter half of the century; by 1900 probably all of the people living in census-defined urban areas (places of 2500 or more) had access to public water of some description (Turneaure and Russell, 1924: 9).

"The first comprehensive sewerage project of the country" was Chicago's system of tunnels which emptied 30 feet below lake level. By

1866, two years after installation, only an eighth of the city was served by sewers, and the water was still contaminated (Bacon, 1942: 118; Martin, 1940: 242-243). Even in the largest cities, sewers were usually improperly ventilated or otherwise defective. Poorly designed and improperly installed house fixtures leaked sewer gas into dwellings and public buildings (Bayles, 1878: 23-43). Due to the public health movement at the end of the century, cities spent a good deal of money on these problems. About one-third of Boston's total city budget in the last third of the century was devoted to sanitary projects. Speculators and subdividers of that city's suburbs extended sanitary services to the middle class, grading streets so that the city would do the initial work before housing was built (Warner, 1962: 30, 61, 121-122, 138). But, as so much Progressive writing demonstrated, sanitary conditions for the urban poor remained outrageously bad.

By the beginning of the Civil War, toilets, sinks, and bathtubs were still luxuries, but not total oddities, in American cities. Edgar Martin reports that Boston had 31,098 sinks, 3,910 bathtubs, and 9,864 water closets in 1860, when the population was 177,840. These figures are considerably higher per capita than those for New York, Albany, or Baltimore. Many households were connected with urban water mains but lacked fixtures. As Martin writes, "Most of these figures come from reports of city water departments, where they appear because baths and water closets were charged for in addition to the normal water rates—itself a suggestive fact" (Martin, 1940: 111-112, 127). Still other households, both urban and rural, did have fixtures, but they were connected to cisterns, wells, and springs.

The range of possibilities for household plumbing during the latter half of the century was broad. Water could come into households from private wells or springs, from rivers or streams, from fixtures connected to public water mains, from hydrants on the streets, or from barrels filled from water-hauling carts. At the end of the century, Sears supplied both those with and without indoor plumbing. They offered sinks, wash basins, and urinals fitted for plumbing pipes, as well as chamber pails. Toilet sets (the pitchers and bowls we now see in antique stores) came with or without slop jars and covers (Sears, 1968: 55-56, 134, 682-683). The Lynds maintain that in 1890 only about one-eighth to one-sixth of Muncie's families "had even the crudest running water—a hydrant in the yard or a faucet at the iron sink. . . . For the most part, Middletown pumped its water to the back door or kitchen from a well or cistern. By 1890 there were not over two dozen complete bathrooms in the entire city" (Lynd and Lynd, 1929: 27). In larger cities, plumbing was more common, but the 1893 report of the Commissioner of Labor maintained that 53 percent of New York families, 70 percent of Philadelphia's, 73 percent of Chicago's, and 88 percent of Baltimore's had access only to an outside privy (U.S. Department of Labor, 1959: 64).

Household routine depended on the state of the plumbing. Dishwashing was the daily task most affected. A "full supply of conveniences" included a swab, two or three towels, three dishcloths, two large tin tubs, a "large old waiter tray, on which to drain the dishes," a soap dish, hard soap, a slop pail, and two water pails (Beecher and Stowe, 1869: 372-373). Dish-draining racks were unavailable: Neither Beecher nor Campbell mentions one, and none appears in the Sears catalogue as late as 1897. Pots were generally cleaned with sand, though Campbell suggests a "wire dish cloth" (Campbell, 1881: 89). Commercially made soap was increasingly popular, but available only in bars; it had to be scraped for dishwashing.[12] The procedure is basically familiar: scraping, washing, rinsing, wiping, and putting away. Dishwashing required carrying an enormous amount of water—cold water to the stove, hot water to the dishpans, dirty water to the drain or back porch. Every one of these loads was necessary even in a house equipped with indoor pumps.

Indoor plumbing was to make even greater changes in laundry, "the most trying part of domestic labor," according to Catharine Beecher, who advocated its removal from household routine. This may be taken as an indication of just how trying it was, since communalization and industrialization of housework, the removal of labor from the home, was inconsistent with Beecher's other goals (for a discussion of Beecher's goals, see Strasser, 1977: 116-149). This point—that laundry could not or should not be a one-woman job—was made by many writers. Solutions varied, but even people of limited means sought relief in the form of washerwomen and commercial laundries. Almost unknown in 1860, commercial laundries were a substantial business by 1909, when power laundries grossed over $100 million, an average of $5.30 per household (Hartmann, 1974: 287). One study of urban working-class families at the turn of the century found that 44 percent of even the poorest group spent some money for laundry, and proposed $.05 weekly in its model budget (Chapin, 1909: 165, 179; see also More, 1907: 99, 103, 106). But $.05 a week provided for only the heaviest linens. Although some help with laundry work was available to and used by all classes, at least in the cities, it seems clear that for most of the century most laundry was done at home by housewives.

The process, from start to finish, was staggering. Campbell suggested overnight soaking first, with separate tubs for "fine things," bed linen, table linen, and coarse or soiled outerwear. The next morning, this water was to be drained off, and warm soapy water added. Then came the rubbing and a rinse. From there the clothes went to the boiler, to be covered with cold water and "boiled up": "Once will be sufficient for fine clothes." Then they were put into cold water, and from there into water with bluing. From this last rinse "they must be wrung out very dry, and hung out, always out of doors if possible." Collars and cuffs were dipped into home-made starch, then everything was dampened for ironing. Although many women undoubtedly used fewer rinses than Campbell suggested, even the most basic laundry work required an enormous amount of hard, hot, heavy work: lifting tubs full of cold and hot water, rubbing, wringing, and hanging on the line (Campbell, 1881: 54-59).

Technological devices did not help much. There were plenty of ideas for washing machines: Nearly 2,000 had been patented by 1869. But most of the ones produced were for commercial laundries, and even the rare domestic machines saved little time and not much labor. Sears offered six wringers in 1897; even the most expensive had no safety releases. Its four washing machines included one "steam washer" which had the "decided advantage" of a "faucet attached to the boiler for removing the water without lifting the boiler from the stove." It cost over twice as much as the other three. The work involved was formidable, and the time almost identical to hand washing:

> On the evening before wash-day place all the clothes you wish to wash in a tub, fill the same up with water . . . so that they may be thoroughly soaked over night. On the following morning fill your wash boiler three-fourths full of rain water, put the same to boiling and cut into it one-half bar of hand soap and one teacupful of washing fluid, the recipe of which is found below. [It was made of potash, salts of tartar, ammonia, and water.] When boiling put in your clothes and boil from 10 to 15 minutes, after which wring them out, place them in the machine, work them from 5 to 10 minutes in the same, wring your clothes into the basket, rinse them through clear water, blue and hang on the line.

> Do not put over five shirts or four sheets at a time into the machine, and see that the same is kept well filled with soap suds [Sears, 1968: 139].

Mechanical scrubbing could not by itself make light work of laundry.

Houses without plumbing required other disagreeable work. Most ice-boxes had no drains, so water pans had to be emptied; those with drains were rarely connected to other drainage systems, because sewer gas might back up into the icebox. Households without toilets had chamber pots and slop jars; emptying them constituted "the most disagreeable item in domestic labor" (Beecher and Stowe, 1869: 403). The other choice, of course was to go outside.

Indoor plumbing eventually saved time and labor by removing water carrying and slops carrying from household routine. Throughout the nineteenth century, the urban working classes and people outside towns had to carry water for all cleaning, drinking, and cooking. The aggregate labor involved was huge. A North Carolina Farmer's Alliance paper, anxious to attract women to meetings, wrote about their labor:

> 'Have you a well or a spring?' 'I have a spring—as good water as ever flowed out of the ground,' said he. 'And how far is it from your house,' we inquired. 'About sixty yards,' he replied. 'How long have you lived there?' 'About 41 years.' 'How many times per day throughout the year does the water have to be brought?' After a moment's reflection he said: 'I should say eight or ten times a day on an average.' 'Well suppose we figure a little . . . and we will put it at six instead of eight or ten times a day. Sixty yards at six times a day is 720 yards' [Progressive Farmer, 1886: 4].

That figured to 6,068 miles in 41 years. More to the point, it was nearly half a mile a day at a pound per pint.

Conservation measures lightened the load. People without plumbing changed clothes and linens less often than the wealthy, who had better equipment, paid help, and more clothes. Dishwater and bathwater were reused, perhaps supplemented with additional hot water. Indoor plumbing and the abandonment of these measures meant cleaner dishes, cleaner clothes, and cleaner and healthier bodies. Even without fixtures or complete systems, the establishment of waterworks increased the use of water. In Philadelphia, consumption of water per subscriber doubled between 1823 and 1837. It had more than doubled again by 1850 (Warner, 1968: 107-108).

THE STANDARD OF LIVING

More water meant more washing—just one element in the higher standard of living which nineteenth-century technology did bring to households even while the work there remained substantial. Similarly, the increasing availability of gas and the improvements in kerosene led to a vast increase in the amount of illumination employed in households. One writer estimates that the increase was twentyfold and points out that they ended "almost a campfire situation, in which space was . . . focused around the lamp as much as framed by the walls of the room" (Banham, 1969: 55). Central heating, while considerably less widespread, did the same thing. A central coal furnace still required fire maintenance and hopper filling; vigilant cleaning was especially necessary in houses heated with air forced from coal furnaces. But the nature of family routine and the possibilities for privacy within the family were vastly altered. Without it, one woman recorded her relief at warm weather, when spinning was moved to a room "where it escaped the espionage of the curious eyes and gossiping tongues that during the winter had at times been excessively annoying" (Flaherty, 1972: 73 n). Later, a midwestern home economist advised farm women that, while a furnace should not be a high priority, "the common farm practice of abandoning the rest of the house for a three-months retreat in the kitchen" should be ended by heating a "cozy end" of the dining room (Delgado, 1973: 11-12).

Perhaps the most significant change in the standard of living came in the kinds of food available. Improved transportation and refrigeration—and, especially, the combination of the two in refrigerated railroad cars and steamships—lengthened the seasons for fresh fruits and vegetables, made meat shipment possible over long distances, and provided cheaper food with more variety to all classes. For most of the century, the lack of variety in working people's diets was a significant health problem, especially in rural districts where they lacked spending money and could get food only by growing it. Totally dependent on natural growing seasons, poor people probably suffered more from vitamin deficiencies than from protein shortages. Meat was a staple in the nineteenth-century diet, but early in the century most of it was smoked, salted, or pickled. After the invention of the ice cutter in 1827, and with continued innovation in commercial refrigeration, most urban meat markets by 1860 were using ice to store fresh meat (Cummings, 1940: 36-39; Martin, 1940: 29).

Dairy products and fresh produce were notably lacking, all year in the cities and in winter in the country. Improved transportation extended the market and increased both demand and production, bringing added variety and reduced prices on perishable goods. Milk consumption in New York, for example, tripled or quadrupled during the 1840s, following the construction of the Erie Railroad. Railroads also stimulated truck farming in districts outlying the cities, bringing fresh fruits and vegetables to urban areas (Cummings, 1940: 53-57; Martin, 1940: 29). After the Civil War, refrigerated railroad cars brought produce from the South, and steamships had carried Caribbean fruit even earlier, but these were luxury items. Urban workers did not receive the full benefits of improved transportation and refrigeration until the end of the century. Still, technology did narrow the gap between food for the rich and for the poor, even though it remained greater throughout the century than it is today. And the cost of food in relation to wages fell in mid-century: The percentage of a Massachusetts laborer's weekly wage spent on a "market basket" list of items fell from 86.8% in 1830 to 76.1% in 1860. Workers probably tended to buy more expensive (and more nutritious) food, rather than increasing the quantity of cheaper foods (Cummings, 1940: 244, 77; Bacon, 1942: 74-76).

Although the major part of wages was still spent on food, these improvements did begin to leave some money for nonfood consumption goods, especially textiles and ready-made clothing. The sole area in which work really was removed from the nineteenth-century household, clothing, also serves as another indicator of a raised standard of living. Because the ready-made industry cheapened clothes, one of its major results was a vast increase in demand. Working people in the early nineteenth century had few changes in clothing, whether they bought or made their garments. By the end of the 1850s, commentators speculated that the sewing machine would mean more clothes for more people:

> The needle will soon be consigned to oblivion, like the [spinning] wheel, and the loom, and the knitting needle. . . . People will dress better, change oftener, and altogether grow better looking. . . . The more work can be done, the cheaper it can be done by means of machines—*the greater will be the demand.* Men and women will disdain the soupcon of a nice worn garment, and gradually we shall become a nation without spot or blemish [Kidwell and Christman, 1974: 79].[13]

The prediction was not totally realized by 1900, but people did have more clothes, and the "nation without spot or blemish" was clearly on its way.

TECHNOLOGICAL DEVELOPMENTS AND WOMEN'S WORK

Most of the work for the sewing establishments was done by women at home. The putting-out system remained a major force in the clothing industry at least until the influx of Eastern European immigration after 1880, largely because of two new marketing techniques introduced along with the sewing machine. Installment selling and the trade-in allowance were introduced by Isaac Singer's partner, Edward Clark, about 1856; Singer's competitors soon used them as well (Scull with Fuller, 1967: 184-187). Probably no other household commodity ever caught on as fast as the sewing machine. But it was unlike other innovations: Women bought machines on the installment plan not only to make clothes for their families but also to provide themselves with incomes. The sewing machine did not so much revolutionize the ready-made industry as allow it to increase production while operating in time-honored patterns.

Taking in sewing, whether for individuals or manufacturers, was an important way for many women to make money without leaving home. Others took in laundry and boarders. Work of this nature has always been undercounted in published statistics of women's work. For the many women who did it, as for those who did unpaid housework, the work situation was quite unlike that in the factories.

While technological change was revolutionizing work outside the household, it made even fewer inroads on the organization of housework than it did on the amount of time and labor involved. Whereas factory work was timed by the clock, home work was task-oriented labor (on task-orientation, see Thompson, 1967: 60). Task-orientation was the essence of piecework done for manufacturers as well as of housework. Married women were not under the direct supervision of bosses. They could plan their own work and suspend a task to care for a crying baby or stir the soup. While their husbands increasingly worked with others in factories, women continued to work alone or in very small groups. Industrial organization was impossible for them during a time when workers' organizations were growing, and factories were often arenas for political discussion.[14]

Married women worked outside the definitions of an economy based on money and profit. The household was not operated for profit, and housewives did not work for wages. Even women who made money in the home—domestic servants, pieceworkers, laundresses, seamstresses, and landladies—were not, strictly speaking, wage workers. Their hours were indefinite, they lived in their workplaces, and their jobs were not defined by contract (for a discussion of these distinctions as they applied to domestic service, see Strasser, 1978). Meanwhile, men went out to work in increasing numbers: by 1870, about two-thirds of gainfully employed workers were wage earners, dependent for their survival on selling their labor power to others (Montgomery, 1967: 29-30). Men's work was controlled by their employers and defined either by contract or by verbal agreement. The primacy of wage labor meant that class became an increasingly important social category, but it remained obscured within households, where the nature of work was defined by sex.

This is not merely a description of the sexual division of labor during the nineteenth century. Rather, it is a suggestion that, during the transition to industrial capitalism, half the population were active participants, while the other half had no clearly defined role in the new order.[15] The transfer of production from the home to the factory was clearly under way, yet housewives were not yet even defined as consumer participants in the economy.[16]

Technological change, which so impressed nineteenth-century people, did make inroads into household life by raising the standard of living. Patents abounded for household innovations. The wealthy bought them and, as one archhitectural historian has pointed out, by the middle of the century dwellings coexisted which, "in terms of amenities, were literally centuries apart" (Fitch, 1966: 88). But technology had little impact on most women's working life. Indoor plumbing and the new fuels, which were to become nearly universal in urban areas by 1920 and in small towns by 1930, were still just technological possibilities at the turn of the century. Still burdened by household chores which technology had failed to change, not yet able to take advantage of the expensive technological aids which did exist, most married women remained isolated in the traditional household, outside the leading sectors of economic life and with little share in the "wealth of an enlarged human existence."

NOTES

1. For others who make the same point on similarly flimsy evidence, see Cummings (1940: 39) and de Rochemont (1976: 148) and their quotation from Daniel Boorstin.

2. For the definitive work on the earlier period, see Cummings (1949).

3. For lists of equipment, see Campbell (1881: 267-269); Beecher and Stowe (1869: 373-376); Beecher (1845: 319; 1848: 260-267). The last list was illustrated.

4. This is the date of Elias Howe's patent, the fifth U.S. patent to be issued for a sewing machine. For the definitive work on this invention, see Cooper (1968).

5. For a discussion of changes in flour quality due to changes in milling processes, see Giedion (1948: 188-190). For impurities, see Beecher (1848: 130). For flour drying, see Emerson (1808: 63) and Rundell (1807: 213-214).

6. Bacon makes this point emphatically: "It is hard to know how widely [canned foods] were used in 1865, but remarks of magazine writers and authors of cook books would indicate that canned foods were bought for special occasions when out of season or for use inland, as in the case of fish. In most instances prices were too high for the ordinary pocketbook" (Bacon, 1942: 15-16).

7. Even after stoves became popular, some fireplace cooking continued. As late as 1885, one cookbook differentiated between roast beef, made at a fire, and "baked beef," roasted in the oven (Washington, 1885: 85, 87). *The White House Cook Book,* coauthored by the steward of the White House in 1887, gave directions for roasting beef in the oven, without apologies, but suggested that, "If convenient, [potatoes] may be baked in wood-ashes, or in a Dutch oven in front of the fire" (Gillette And Ziemann, 1889: 175).

8. The phrase is from Campbell (1881: 60-62). See also Lynd and Lynd (1929: 171 n), for a description of a seven-day "household earthquake" at the end of the century.

9. For a discussion of these innovations, see Martin (1940: 84-86) and Editors of the Pyne Press (1972: 3-45).

10. For comments on the unpleasant nature of this work, see Campbell (1881:

50) and Beecher and Stowe (1869: 364).

11. For descriptions of the water gas production process, see Bacon (1942: 104-105) and Clark (1928: 516).

12. Martin (1940: 216) suggests that the use of commercial soap outside cities was rare in 1860. Neither Campbell's 1880 manual for country women nor Beecher's 1869 manual for urban and suburban households has directions for making soap.

13. This is a quote from a New York *Tribune* editorial. For a similar comment, from the first annual report (1869) of the New York Chamber of Commerce, see Feldman (1960: 111).

14. See, for example, Edith Abbot's (1910: 161) discussion of Massachusetts women shoe binders' isolation from the political discussions in the shoe factories.

15. This ties into Tamara Hareven's (1976) suggestion that any model of family change must account for the possibility that workers might be "premodern" at home at the same time as they were "modern" at work.

16. European travelers often commented that men (even of the wealthiest classes) did the food marketing in the 1820s and 1830s, usually before they went to work in the morning (see Trollope, 1960: 85, 419; Martineau, 1962: 302). Until late in the century, household advice manuals did not include education for consumption; none of Beecher's books, for example, contains a chapter or even a section on choosing food.

REFERENCES

ABBOTT, E. (1910) Women in Industry: A Study in American Economic History. New York: Appleton-Century-Crofts.

ANDERSON, O. E. (1953) Refrigeration in America: A History of a New Technology and its Impact. Princeton: Princeton University Press (for the University of Cincinnati).

BACON, E. M. (1942) "The growth of household conveniences in the United States from 1865 to 1900." Ph.D. dissertation, Radcliffe College.

BANHAM, R. (1969) The Architecture of the Well-Tempered Environment. Chicago: University of Chicago Press.

BAYLES, J. C. (1878) House Drainage and Water Service, in Cities, Villages, and Rural Neighborhoods, with Incidental Consideration of Causes Affecting the Healthfulness of Dwellings. New York: David Williams.

BEECHER, C. E. (1845) Treatise on Domestic Economy for the Use of Young Ladies at Home and at School. New York: Harper & Row.

――― (1848) Miss Beecher's Domestic Receipt Book: Designed as a Supplement to her Treatise on Domestic Economy. New York: Harper & Row.

――― and H. B. STOWE (1869) The American Woman's Home; or Principles of Domestic Science; Being a Guide to the Formation and Maintenance of Economical, Healthful, Beautiful, and Christian Homes. New York: J. B. Ford.

BUEHR, W. (1965) Home, Sweet Home in the Nineteenth Century. New York: Thomas Y. Crowell.

BURLEND, R. (1969) "A Yorkshire family settles in Illinois," pp. 66-84 in D. B. Greenberg (ed.) Land that Our Fathers Plowed. Norman: University of Oklahoma Press.

BYRN, E. W. (1900) The Progress of Invention in the Nineteenth Century. New York: Munn.

CAMPBELL, H. (1881) The Easiest Way in Housekeeping and Cooking, Adapted to Domestic Use, or Study in Classes. New York: Fords, Howard, & Hulbert.

CHAPIN, R. C. (1909) The Standard of Living Among Workingmen's Families in New York City. New York: Russell Sage.

CLARK, V. S. (1928) History of Manufactures in the United States, 1860-1914. Washington, D.C.: Carnegie Institution of Washington.

——— (1929) History of Manufactures in the United States. 3 vols. New York: McGraw-Hill (for the Carnegie Institution of Washington).

COLLINS, J. H. (1924) The Story of Canned Foods. New York: E. P. Dutton.

COOPER, G. R. (1968) "The invention of the sewing machine." U.S. National Museum Bulletin 254.

CUMMINGS, R. O. (1940) The American and His Food: A History of Food Habits in the United States. Chicago: University of Chicago Press.

——— (1949) The American Ice Harvests: A Historical Study in Technology, 1800-1918. Berkeley: University of California Press.

DELGADO, J. H. (1973) "Nellie Kedzie Jones's Advice to Farm Women: Letters from Wisconsin, 1912-1916." Wisconsin Magazine of History 57 (Autumn): 3-27.

DEVOE, T. F. (1867) The Market Assistant: Containing a Brief Description of Every Article of Human Food Sold in the Public Markets of the Cities of New York, Boston, Philadelphia, and Brooklyn. New York: Riverside Press. (Privately printed.)

Editors of the Pyne Press (1972) Lamps and Other Lighting Devices, 1850-1906. Princeton: Pyne Press.

EMERSON, L. (1808) The New-England Cookery, or the Art of Dressing All Kinds of Flesh, Fish, and Vegetables, and the Best Modes of Making Pastes, Puffs, Pies, Tarts, Puddings, Custards and Preserves, and All Kinds of Cakes, from the Imperial Plumb to Plain Cake, Particularly Adapted to this Part of Our Country. Montpelier: Josiah Parks.

FARMER, F. M. (1943) The Boston Cooking School Cook Book (W. L. Perkins, ed.). Boston: Little, Brown.

FELDMAN, E. (1960) Fit for Men: A Study of New York's Clothing Trade. Washington, D.C.: Public Affairs Press.

FITCH, J. M. (1966) American Building. I: The Historical Forces that Shaped It. Boston: Houghton Mifflin.

FLAHERTY, D. H. (1972) Privacy in Colonial New England. Charlottesville: University Press of Virginia.

FRIEDMANN, K. J. (1973) "Victualling colonial Boston." Agricultural History 47 (July): 189-205.

GIEDION, S. (1948) Mechanization Takes Command: A Contribution to Anonymous History. New York: W. W. Norton.

GILLETTE, F. L. and H. ZIEMANN (1889) The White House Cook Book: Cooking, Toilet and Household Recipes, Menus, Dinner-Giving, Table Etiquette, Care of the Sick, Health Suggestions, Facts Worth Knowing, etc., etc., the Whole Comprising a Comprehensive Cyclopedia of Information for the Home. New York: J. A. Hill.

HALE, S. J. (1844) The Good Housekeeper, or the Way To Live Well, and To Be Well While We Live, Containing Directions for Choosing and Preparing Food, in Regard to Health, Economy, and Taste. Boston: Otis, Broaders.

––– (1852) The Ladies' New Book of Cookery: A Practical System for Private Families in Town and Country, with Directions for Carving, and Arranging the Table for Parties, etc. Also, Preparations of Food for Invalids and Children. New York: H. Long.

HAREVEN, T. K. (1976) "Modernization and family history: Perspectives on social change." Signs 2 (Autumn): 190-206.

HARTMANN, H. (1974) "Capitalism and women's work in the home, 1900-1930." Ph.D. dissertation, Yale University.

KENNEDY, J. C. et al. (1914) Wages and Family Budgets in the Chicago Stockyards District, with Wage Statistics from Other Industries Employing Unskilled Labor. Chicago: University of Chicago Press.

KIDWELL, C. B. and M. C. CHRISTMAN (1974) Suiting Everyone: The Democratization of Clothing in America. Washington, D.C.: Smithsonian Institution.

LYND, R. S. and H. M. LYND (1929) Middletown: A Study in Modern American Culture. New York: Harcourt Brace Jovanovich.

LYNES, R. (1963) The Domesticated Americans. New York: Harper & Row.

MARTIN, E. W. (1940) The Standard of Living in 1860: American Consumption Levels on the Eve of the Civil War. Chicago: University of Chicago Press.

MARTINEAU, H. (1962) Society in America (S. M. Lipset, ed.). Gloucester, MA: Peter Smith.

Massachusetts Bureau of Statistics of Labor (1901) Comparison of the Cost of Home-Made and Prepared Food, Published by the Massachusetts Bureau of Statistics of Labor from Information Collected by the Boston Branch of the Association of Collegiate Alumnae annd the School of Housekeeping, Boston, Massachusetts. Boston: Wright & Potter.

MONTGOMERY, D. (1967) Beyond Equality: Labor and the Radical Republicans, 1862-1872. New York: Vintage.

MORE, L. B. (1907) Wage-Earners' Budgets, a Study of Standards and Cost of Living in New York City. New York: Holt, Rinehart & Winston.

New York City Bureau of Standards (1915) Report on the Cost of Living for an Unskilled Laborer's Family in New York City. New York: Author.

Progressive Farmer (1886) "Farmers' wives sadly overworked." December 8: 4.

RANDOLPH, M. (1824) The Virginia Housewife: Method Is the Soul of Management. Washington, D.C.: Davis & Force.

Reed College Bulletin (1925) "Cost of living survey–Portland, Oregon." January.

de ROCHEMONT, R. and W. ROOT (1976) Eating in America: A History. New York: Morrow.

ROMBAUER, I. S. and M. B. BECKER (1964) The Joy of Cooking. Indianapolis: Bobbs-Merrill.

RUNDELL, M. E. (1807) New System of Domestic Cookery, Formed upon Principles of Economy, and Adapted to the use of Private Families. Boston: Andrews & Cummings, & L. Slake.

SCULL, P. with P. C. FULLER (1967) From Peddlars to Merchant Princes. Chicago: Follett.

Sears, Roebuck & Co. (1968) 1897 Sears Catalogue (F. L. Israel, ed.). New York: Chelsea House.

SMUTS, R. W. (1971) Women and Work in America. New York: Schocken.

STRASSER, S. M. (1977) "Never done: the ideology and technology of household work, 1850-1930." Ph.D. dissertation, SUNY at Stony Brook.

――― (1978) "Mistress and maid, employer and employee: domestic service reform in the United States, 1897-1920." Marxist Perspectives 1 (Winter): 52-67.

THOMPSON, E. P. (1967) "Time, work discipline, and industrial capitalism." Past and Present 38: 56-97.

TROLLOPE, F. (1960) Domestic Manners of the Americans (D. Smalley, ed.). New York: Vintage.

TRYON, R. M. (1917) Household Manufactures in the United States, 1640-1860. Chicago: University of Chicago Press.

TURNEAURE, F. E. and H. L. RUSSELL (1924) Public Water-Supplies: Requirements, Resources, and the Construction of Works. New York: John Wiley.

U.S. Department of Labor (1959) How American Buying Habits Change. Washington, D.C.: Author.

WARNER, S. B. (1962) Streetcar Suburbs: The Process of Growth in Boston, 1870-1900. Cambridge: Harvard University Press and MIT Press.

――― (1968) The Private City: Philadelphia in Three Periods of Its Growth. Philadelphia: University of Pennsylvania Press.

WASHINGTON, Mrs. [pseud.] (1885) The Unrivalled Cook-Book and Housekeeper's Guide. New York: Harper & Row.

2

HOUSEWORK TECHNOLOGY AND HOUSEHOLD WORK

JOHN P. ROBINSON

One cornerstone of the argument that technology has improved the quality of life in the United States over the last 50 or 100 years has been the increase of the population's discretionary time. For example, it is usually assumed that advances in technology have been responsible for the decrease of the formal workweek from over sixty hours at the turn of the century to today's forty hours or less. This in turn has given Americans greater control over how they spend their time, particularly their ability to participate in leisure and other nonwork activities that represent an increase in the quality of their lives (DeGrazia, 1962).

Somewhat the same beneficial assumptions about technology have often characterized speculations about relieving the burdens of housework—from the first stoves and refrigerators to today's more sophisticated appliances such as dishwashers and microwave ovens, and the fast foods and minimal care clothing that have become a common feature of our daily life. Combined with her higher education, today's woman is usually thought to be better able to use this technology to organize her time more efficiently, particularly to minimize the routine, repetitive, and mundane aspects of housework. Indeed, it is often suggested that it is these very characteristics of housework, and the ability of technology to reduce them, that have been responsible for so many more women being able to enter the paid labor market.

Technology, of course, can be a mixed blessing as far as time is concerned. The greater variety of products (and the increasing rate of product innovation) make the trip to the marketplace more time-con-

suming, especially when shopping centers are located at increasing distances from the household. Once technology enters the home, individuals
may find themselves using it to produce output never possible before: e.g.,
a more varied wardrobe with wash-and-wear fabrics, more ambitious meals
with Cuisinarts or microwave ovens; and, as Linder (1970) noted, the more
technology in the household, the more time will be required for its
acquisition, maintenance, and repair.

In the 1960s, suitable large-scale empirical data on how much time
women actually spend doing housework began to become available.
Results of these studies challenged the characterization of technology
shrinking the demands of housework. Morgan et al. (1966: 111-113)
found families with more automatic home appliances estimating more
hours of housework than those with fewer appliances, particularly in
families with preschool children and two or more appliances. Robinson et
al. (1972: 126) found employed women in the United States with much
higher ownership of appliances spending only about four fewer hours per
week on housework than employed women in Yugoslavia or Poland, and
more time doing housework than employed women in Bulgaria or Peru.
Despite their much lower employment rate in 1965, then, women in the
United States reported less than 10 percent less housework than women in
other countries in the survey.

The results dovetailed with historical comparisons made with results of
earlier, usually cruder, time-use studies. Women both in and out of the
labor market reported virtually the same amount of time doing housework
in the 1960s as they had ten, twenty, or forty years previously, when
much less technology was available. Walker (1969) found employed
women in 1967-1968 spending 7.4 hours per day on housework compared
to only 4.1 hours in 1958; housewives also reported more housework (8.0
hours) in 1967-1968 than in 1958 (7.4 hours). Robinson et al. (1972)
found women in a 1965-1966 national survey reporting 6.5 hours per day
of housework compared to 6.7 hours in a 1954 national survey in which
only two-thirds as many women were employed in the paid labor market;
compared to a 1932 survey, they found both employed women and
housewives doing over 2 hours more housework per day. Using different
earlier data bases, Vanek (1974) found the number of weekly hours on
housework by housewives to vary only from 51 hours in 1926 to 52 hours
in 1929, 1936, and 1943 to 53 hours in 1953 and 55 hours in 1965-1966.

Both single-time and cross-time analyses, then, suggest a certain invari-
ability or constancy of housework not only in relation to technology but
in terms of the demands of the household. They further suggest a sort of
Parkinson's Law that keeps women's housework at a constant level despite

the time savings possible with technology—although the cross-time analyses of both Walker and Vanek indicate that the changes over time do show a tradeoff of more routine and repetitive housework (like laundry and meal cleanup) to managerial activity rather than a matter of filling up time that is available simply because it is not being devoted to other activities.

Analyses of other uses of time suggest much the same homeostatic mechanisms to be in operation. Thus, little change in the workweek has been noted over the last few decades (Wilensky, 1961; DeGrazia, 1962; Owen, 1976) and some tendency for workers given shorter workweeks to take on second jobs or to work overtime to compensate has been observed (Swados, 1958; Wilensky, 1961; Maklan, 1976). There also seems to be a limit of time (about 20 percent of that reported by women) that men devote to housework, such that it does not increase significantly when their wives take on employment or have additional child care responsibilities, or when technology is available (Meissner et al., 1975; Robinson, 1977). The technology of the automobile makes a faster commute to work possible, but the automobile also makes it possible to live further from work, so that the total travel times of automobile owners and nonowners are roughly equivalent (Robinson, et al., 1972). The same type of homeostatic tradeoffs also appear to characterize the impact of television (Coffin, 1955; Weiss, 1969), with television replacing mainly those mass media with the most similar content—radio, movies, and the reading of fiction.

The present report indicates that the homeostatic mechanisms that have governed time use may be undergoing processes of change. This is particularly true with regard to housework since 1965, the date of the last comprehensive source of national data on how people spend time. This decline in housework, moreover, has occurred during a decade of remarkable diffusion of household technology. While such basic technology as refrigerators, stoves, and running water were already household "universals" in 1965, significant gains in ownership of such potentially time-saving applicances as washers (from 57 percent to 70 percent), dryers (from 26 percent to 58 percent), dishwashers (13 percent to 38 percent), disposals (14 percent to 39 percent), and freezers (27 percent to 44 percent) had occurred by 1975 (U.S. Bureau of Census, 1978). Practically no households in 1965 had a microwave oven, but by the time of our 1975 national survey, ownership was reported by over 5 percent of households interviewed. These shifts, then, could well be large enough to account for any observed decline in housework.

The changes in time use since 1975 are, however, ones that took place when several important changes were occurring in the composition of society besides the further diffusion of household technology: the increased entry of women into the labor force; the increase in the number of unmarried women; the increased number of childless couples; the prominence of the women's movement, with its emphasis on increasing the values of women's time and the sharing of household responsibilities by men; the increased education of women; the increased incomes of families, making possible the purchase of technology or outside help; and the decreased size of housing units and increased use of rental units and apartments, which require less care. The possible impact of several of these factors will be examined first in the analysis which follows, prior to analysis which examines the possible impact of the diffusion of household technology over the same time period.

DATA SOURCE

The main data source for analysis is the 1975 study of *Americans' Use of Time* conducted by the Survey Research Center at the University of Michigan. In this study, a national probability sample of 1519 people aged eighteen years and older provided a complete accounting of all their activities for a single day during the fall of 1975.[1] The sample days were scattered across the various days of the weeks, although not at random, and the analyses which follow adjust the data to ensure that the various days of the week are equally represented.

Individuals in the survey reported a diary of their separate activities in sequence from midnight to midnight for the particular day in question, describing the activity itself, how long it took place, and where it took place as well as other details of each activity. On the average, respondents in the survey reported 22.7 activities in their diaries. Previous research has shown that the activities people report in this way do provide reliable and valid accounts of how people spend their time; that is, different investigators derive similar estimates of activities using this diary method, and the obtained diary results also correlate highly with estimates of how time is spent using more observational methods of daily behavior (Robinson, 1977: 9-21).

Each diary activity reported by respondents was then coded into one of the mutually exclusive and exhaustive 96 categories of activity described in Szalai et al. (1972). Included in these codes are designations for several activities related to the major headings of household production, child care, and shopping, and its associated travel.[2] It is these family care activities that we will examine extensively in this report. "Secondary activity" family care—that is, family care done to the accompaniment of other activities—was recorded but is not included in the present analyses; it amounts to about three hours per week for child care and one hour a week of other family care for women in the present surveys.

Identical procedures had been used in a national survey of time use conducted by the Survey Research Center ten years earlier. However, the sample base in 1965-1966 was restricted to the nonrural population, in places of over 50,000 population, and to persons aged 18-65 in households where at least one person (male or female) was employed in the labor market for over ten hours per week.[3] In order to make cross-time comparisons exact, then, only the diary activities of the 438 female respondents in the 1975 sample who met these qualifications were included for comparison with the 700 female respondents interviewed in the 1965 study. In the analyses which follow, background characteristics (age, employment status, etc.) of respondents that were common to both surveys are examined as predictors of time devoted to family care.

RESULTS

Table 1 shows that women aged 18-65 in urbanized labor-force households reported substantially less family care in the fall 1975 diaries compared to the 1965-1966 diary entries. The per day figure (corrected for different days of the week) in the 1975 diaries was 288.1 minutes compared to 344.6 minutes for the 1965 diaries. Translated to a weekly basis, this would total almost 6.6 fewer hours per week family care in 1975, a 17 percent decline over the decade.

Such a simple comparison, however, obscures the several possible structural explanations for the decline, besides a simple cross-time effect. As noted earlier, women in the 1975 sample were more likely to be in the labor force, to be married, to be young, to have smaller families, to be better educated, to live in rented housing units and so forth. For this reason, it is necessary to analyze whether this decline in family care is simply due to these important structural changes in the composition of the female population.

The higher proportion of 1975 women in the labor market is, of course, the third major variable that needs to be taken into account in explaining the differences from the 1965 figures. Employment status is, moreover, the major predictor of family care (Robinson, 1977: 61-83). Table 1 shows employed women in both 1965 and 1975 reporting just over half of

Table 1   Differences in Women's Family Care Time by
Background Factors (in minutes per day)

(N = 1138)		1965		1975	1965-1975 Difference
	(700)	345	(438)	288	-57
PAID LABOR FORCE					
Employed	(339)	234	(221)	209	-25 min./day
Housewife	(355)	455	(158)	412	-43
Unemployed	(0)	NA	(44)	266	---
Student	(6)	71	(15)	207	+136
ADULTS IN HOUSEHOLD					
One	(114)	215	(122)	240	+25
Two	(492)	380	(263)	320	-60
Three +	(94)	310	(53)	235	-75
AGE					
18-29	(200)	322	(128)	269	-53
30-39	(158)	432	(124)	312	-80
40-49	(173)	338	(75)	334	-4
50-65	(166)	298	(108)	252	-46
RACE					
White	(638)	354	(365)	297	-57
Non-White	(62)	306	(73)	226	-80
MARITAL STATUS					
Married	(531)	387	(268)	333	-54
Widowed	(48)	247	(70)	224	-23
Divorced	(51)	268	(44)	249	-19
Single	(69)	146	(56)	184	+38
CHILDREN					
None	(277)	242	(132)	214	-28
One, over 4 years	(81)	428	(54)	343	-85
One, under 4 years	(36)	319	(25)	249	-70
Two, over 4 years	(146)	408	(81)	336	-72
Two, under 4 years	(80)	459	(50)	393	-66
Three +, over 4 years	(27)	440	(19)	379	-61
Three +, under 4 years	(44)	522	(15)	553	+31

Table 1   Differences in Women's Family Care Time by
Background Factors (in minutes per day) (cont'd)

		1965		1975	1965-1976 Difference
HOME					
Owner	(469)	365	(253)	321	-44
Renter	(209)	306	(147)	262	-44
Both	(17)	258	(8)	183	-75
Not Known	(5)	NA	(30)	164	---
RELIGION					
Catholic	(316)	347	(275)	283	-64
Protestant	(431)	348	(132)	295	-53
Jewish	(40)	308	(10)	351	+43
None/Other	(13)	325	(21)	279	-46
EDUCATION					
Grade School	(83)	365	(44)	259	-106
Some High School	(128)	331	(59)	330	-1
High School Grad	(296)	358	(211)	290	-68
Some College	(102)	330	(74)	272	-58
College Grad	(85)	324	(49)	279	-45
INCOME (1965)					
Under $3000	(74)	279	(62)	242	-37
$3000-5999	(120)	335	(38)	258	-77
$6000-9999	(125)	382	(46)	251	-131
$10,000-14,999	(139)	362	(79)	294	-68
$15,000 +	(226)	341	(165)	327	-14
Refused	(38)	339	(48)	285	-54

NA = No appropriate data collected in 1965.

the family care reported by women not in the paid labor force. None-theless, these analyses also reveal that this employment factor does not greatly affect the basic 1965-1975 differences. As shown in the first two columns of Table 1, employed women in 1975 still report three fewer hours in family care per week than in 1965 and housewives about five fewer hours per week.

The second most important predictor of family care, presence of children, makes a further difference in the results. Women with children under age 18 spend half again as much time on family care as those without children, and twice as much time if there are more than two children in the household, at least one of whom is of preschool age.[4] Data in the first two columns of Table 1 show that women without children in 1975 spent only three fewer hours in family care per week than their 1965 counterparts, but those with children over seven fewer hours a week.

More women in the 1975 sample were divorced, widowed, or single than in 1965 but marital status per se has relatively little influence on the combined 1965-1975 family care times. Married women in 1975 spent about six fewer hours per week on family care than in 1965-1966 but women who were not married spent only about two fewer hours a week.

Women in the 1975 sample were also younger than those in the 1965 sample, and women under age 30 spend less time on family care than those aged 30-65 in both years. Moreover, women under age 30 reported greater (6 hours per week) declines in family care over the decade than did women aged 40-65 (just over 2.5 hours per week).

There is no linear relation between education and family care time, and this factor shows little systematic differential in cross-time differences. Much the same is true for the predictors of number of adults in the household, home ownership, race, and religion.

Finally, there is the important factor of income. Despite the fact that higher income makes individuals more able to afford labor-saving technology and paid outside help (factors not taken into account in the present analysis), income is not systematically related to family care time in either the cross-time differences or the static single-year comparisons. This implicit lack of relation between housework and technology will be examined more directly shortly.

While the 1965-1975 differences in Table 1 do vary for each variable, none of them fully explains nor accounts for the overall decline. What then is the composite effect of all of these third variables on the time women spend on family care in 1975 compared to 1965?

In order to determine the effect of these structural variables, the 1965 and 1975 data sets were combined and entered into a multivariate regression program with family care time as the dependent variable. In addition to the two years of the study, all the Table 1 factors were entered into this regression equation as independent (predictor) variables. Since many of these variables are measured on nominal or categorical scales (e.g., year of study, family composition, race) rather than on ordinal, interval, or ratio scales (like education, age, or income) a dummy-variable regression program had to be employed. The particular regression program applied here was Multiple Classification Analysis (MCA) developed by Andrews et al.

(1969) for analysis of complex survey data sets with predictors on both nominal and higher-scale levels. The MCA program provides estimates of the mean value of a variable for each *category* of each predictor (whether on a categorical, ordinal, or interval scale) rather than a single parameter expressing the extent of linear relation between variables (such as the beta coefficient in traditional multivariate regression programs). In other words, it provides mean values of family care time for each age group, each racial group, each education group, and so on, corrected for the effects of all other factors in the dummy variable regression. The categories of each predictor variable are shown in Table 1.

Based on the MCA results, once the higher employment status, lower marital status, fewer children, youth, higher education, higher income, and the like of the 1975 sample are simultaneously taken into account, women in this latest sample spend 22 fewer minutes of family care per day, or about 2.5 fewer hours per week. This difference is statistically significant at the usual .05 confidence level (t = 2.15, p < .05) and, while not as great a factor as many of the predictor variables in Table 1, it is clearly divergent from the "constancy of housework" phenomenon reported in previous cross-time comparisons. As noted above, it is the corrections for employment, lack of children, and marital status which have the most effect on narrowing the cross-time gap, but the declines are still found within each of these categories of women.

Nor are the differences apparently due to any greater sharing of family responsibilities by the males of the household. Analyses parallel to those in Table 1 for males also reveal a decline (of about 5 percent) in male housework between 1965 and 1975 after other structural factors have been taken into account. Moreover, women's family care time was *higher* in households where husbands also reported more family care time.[5]

SPECIFIC ACTIVITIES AFFECTED

In the preceding analyses, family care has been defined in rather global terms, and it needs to be pointed out that the changes do not apply for all its components. In Table 2, five components of family care are identified and examined separately, again after correction by the various factors in Table 1.

It can be seen that the decline in housework is mainly concentrated in the routine cleaning and maintenance activities that should be affected by technology. Shopping also shows a decline, and there is also a small drop in time spent with children, even after correction on a per child basis. This increase in cooking time after correction stands in marked contrast to the

Table 2   Changes in Components of Family Care (in minutes
per day; before and after correction by MCA)

	1965 (N=700)	1975 (N=438)	Change 1965–75 Uncorrected	Change 1965–75 Corrected
Cooking	71 m/d	66 m/d	-5 m/d	+4 m/d
Cleaning-Dishwashing,				
Chores, Laundry	137	103	-34	-14
Repairs, Gardening				
Bills, Etc.	23	15	-8	-6
Child Care, Including				
Travel	54	51	-3	-2
Shopping, Including				
Travel	60	53	-7	-4
	345 m/d	288 m/d	-57 m/d	-22 m/d

decline in the four other components of housework and indicates that this
activity continues to maintain some intrinsic merit even in the age of the
fast-food restaurant.

THE ROLE OF TECHNOLOGY

The above analyses cannot reflect the factor of technology directly
because no information on appliances in the household was collected in
the 1965 survey. However, such information was collected in the 1975
survey and the time-use comparisons of owners and nonowners should
indicate how significant its impact on family care time has been on a static
basis, once other factors are held constant. For this reason, additional
analyses of the relation between housework time and technology ownership were undertaken on the 1975 data to examine its apparent impact,
using the same set of predictor variables in Table 1.

Table 3   Differences in Women's Housework Time as a
Function of Ownership of Technology (after control by MCA)[a]

TECHNOLOGY (N = 597)		AMOUNT ABOVE OR BELOW MEAN
Microwave Oven	(44)	-10 min./day
Dishwasher	(244)	+1
Washer	(506)	+4
Dryer	(454)	-5
Freezer	(294)	+6
Vacuum Cleaner	(565)	-1
Sewing Machine	(481)	+1
Garbage Disposal	(166)	0

[a]1975 data only—see note 1 for sampling definition.

The results shown in Table 3 update those of Morgan et al. (1966) with more careful measures of time use and a broader range of appliances in use in 1975. In brief, Table 3 shows no systematic tendency for women with household technology to spend less time doing housework. The only appliance for which a clear difference is found is microwave ovens, and even this single largest difference is associated with only a 5 percent decline and is not statistically significant ($t = 1.1$, n.s.) Moreover, the decline holds only for that 5 percent who had this piece of technology in their household. Furthermore, parallel analyses more closely matching the appliance to the task in question (e.g., dishwashers with meal cleanup) do not alter this conclusion. Table 3 then replicates the earlier studies, indicating minimal reductions in housework where household technology is present (Morgan et al., 1966), which should lead to a serious reconsideration of the simple proposition that greater availability of household technology will lead to declines in housework. Moreover, much the same conclusions emerge when the relation between technology and housework are examined for the male portion of this sample.

Nonetheless, the test is static and indirect, and technology needs to be analyzed in the dynamic cross-time context of a Table 1 analysis to be definitive. These results, however, are consistent with those found for the relation between income and family care. Higher-income women do not appear to spend this important resource of money in ways that will bring the time necessary to complete these duties below that required by women with much less money available to spend. Separate analyses of these data do show that income is the major predictor of owning such appliances and having them available in the household; but this may mean that higher-income women simply have or set more ambitious goals for what housework can be accomplished in the time available. As Linder (1970) suggested, the more appliances to take care of, the more time will be required for their upkeep. Higher-income people not only own more appliances, but also live in larger households with a larger stock of household goods to maintain.

SUMMARY AND CONCLUSIONS

Women in a 1975 national study of time use reported doing less housework and other family care than women in a comparable 1965 study. While this is in large part due to several demographic shifts (particularly in employment status and in children to care for) in the status of women over that time period, this difference is still statistically significant after these factors are controlled. This finding departs from previous cross-time studies supporting a historical "constancy of housework" hypothesis.

Consistent with previous cross-time studies, however, little evidence could be found to support the hypothesis that household technology has been responsible for these declines in housework. It may well be that this technology has made it possible for women to take on the housework-reducing role of paid employment, as Stafford and Duncan (1978) suggest, but its direct effect on reducing their housework cannot be demonstrated on the basis of diary records of the housework performed by women (or men) with various pieces of household technology. There is little doubt that an individual housewife *can* save time using a dishwasher or clothes dryer instead of doing these chores by hand. In the long run amid the press of all other household tasks that have to be performed, however, the mere presence of the machines makes little difference in housework time.

There are several plausible explanations for the decline in time devoted to housework that could not be accounted for by this analysis. First, household cleaning activities identified in Table 2, for example, rank near the bottom of activities that women said they enjoyed doing in the 1975 survey, so there is little doubt about the attraction to many women of minimizing time in such unpleasant activities. Moreover, the rated enjoyment for cooking is well above the average for the household production activities, so there is a reassuring correspondence in line with the hypothesis that people will seek to maximize time on activities that they do enjoy, and to minimize time on unenjoyable activities.

Another explanation for the decline is that women's norms for household production and/or cleanliness have relaxed over this decade. In other words, today's woman could find a less tidy household more tolerable than ten years previously. Nonetheless, few women in our 1975 survey expressed dissatisfaction with the internal order of their households and fewer than 10 percent were rated as in serious disarray by the interviewers.

Thus, a more positive alternative explanation is that women have become more efficient in achieving acceptable levels of household "output" with lower investments of time. There is again some semblance of Parkinson's Law in the finding that even after controlling for the various factors that distinguish women in and out of the labor force, employed women are able to complete their housework in less than two-thirds the time required by women who are not employed. Is it the case that they are only able to accomplish two-thirds as much output or that their households are only two-thirds as clean or productive? By their own rating standards in the 1975 study, in fact, they differ little from women not in the labor force in their rated satisfaction with household cleanliness, meal quality, and other "output" (again taking most of the other Table 1 factors into account).

Perhaps the most promising overall result of their decreased housework (along with decreases in the average length of the workweek) is that women in 1975 had almost 20 percent more free time available than they did in 1965. The desire for more free time, of course, provides another plausible nondemographic explanation for the 7 percent decline in housework time.

Given continued declines in the birthrate and increased female participation in the labor market, time devoted to housework (and hence available for leisure) should continue to decline in the future. The increased diffusion of household technology may continue apace. However, the present analysis suggests that the two trends will occur largely independently of one another.

NOTES

1. These data were made up of the first of four waves of data collection with this sample across the year. The diaries in the additional waves were used to construct more stable estimates of time use for individuals, and these expanded data bases are employed in "static" analyses of the 1975 data as in Table 2. The declines in housework were noted in the winter, spring, and summer surveys of 1976, as well as in the fall 1975 survey in comparison to the 1965-1966 data.

2. Family care includes all meal preparation and cleaning; indoor and outdoor cleaning related to household operations; maintenance, repairs, and paper work; all care and attention to children and other adults in the household; all shopping and errands (including for personal care); and all related travel. A complete listing of such activities appears in the Appendix. Other headings of time use in the coding scheme include paid work, personal care (including eating and sleeping), study, organizational participation, social life, active leisure, and passive leisure (including television and other mass media usage). Travel associated with each of these major headings of activities was coded with the related activity—e.g., the job commute was coded with work and the trip to class with study.

3. Thus, the comparisons in Tables 1 and 2 refer to national cross sections of women in urban areas, aged 18-65 in labor-free households. Numbers of employed and nonemployed, married and unmarried, with and without children are, then, roughly proportionate to their percentages in the popualtion in both years. Most of the 1965-1966 interviews were conducted in the fall of 1965, the rest in the early spring of 1966. Only marginal differences were found across these seasons. For this reason, we refer to the study simply as the 1965 data in the later tables and discussions.

4. Not all this greater family care time is spent on child care. Housework also increases for women with children, up to five hours per week if more than three children are in the household. While *number* of children has more effect on this "hard-core" housework, it is the *age* of the children that has more effect on how much time is devoted to child care (Robinson, 1977: 65-75). While it is possible for both women without children and women with older children to have lower family care time, such effects are controlled by the MCA procedure which operates similarly to a multivariate cross-tabulation; MCA does not identify important interaction effects, however.

5. Over this period there was in an increase of 10 percent (from 19 percent to 29 percent) in the proportion of women who said they wanted their husbands to "help with the housework." This indicates mounting attitudinal pressure in the household for men to take a greater share of family responsibilities, which may or may not be successful in the years ahead.

REFERENCES

ANDREWS, F., J. MORGAN, and J. SONQUIST (1969) Multiple Classification Analysis. Ann Arbor, MI: Institute for Social Research.

COFFIN, T. (1955) "Television's impact on society." American Psychologist 10 (October): 630-641.

DeGRAZIA, S. (1962) Of Time, Work and Leisure. New York: Twentieth Century Fund.

JUSTER, T. (forthcoming) Studies in the Measurement of Time Allocation. Ann Arbor, MI: Institute for Social Research.

LINDER, S. (1970) The Harried Leisure Class. New York: Columbia University Press.

MAKLAN, D. (1976) "The four day workweek." Ph.D. dissertation, University of Michigan.

MEISSNER, M. et al. (1975) "No exit for wives: sexual division of labor and the cumulation of household demands." Canadian Review of Sociology and Anthropology 12: 424-439.

MORGAN, J., I. SIRAGELDIN, and N. BAERWALDT (1966) Productive Americans. Ann Arbor, MI: Institute for Social Research.

OWEN, J. (1976) "Workweeks and leisure: an analysis of trends, 1948-1975." Monthly Labor Review (April): 3-8.

ROBINSON, J. (1977) How Americans Use Time. New York: Praeger.

———— P. CONVERSE, and A. SZALAI (1972) "Everyday life in the twelve countries," in A. Szalai et al. The Use of Time. The Hague: Mouton.

STAFFORD, F. and G. DUNCAN (1978) "The use of time and technology by households in the United States." University of Michigan, Department of Economics, Ann Arbor. (unpublished)

SWADOS, H. (1958) "Less work—less leisure." Nation 22 (February): 155-160.

SZALAI, A. et al. (1972) The Use of Time. The Hague: Mouton.

U.S. Bureau of the Census (1978) Statistical Abstract of the United States. Washington, D.C.: Government Printing Office.

VANEK, J. (1974) "Time spent in housework." Scientific American (November): 116-120.

WALKER, K. (1969) "Homemaking still takes time." Journal of Home Economics 61 (October): 621-624.

WEISS, W. (1969) "Effects of the mass media on communication," pp. 77-195 in G. Lindsay and E. Aronson (eds.) The Handbook of Social Psychology, Vol. 5. San Francisco: Chandler.

WILENSKY, H. (1961) "The uneven distribution of leisure: the impact of economic growth of free time." Social Problems 9 (Summer): 32-56.

Appendix   Activities Coded as Family Care

HOUSEWORK (Code activities of household maids, etc. under WORK)

    109) Preparing and cooking food (for babies code 209)

    119) Doing dishes, cleaning up after meals

    129) Indoor cleaning (sweeping, washing, bedmaking)

    139) Outdoor cleaning (sidewalk, garbage)

    149) Laundry, ironing

    159) Mending or upkeep of clothing, shoes

    169) Other repairs and home operations (snow removal, painting)

    179) Gardening, animal care

    189) Upkeep of heat and water supplies

    199) Other (household bills, paperwork, etc.)

CHILD CARE

    209) All baby care (under 5 years) -- including meals

    219) Care to older children (over 5 years) -- dressing, general supervision,
          getting up

    229) Helping with or supervising schoolwork

    23*) Reading stories to or talking with children (under 19 years old)

    249) Indoor games or manual instruction

    259) Outdoor games or walks

    269) Medical care (doctor's visits, giving medicine, etc.)

    279) Other child care (e.g. babysitting for someone else, unless codable
          above)

    289) ---

    29*) Trips (including waiting time) related to child care

SHOPPING AND PURCHASING

    30*) Everyday goods and products (food, clothing, etc.)

    31*) Durable goods (cars, appliances, hardware, etc.)

    329) Personal care outside home (barbers, masseurs, etc.)

    339) Medical and dental care outside home

    34*) Government services (post office, civic fees, licenses, etc.)

    35*) Repair and cleaning services (car, laundry, appliances, etc.)

    36*) Waiting for the purchase of goods and services

    37*) Other and professional services (caterer, lawyer, etc.)

    389) ---

    39*) Trips (including waiting time) related to shopping

3

SOCIAL STATUS OF THE HOMEMAKER

CHRISTINE BOSE

Over the last several years stratification studies of women's economic role have focused on the previously ignored occupation of housewife. Yet there is still much disagreement on both the components of the homemaker job and the function this job has in the larger stratification system. Resolution of these questions is important for social mobility studies as well as in occupational studies of this most widely held American job.

This study facilitates both goals by developing a single social status score for the homemaker role, comparing this status to that of other occupational alternatives, and by examining attitudes of several demographic groupings toward the job.

PREVIOUS RESEARCH

In order to accurately understand the status of women, researchers have found that a comparison base is necessary. Thus several early debates began around the relative social mobility of women and men (DeJong et al., 1971; Havens and Tully, 1972; Treiman and Terrell, 1975; Tyree and

AUTHOR'S NOTE: The research reported here was conducted under U.S. Department of Labor, Manpower Administration, Research and Development Grant 91-24-72-44. This chapter is a revision of an earlier paper presented at the 1976 annual meeting of the American Sociological Association in New York. I would like to thank Michael Ornstein, Peter H. Rossi, and other colleagues who read and gave comments on this and previous versions of the chapter.

Treas, 1974). However, most of these studies assumed that the only way in which status was obtained was through a paid labor-force job. "Time out" from the labor force was viewed as a gap in status-gaining roles which caused methodological and measurement problems for mobility studies. While a solution to a male military service gap was found, no one has tried to develop a means of solving the female home-service gap. This is complicated by the fact that many homemakers also have paying jobs. To date, instead of independently measuring the status of housewives, it is often assumed that their status comes solely from their husband's job (Glenn et al., 1974). Authors forget that other kinds of power bases—stocks and bonds, political position, personal strength, or non-labor-force work—contribute to social standing. So it is with the millions of American housewives and thousands of male homemakers whose contributions to the economy at large are often forgotten, never counted in the gross national product, and rarely considered in studies of women's (or men's) social standing.

Several researchers have examined the role attributes of the housewife. Yet there is still much disagreement on how people view the housework role. Helena Lopata (1971) found that women see the role as "*only* a housewife," while Mirra Komarovsky (1962: 49) found that blue-collar women's attitudes toward the role were not so negative.

> We find little evidence of status frustrations among working class wives. They accept housewifery. There is hardly a trace in the interviews of the low prestige educated housewives sometimes attach to their role. . . . This is not to say that [working class] women are all satisfied homemakers. But their discontent is not caused by the low evaluation they place upon domesticity, stemming rather from other frustrations of housewifery.

Ferree (1976) agreed with Komarovsky that working-class housewives were somewhat happier than middle-class housewives, but disagreed with the thesis that working-class women preferred housework to paid work. She found that full-time housewives were more dissatisfied with the way they were spending their lives than either part-time or full-time employed wives. Low self-esteem was associated with housework, and the role was found to be socially isolating and powerless. Vanek's (1976) conclusions were compatible with these results. She found that most wives were satisfied with housework, but that the satisfaction of those with waged jobs was higher than that of those doing full-time housework.

However, in terms of status, Ann Oakley (1974: 70-78) concluded that both working- and middle-class wives generally perceive the housewife's standing to be low. This class convergence was also suggested by Vanek

(1977) who felt the limited existing data indicated that housewives' perceptions of their work were concurring and that status differences in homemaker role content were narrowing. The theory was also implicit in Glazer's (1976) work, which concluded that the primarily social service role of housewife defined women's caste status.

Each of the previous studies gave some sense of what the homemaker's status might be, but none of them had concrete measures of the role's status. Housewife status was first rated when Clara Menger (1932) had a sample of students rank 35 jobs in which women were usually employed. Homemaker ranked at sixteenth place, but there was great disagreement as to its status, since men rated it high and women rated it low. While these results foreshadow later ones, no author knew how housewife would compare with a random sample of all jobs. More recently, Arnott and Bengtson (1970) found faculty wives ranked homemaker in the middle of twenty job options. Similarly Eichler (1976) found housewife was ranked fifty-second out of 93 randomly selected jobs by 180 randomly selected respondents.

In a 1973 study, Bose was able to develop a numerical prestige score for the occupations of housewife and househusband as they would compare to scores for a sample of 108 other occupations. Both the homemaker and labor force jobs were rated by an economically stratified population sample of men and women. Jobs were rated with no incumbent, male incumbents only, female incumbents only, and in a mixed-sex incumbent format. The first treatment, which was most similar to previous National Opinion Research Center prestige studies, resulted in a housewife prestige score of 51 (on a 0 to 100 point scale). The latter treatment provided a direct comparison of the housewife role with other potential labor force jobs which incumbent men and women held. In this treatment, probably most useful for mobility studies, housewife was rated 44. Bose compared housewife status with that of women's traditional labor force jobs, with its other status equivalents, and projected its deserved income from prestige.

Nilson (1978) performed a similar analysis using only 17 occupations and treatments similar to Bose's female incumbent only and male incumbent only formats. In the former treatment, the resulting housewife prestige score was a rather high 70 points. Much of the analysis was devoted to disaggregating rater characteristics which explain variation around the housewife score. Innovatively, Nilson also had respondents rate the general social standing of seven housewives, each of whom was presented as being married to a man in a different occupation. She found that husband's occupation influenced wife's prestige, and that controlling on husband's occupation reduced the variance in housewife prestige.

In sum early social mobility research ignored housewifery as a separate occupational role, later studies showed respondent disagreement on home-maker status, and only a few recent studies have developed concrete measures of housewife prestige. Social mobility studies require more than this. A single prestige score for homemaker, knowledge of how it compares with other roles, and background on the variation in attitude toward it by social subgroups are essential. The research reported below provides these data through an extension of the previous work by Bose (1976), which includes additional analyses suggested by the work of Nilson and others. In particular, the variation in prestige accorded the housewife is examined, and the effects of rater characteristics are explored.

RESEARCH DESIGN

The study, carried out in late 1972, used an experimentally designed survey methodology with a vignette card sort task. Each of the 99 women and 98 men in a Baltimore household sample was presented with a set of IBM type cards. A description or vignette of a hypothetical individual was printed on each card. In the rating task, respondents were asked to place each card in a box having nine slots according to the "social standing accorded to people described" as in the vignette. The slots were labeled from "1" (lowest standing) to "9" (highest standing). Roughly 97 percent of the respondents believed that such a ladder of social standing exists and proceeded to sort the cards in the set. Respondents were free to bring any preconceptions they had about status to this task.

Each respondent was given 110 different vignettes where each vignette represented a separate occupation with either a male incumbent, a female incumbent or with no incumbent designated. Every respondent received the same set of occupations. This set was selected to represent the distribution of men and women in the labor force. Fifty occupations were chosen in proportion to the distribution of men across all detailed census occupations in 1960 and fifty were chosen in proportion to the distribu-tion of women in the 1960 detailed occupations. Eight other occupations were added to the rated sample in order to include high-status jobs which tend to be fewer in number and thus not represented in a proportional distribution. Finally, two roles indicating nonparticipation in the paid labor force were included. The first was Person Living on Welfare, and the second and most interesting was Housewife/Househusband (the latter depending upon the sex of incumbent). Although it was not chosen to represent the distribution of jobs according to its percentage of women, the set of jobs also approximated this type of sample. Obviously, home-maker was at the top of this distribution with nearly 100 percent of its usual incumbents being women. The average percentage of women in the 108 labor force jobs was 37.7 percent, exactly equal to the distribution of women in the 1970 paid work force. On the whole, this occupational sample was advantageous because it allowed a comparison of the home-maker role to a set of fifty largely female occupations, fifty largely male occupations, and eight high-status jobs.[1]

The sex of the actual incumbent in the job was designated with the first and last name of a hypothetical person whose sex was clearly indicated by that name. There are considerable data which show that different sex names are a salient stimulus to use as an indicator of sex (Fidell, 1970). The names were chosen randomly, including primarily Anglo-Saxon sound-ing names and excluding those appearing to have other ethnic connota-tions. The names were used in order to prevent boredom on the part of respondents who would otherwise have to read "female [box packer]," "female [judge]," etc. 110 times. No one name consistently appeared with a given occupation in any of the respondent decks, the names being randomly assigned to an occupation. No one name appeared twice to the same respondent since 110 different names were chosen.

The vignettes were presented in four different experimental treatments according to the sex of the incumbent in the job. One treatment, with no incumbent, was used as a base to see the effect of adding an incumbent, regardless of sex. The next two treatments presented either all female incumbents or all male incumbents. The fourth treatment presented occu-pations with half having female incumbents and the other half having male incumbents.

The first and fourth treatments were most interesting in analyzing the homemaker's status. The four treatments controlled on the effects of the sex of an incumbent and on the overall base of comparison of persons to either men or women. The combination of the four treatments with the two possible values of respondent's sex defined an experimental design with ten cells.[2] Thus the ideal sample size was 200 cases. The actual sample was 197 (99 women and 98 men).

Because occupational prestige scores had proven in past studies to be invariant over major population subgroups (Hodge et al., 1965), it seemed justifiable to use a smaller area sample to generate the scores. Thus, the study relied on a sample drawn from the Baltimore metropolitan area. To ensure the experimental design an equal number of ratings by all types of respondents on each type of vignette was needed. This was accomplished using block quota interviewing, with quotas based on respondent's sex.

Blocks were chosen in proportion to the 1970 income distribution of city census tracts to obtain an economic cross section of participants. Only census tracts with 90 percent or more white population were used in order to reduce interviewing costs.[3]

Once all the cards were rated, the score given each vignette was converted into the standard prestige metric of 0 (low) to 100 (high) using the equation:

$$PRESTIGE = 12.5 (RANK - 1)$$

where RANK is the one through nine rating given to each occupational vignette by a respondent. Occupational prestige is later calculated by finding the mean prestige given a job by all respondents within a given treatment.[4]

STATUS OF HOMEMAKING

Using this design a concrete prestige score can be given to homemaking and its status compared to a wide variety of jobs.

In the no incumbent treatment, where respondents were comparing housewife or househusband with other jobs, the average job was rated at 45. However, respondents rated housewife at 51 on the scale and househusband at 15. The low ranking of the househusband was not unexpected, since the role lacks cultural legitimacy. In fact, such men are so rare that there was no real term for male homemakers, and it was defined for respondents as "someone who keeps house while (his) wife works."

On the other hand, a rating of 51 for housewife at first seemed fairly high, given that an employed housekeeper rated only 25 points. Even though this score (51) was near that of an average job, previous research would lead one to expect a lower evaluation of housewives—an evaluation that would approximate that of a housekeeper. Yet in the past there were no or few job opportunities for women (particularly married women) in the labor force. The higher status of a housewife could be viewed as a substitute reward for staying at home. Although women received no cash wages for their labor in the home, they did receive large amounts of status for staying out of the "rat race" and not competing with men. Ehrenreich and English (1975) stressed that women themselves, at the turn of the century, tried to improve the status of the housewife and to profession-alize the role. The domestic science movement of the period sought to develop an appreciation of the volume of scientific knowledge (such as the germ theory of disease) that was necessary to be a competent homemaker. To a certain extent men accepted this movement, for it channeled the drive for women's access to higher education into the traditional field of home economics, and thus back into the home itself. The rating may also be due to differentially weighting some higher status components of housework, such as child rearing, over other lower-status components, such as scrubbing floors. Thus, the housewife role might be given extra moral status because of its frequent motherhood element.

There was not consensus, however, on the housewife's prestige. When measured across all treatments and respondents, housewife had a variance of 1018 while most occupational variance was in the 300-500 range. The second largest variance (876) was for the artist role, and another dozen occupations fell into the 600 range, including coal miner, and then farmer, househusband, landscape gardener, social worker, and sociologist. The latter group fell at all levels of the prestige scale, so that the lack of consensus on its status could not be attributed to merely falling in the middle where more variation was possible.

The dispersion appeared to be related to confusion over the content of these occupations, making it difficult to place them on a prestige scale. Each of the nine slots in the rating box was used by some respondents in rating the housewife. The modal response was slot 5, but slots 1, 5, 6, 7, and 9 all received ten or more votes and included 71 percent of the respondents. In the absence of further information about the housewife's own education or her spouse's occupation, respondents may have been saying "phooey" (slot 1), "average" (slots 5, 6, 7), or "great" (slot 9). The 51-point rating does not appear to be the result of respondents averaging all possible husband's jobs and attributing this "average spouse" to the wife. Instead, there appears to be substantive disagreement about how to rate housewife and implicitly about which elements of that work role are salient for prestige ratings. Some of this difference in perspective could be accounted for by rater characteristics, as we will see later. For the moment, this chapter will focus on the average (no incumbent) prestige score of housewife and compare it with other occupations.

STATUS EQUIVALENTS OF THE HOMEMAKER ROLE

Housework is work which deserves to be rewarded for its own sake, and not just for keeping women out of the paid labor force. The position minimally involves being a housekeeper, maid, laundress, cook, waitress, practical nurse, elementary school teacher, seamstress, chauffeur, administrative assistant, and so on. These tasks are repeated seven days a week, often for more than eight hours per day, and can include over seventy discrete tasks per day.

One way to determine housewife's prestige might be to compare it with its labor force equivalent. "Housekeeper" alone does not define all of the comparable labor force roles. Housekeeping activities such as cleaning and laundering are involved in housework, but cooking, shopping, caring for children, nursing, and administrative skills are also included. Other aspects, such as straightening up or nurturing have no labor market equivalent. Thus, the housewife role is greater than the sum of its market-defined parts. One can only find a rough labor market equivalent of the role. One way to do so was to select the labor force occupations in this study which best approximate a housewife's role and find the average (no incumbent) status of these jobs. The 15 jobs chosen for this procedure (Table 1) gave us an approximation of what a housewife's status might be were it considered a labor force job. The resulting average was 35 points—16 points fewer than the housewife gets. Are these 16 points a bonus to women for staying out of the labor force? Is this a bonus to women for bearing children, which even male househusbands cannot achieve? Or is the housewife obtaining more status than one would expect?

These may be the wrong questions to ask. More important is that she was and is grossly unrewarded for the significance of the work she does. Recent insurance estimates indicate that a full-time housewife and mother works 100 hours per week. At a minimum wage of $2.80 an hour, the housewife deserves $14,560 per year. Even taking the lower estimates made of the housewife's work week as 55 hours (Vanek, 1974), an $8,008 annual income would be earned.

Another way to approach the question of economic value is to explore the income and educational components of social standing. Blau and Duncan (1967) found that prestige scores, such as the no incumbent ones described here, were related to male education and income by the equation:

$$\text{PRESTIGE} = .59\,X_2 + .55\,X_3 - 6.0$$

where X_2 is the percentage of men in a job with greater than $3,000 earnings per year and X_3 is the percentage of men with a high school diploma or more education. Using this equation for female homemakers, we substituted for X_3 the 52.3% of all working women who had at least four years of high school education and replaced X_2 with the $0.00 earnings of housewives. The result was the low status of 23 prestige points. Substituting, instead, for X_3, assuming a status of 51 points for housewife, and then solving for X_2, we found that 48 percent of all housewives

Table 1   Average Status of Jobs (no incumbent) Roughly
Approximating Duties of a Homemaker

Occupation	Prestige
Boardinghousekeeper	24
Housekeeper	25
Maid	12
Laundry Worker	15
Textile Machine Operator (e.g., Seamstress)	28
Short Order Cook	22
Pastry Chef	39
Waitress	22
Hairdresser	39
Delivery Truck Driver (An approximation of Chauffeur)	27
Babysitter	18
Grade School Teacher	65
Social Worker	63
Practical Nurse	56
Administrative Assistant	68
Average of Above Occupations	35

should be earning more than $3,000 per year. These projected earnings are close to, but below, the current claims of pay due housewives. Note that they were based on conversion factors for *men* of income and education into prestige.[5] Nonetheless, the female homemakers did receive more

Table 2   Women's Occupations with Prestige (no incumbent)
Higher Than Housewife or 51

Occupation	Prestige
Office Secretary	51
Inspector in a Manufacturing Plant	51
Stenographer	53
Dental Assistant	55
Practical Nurse	56
Floor Supervisor in a Hospital	60
Private Secretary	61
Hospital Lab Technician	63
Social Worker	63
Hotel Manager	64
Grade School Teacher	65
Administrative Assistant	68
High School Teacher	70
Registered Nurse	75

status than those holding equivalent labor force roles and less pay than
those with equivalent status.

STATUS ALTERNATIVES TO THE HOMEMAKER ROLE

The disagreements among researchers on the status of the housewife
may stem not from a variation in the perceived status of housewife, but
from the variation in the other status options available to women. Table 2
presents a listing of women's occupations with higher (no incumbent)
prestige than that of housewife. In this case, all 108 jobs were reclassified

in order to redefine women's occupations as those in the job sample with more than 38 percent women normally holding them. Since this was the percentage of women in the 1970 labor force, any job with greater than this percentage had more women job holders than one would expect if workers were randomly distributed across all jobs.

The 51 status points of a housewife may be close to the average rating of all jobs, but it is quite high as compared to the status of jobs that most women enter. Women are rarely in the high-status jobs of lawyer, doctor, and congressional representative. As shown in Table 2, the highest-ranking women's job was registered nurse at 75 points. In fact only 30 percent of the women's jobs ranked higher than housewife. To obtain status higher than housewife, women can go into any of the traditional female fields of secretary, nurse, teacher, lab technician, or social worker. Or they must try to fight opposition in a male job. All these jobs require a good deal of training and the money available to spend on education. Not all families can afford to supply this training. So the housewife status could be an attractive alternative to women who cannot afford the educational investment. This explains why working-class women accept the housewife status, as described by Komarovsky (1962). Blue-collar wives may feel trapped or bored with the housewife tasks, but they do value the role. This makes sense for two reasons. First, the cleaning, shopping, and other household tasks they perform are not very different from the manual tasks their spouses do at work. Second, without further education, they could not obtain a job with higher status than that of housewife. Thus, the housewife's status, near an average job, is attractive to working-class women.

Middle-class college-educated women or women who have held professional jobs at one time, such as those described by Lopata (1971) and by Oakley (1974), would feel housewife status to be a low one, even at an average of 51 points. Their perspective on the same homemaker role is different because they have the education which gives them access to higher-status positions in the labor force. If they want to have the most status possible, they should be in the labor force and not in the home. So it should be no surprise that middle-class women report dissatisfaction with the housewife role. This tendency is not reflected, however, in a depression of the actual prestige score attributed to housewife. In fact, those respondents ranking housewife in the mid to upper levels were those from higher-prestige families. (Families with prestige of less than 42 rated housewife at an average of 41 and variance of 1193; families with prestige greater than or equal to 42 rated housewives at 59 with variance of 635.) Therefore we are sure that middle-class women are looking down on housewifery only as it compares with their other role options. In fact, even at 59 points, housewife looks better than many more labor force options than it did at 51 points.

Only 25 percent of women in traditional women's jobs have higher status than a housewife. Why do so many women choose jobs having lower status than housewife? There are several answers. First, and most obvious, is that status is not the major motivation in making decisions. Women often work to provide needed income for a family. Sixty percent of women who work are single, widowed, divorced, or have spouses whose income is inadequate to support a family. Second, education level predicts when women will enter the labor force, with those having higher education being more likely to use it. Third, although there are intrinsic rewards as well as status bonuses for a housewife, worth in our society is primarily defined by economic gain. There are no direct economic gains paid to a housewife unless she enters the labor force. An outside job also allows women to meet more people and to have a greater variety of tasks to perform. Once children are in school there is less to occupy one's time in the home. Then the labor force becomes an attractive alternative, regardless of the job. Thus, working-class and single women are likely to work for money and middle-class women to work to use their educational training. Both groups are more likely to seek employment if previously employed themselves or if their mothers held paying jobs. Both groups work for job satisfaction and to reduce social isolation.

Interestingly, men do not have the slight status alternatives that women have. Househusband, the equivalent of housewife for men, received fifteen status points. The only male jobs falling below this level in our sample were rag picker (five points), parking lot attendant (eight points), bellhop (eleven points), and janitor (twelve points). The predominant ideology stresses that all men should work in the labor force unless physically incapable of doing so. The homemaker position is allotted to millions of women capable of paid employment. Yet, if a man is a homemaker, it is assumed that he could and should be holding a paid position and that he is shirking his duties. He therefore is not given much status for being a househusband. In order to obtain either income or status men must be in the labor force.

EFFECTS OF RESPONDENT CHARACTERISTICS

Since the roles of housewife and househusband (sex of role incumbent) were so differently evaluated, the obvious next step was to ascertain if the sex of the respondent affected the rating given to the homemaker role.

Table 3   Mean Score of the Homemaker Roles by Sex of
Respondent for No Incumbent Treatment (n = 10 per cell)

| | Sex of Respondent | |
	Female	Male
Housewife	61	41
Househusband	14	15

Table 3 indicates that there were significant effects caused by the sex of the rater. These differences for the housewife were much larger than those found for any other job, while there was almost no fluctuation in the status of the househusband.

The 51.0 average score for housewives was caused by a high rating given to the role by women and a rather low rating given by men. While a definite interpretation of this result was not allowed by our data, it can be hypothesized that when no incumbents were present, women were able to bring non-labor-force considerations to their ratings of the housewife role. For example, they may have included the positive cultural aspects of motherhood. In this treatment, women were not clearly presented in other jobs, and the positive rewards of the home were perhaps not brought into direct comparison with the economic rewards of the job market.

Other treatments help to test this thesis. In the treatment where every job was presented with a female incumbent, women respondents dropped their rating of the housewife by 10 points to 51. In the fourth treatment in which half the incumbents were male and half were female, women's ratings of the role dropped another 14 points to 37. At the same time, men raised their estimation of the role to 50.0, as can be seen in Table 4. Apparently, women rated housewives highly in the abstract situation, but when forced to compare homemaking to a mixed-sex labor force in which they would have a myriad of job options, women then dropped their rating of the role to 37. This score was roughly the same as the status of 35 obtained by averaging the labor force components of homemaking. The contextual effect was extremely important in determining the status women accord housewives. It was primarily the women's change in perceptions that caused the drop in housewife's status between the no incumbent and mixed incumbent treatments. In fact male respondents prevented the score of housewife from dropping much below the mean of all occupations

Table 4   Mean Score of the Homemaker Roles by Sex of
Respondent for Mixed-Sex Incumbent Treatment (n = 20 per cell)

| | Sex of Respondent | |
	Female	Male
Housewife	37	50
Househusband	26	22

in the mixed incumbent treatment. This mixed incumbent finding is similar to earlier research such as that of Clara Menger (1932), who discovered that although housewife ranked in the middle of her occupational sample, there was great disagreement as to the status of the role, with men rating it high and women rating it low.

For the purposes of mobility studies, the mixed-sex treatment probably presents the most accurate picture in which the housewife role is compared as a job to paid labor force roles. In this case the average score assigned by men and women is 44, with men slightly overrating the job and women underrating it. However, the low rating given by women does seem to reflect accurately the lower status of housewifely tasks when performed for pay. In this treatment, the status of househusband was fairly stable, but was slightly higher than in the no incumbent situation. It appeared still to maintain an element of social opprobrium, but began to approximate the composite labor force homemaker score of 35.

Although respondent's sex clearly influenced the rating given to housewives, multivariate analyses resulted in the disappearance of its effects when controlling for other related variables. Regressing housewife prestige ratings given by respondents of both sexes on their demographic and attitudinal attributes, only age and status of household head contributed significantly at a .05 F-test level. Older respondents and those households headed by high-prestige occupation holders appeared to rate housewives higher. Although not statistically significant, housewives and those with high education also valued the role. As noted above, the mixed incumbent context lowered housewife prestige. But, surprisingly, married persons rated housewife fully 11 points lower than nonmarrieds.

The exact effects of household head's status are difficult to decipher. As indicated above, ratings of housewife tended to clump around the two

Table 5 Regression of Housewife Rating on Respondent Characteristics (n = 97)

Variable	Unstandardized Coefficient	Beta
Age	.52	.28*
Household Status[a]	.51	.25*
Marital Status[b]	−11.51	−.17
Treatment 4 [c]	− 7.35	−.11
Years of Education	1.05	.13
Housewife [d]	5.92	.09
Intercept	2.69	

R^2 = .20
* = significant at .05 or better

a. Prestige of head of household
b. Coded 1—married, 0—single, separated/divorced, widowed
c. Dummy variable for effect of mixed incumbent treatment where 1—mixed treatment, 0—all other treatments
d. Response to question, "Are you working?" coded 1—full-time housewife, 0—all others

ends and the upper middle of the prestige scale. Those people ranking housewife low tended to be of low status themselves, and those rating housewife higher tended to have higher occupational standing. However, a distribution of average household status according to attributed housewife rank showed the relationship not to be directly linear. Lower-status respondents showed the most confusion or dispersion in their judgment. As indicated earlier, if we divide the sample at its mean status of 42.5, we find that household heads with less status rate housewife at 41 with variance of 1193, while household heads with greater status give the role 59 points with variance of 635. Thus middle-class people rated housewife high and working-class people tended to rate housewife low, but some also rated it high as well. Nilson suggested that the role may be a luxury in a time when most families need two incomes, and thus it was rated high. Full-time housewifery will be more of a luxury for working-class people who seem to be torn between rating a working-class housewife as low as her comparable labor force options and rating her high since she represents such a luxury. Thus, Nilson's analysis seems to explain lower-class respondents' variance in housewife status.

Since some of the variables in Table 5, such as housewife status, varied with sex, separate regression analyses for male and female respondents were performed. For men, only age significantly affects ranking of housewife. The prestige of their own jobs, marital status, and education all have no effect. For women, having a current or past job is the most important predictor of the housewife's score. In these circumstances the score dramatically drops 41 points. Years of education, household head's status, age, and marital status proved insignificant for women, though married women still tended to rate housewifery low. Further analyses showed that while absolute prestige level of a woman's labor force job did not affect her ratings of the housewife role, it was more important than level of spouse's prestige.

Thus, while both age and occupational considerations are important in the overall rating process, there are sex differences in their relevance. For women, respondent characteristics explained more of the variance than did comparable variables for men (35 percent vs. 18 percent).

In summary, women who have held labor force jobs are greatly affected by employment experience, no matter what the status, and thus rate the housewife role lower than those who have remained at home. However, the higher the status of the job held (or the higher class background a women has), the more positively she will see housewifery. Nonmarried women and housewives themselves did rate the role high.

CONCLUSIONS

A single numerical social prestige score has been assigned to the roles of househusband and housewife through this research. In general, the score of 51 out of 100 prestige points can be assigned to the housewife; and for purposes of comparison with labor force roles (such as for social mobility studies) the score of 44 seems appropriate, as derived from the fourth treatment rating situation. Similarly, househusband may be assigned a score of 15 or of 24.

Exactly how a woman views this role depends on her other job options and need for income, such that the status of housewife is higher than most working-class women's jobs, but lower than most middle-class women's jobs. So the former are likely to be satisfied with the role and the latter to be dissatisfied. Further, those who have been in the paid labor force are likely to be so dissatisfied as to lower their ratings of housewife. Although status maximization is not a major motivation for everyone, it does influence decisions and perceptions of one's options. Exactly how men view the role depends primarily on their age.

A housewife's status is higher than recent writers would lead us to expect and certainly is higher than labor force equivalent jobs such as housekeeper. This positive tradeoff can act as an incentive for women not to compete for scarce labor force occupations or as a reward for a household not needing a second wage earner, while the low status of a house-husband can force him to enter the labor force to gain either prestige or income. Women do achieve more status than one would expect, perhaps because of childrearing, but they also receive no income for their roles. Thus, they gain status in compensation for the loss in income. Whether or not the status gain is actually given for motherhood is a task for future research. This hypothesis could be tested by analyzing the variance in prestige received by housewives with various numbers and ages of children.

The status of a housewife is high, but few women achieve higher status when entering the labor force, especially since the prestige range of women's occupations is limited. Thus, the social status of homemaker is a stick to men and a carrot to women. It can cut competition for a limited number of jobs and can help obtain much work in the home needed for society, without having to pay for it.

Certainly homemaking is work, but the contextual effects of the work help determine exactly what status it is accorded. For example, when it is compared to a labor force job, its status drops. The status of the home-maker could change. If many of a housewife's tasks (such as laundry, food preparation, or child care) were taken over by others in the paid labor force, leaving primarily consumption and nurturing work in the home, it seems likely that the status of housework would drop. Although consumption and family support are important to the U.S. economy, they are not recognized as complex and productive work. If a household's tasks were actually shared among its members, the housewife/husband role might disappear. However, lack of any real change in recent household division of labor makes this unlikely. As real wages decline in the United States, an increasing number of women are entering paid work while continuing to do housework. Therefore, it seems reasonable to expect that there will indeed be an increasing class convergence in how housework is viewed. Future research can also be anticipated to determine if the status of part-time housework, when combined with paid work, may be lower in prestige than full-time housewifery.

NOTES

1. When occupations are drawn in proportion to the distribution of women (or men) in them, those occupations with more women (or men) have a greater likeli-

hood of being included in the sample, while those occupations with only a few women (or men) have a lower probability of being included. Nonetheless, at a low probability, it is possible for a job with few women (or men) to be drawn for the sample of female (male) jobs. Therefore the jobs are only largely female or largely male. However, the advantage is that the total sample of 100 jobs will represent the way in which women and men are distributed throughout all occupations. The eight additional high-status jobs added were College Professor, Architect, Physician, Lawyer, Stockbroker, Manager of a Supermarket, Manager of a Factory Employing 2000 People and Owner of a Factory Employing 2000 People.

2. Five treatments exist when one counts men in the mixed-incumbent situation and women in the mixed-incumbent situation as two separate treatments.

3. Funds were not sufficient to double the sample size in order to include a black population subsample. We hope to extend this analysis in the future to black and ethnic respondents and incumbents.

4. The figure 12.5 is a constant allowing one to expand the 0-9 scale to a 0-100 scale. For example, if a respondent rated Lawyer at 7, the prestige score would be $12.5(7 - 1) = 75.0$. If a second respondent gave Lawyer the top status of 9, the prestige score would be $12.5(9 - 1) = 100.0$. The average occupational prestige for Lawyer, across these two respondents, would be 87.5.

5. This basis assumes that women earn prestige from their incomes and education in the same way that men do. This assumption is probably false, especially because of the low variance in women's income. It does, however, give housewives all the advantages of men in the paid labor force. If we use the prestige scores of all 108 labor force occupations in the mixed incumbent treatment (for female incumbents) to develop a new equation usable for women, we find this relationship:

PRESTIGE of JOB = 5.54 x (Median Education of Women in Job)
+ .0048 x (Median Income of Women in Job) - 34.4.

Substituting the mixed incumbent treatment housewife prestige of 44, we find that the housewife's income should be a median of $2292 (1960). Given current inflation the 1970 figure would probably fall between $3000 and $4000.

REFERENCES

ARNOTT, C. and V. BENGTSON (1970) " 'Only a homemaker': distributive justice and role choice among married women." Sociology and Social Research 54, 4: 495-507.

BLAU, P. and O. D. DUNCAN (1967) The American Occupational Structure. New York: John Wiley.

BOSE, C. (1973) Jobs and Gender. Baltimore: Johns Hopkins University Center for Metropolitan Planning and Research.

----- (1976) "Social status of the homemaker." Presented at the annual meeting of the American Sociological Association, New York, August.

DeJONG, P. Y., M. J. BRAWER, and S. S. ROBIN (1971) "Patterns of female intergenerational occupational mobility: a comparison with male patterns of intergenerational occupational mobility." American Sociological Review 36, 6: 1033-1042.

EHRENREICH, B. and D. ENGLISH (1975) "The manufacture of housework." Socialist Revolution 5, 4:5-40.

EICHLER, M. (1976) "The prestige of the occupation housewife." Presented at the Symposium on 'The Working Sexes,' University of British Columbia, Vancouver.

FERREE, M. M. (1976) "Working-class jobs: housework and paid work as sources of satisfaction." Social Problems 23 (April): 431-441.

FIDELL, L. S. (1970) "Empirical verification of sex discrimination in hiring practices in psychology." American Psychologist 25, 12: 1094-1098.

GLAZER, N. (1976) "The caste position of women: housewifery." Presented at annual meeting of the American Sociological Association, New York, September.

GLENN, N., A. ROSS, and J. C. TULLY (1974) "Patterns of intergenerational mobility of females through marriage." American Sociological Review 39, 5: 683-699.

HAVENS, E. M. and J. C. TULLY (1972) "Female intergenerational occupational mobility: comparisons of patterns?" American Sociological Review 37, 6: 774-777.

HODGE, W., P. SIEGEL, and P. H. ROSSI (1965) "Occupational prestige in the United States: 1925-1963." American Journal of Sociology 20 (November): 286-302.

KOMAROVSKY, M. (1962) Blue-Collar Marriage. New York: Random House.

LOPATA, H. Z. (1971) Occupation: Housewife. New York: Oxford University Press.

MENGER, C. (1932) "The social status of occupations for women." Teachers College Record 33: 696-704.

NILSON, L. B. (1978) "The social standing of a housewife." Journal of Marriage and the Family 40, 3: 541-548.

OAKLEY, A. (1974) The Sociology of Housework. New York: Pantheon.

TREIMAN, D. J. and K. TERRELL (1975) "Sex and the process of status attainment: a comparison of working women and men." American Sociological Review 40, 2: 174-200.

TYREE, A. and J. TREAS (1974) "The occupational and marital mobility of women." American Sociological Review 39, 3: 293-307.

VANEK, J. (1974) "Time spent in housework." Scientific American 231, 5: 116-120.

—— (1976) "Job satisfactions: the case of housework." (unpublished)

—— (1977) "Social status and housework over time." (unpublished)

4

SATISFACTION WITH HOUSEWORK:
THE SOCIAL CONTEXT

MYRA MARX FERREE

Although it could justly be claimed even a few years ago that housework was one of the most neglected sectors of the economy, recent years have witnessed a rapid expansion of interest in the topic. In the first place, there is a growing recognition that housework is work. Even in industrial or "postindustrial" societies such as our own, the home is a workplace in which a large proportion of the population labors. Understanding the economy is seen to require consideration of this large nonmarket sector (Gauger, 1973; Morgan et al., 1966). Moreover, society's allocation of housework to women is increasingly acknowledged as a crucial part of the mechanism of gender stratification. Housework itself is not only a task that is inequitably assigned to women and undervalued by society as a whole, but also plays a substantial part in disadvantaging women in the rest of the economy (Glazer, 1976; Sweet, 1973). Finally it is noted that for many, if not most, women housework constitutes a major aspect of their lives and shapes much of their daily experience of the world. Thus, in addition to its economic and political importance, housework is of major social-psychological significance to women (Ferree, 1976a; Birnbaum, 1975; Oakley, 1974b). For all these reasons, housework has become a key issue in the reconstruction of the social sciences from a feminist perspective.

This chapter attempts to consider the third, the social-psychological, aspect of housework in the socioeconomic context in which housework

AUTHOR'S NOTE: My thanks are extended to Sarah Fenstermaker Berk, Christine Bose, and Frances Boudreau for their criticisms of an earlier draft. Their suggestions have been invaluable.

occurs. This consideration will touch on several distinct issues. The psychological meaning of housework is first viewed in relation to certain historical changes in the social context in which the work is performed. Second, attention is directed to the ways in which satisfaction with housework has been conceptualized and what these various formulations reveal about the ways in which housework itself has been understood as an occupation. Finally, a question is raised about the nature and extent of class differences in either the objective or subjective experience of housework. Although to some extent independent of each other, the three issues are related in their explicit consideration of the conditions under which houseworkers are or are not expected to be satisfied with their work. Expectations based on class are contrasted with expectations which focus on general trends in our society, such as isolation or prior work experience.

THE CONTEXT OF HOME EMPLOYMENT

THE COLLECTIVE CONTEXT

The changes in the nature of housework over the past century are not only technological (Vanek, 1978; Bose, 1978) but social. Housework in contemporary American society is an increasingly isolated task. This isolation began to be remarked upon shortly after World War II. The decreasing size of private households and the increase in individual ownership were seen as partially responsible for this trend (Zweig, 1952; Myrdal and Klein, 1956). Rossi (1964) noted that the effect of suburbanization on houseworkers was to physically separate them in their individual homes and to tie them to their individually owned appliances. Suburbs also systematically undermined the park-sidewalk-and-corner-store communities which had previously brought women together, at least to interact if not actually to work together.

High geographic mobility in nuclear families has also served to cut women away from other women. Traditional societies assigned the home maintenance tasks to women collectively, and the work was shared within a community of women. Even up through World War II, the ties between women and their female kin and childhood friends were close, lifelong, and of central importance in the lives of most women (Bott, 1957). Within these interacting networks the labor and frustrations of full-time housework could be shared. Mothers and daughters, in particular, remained close. The expectation of geographic mobility, as well as the moves themselves, now serve to disrupt and attenuate these ties. Women may well find themselves with no one near them in whom they can confide or on whom they can call for actual assistance in their work.

A third and, I contend, most critical factor contributing to the increasing isolation of women who work in the home is the steady increase in the number of women who also hold outside employment. By 1978, slightly over 50 percent of all women age sixteen and over were in the labor force and, conversely, fewer than half of all adult women were full-time housewives. This is a dramatic change when compared to typical levels of labor force participation prior to World War II (29 percent in 1940) or even in comparison to the post war years (33 percent in 1950) (U.S. Department of Labor, 1978, 1975). Although in the period from 1940 to 1960, the greatest expansion in labor force participation was among married women whose children were in school or grown, the growth in aggregate female labor force participation since 1960 can be largely attributed to the increasing proportions of mothers of young children who hold paid jobs (Oppenheimer, 1973). This means that regardless of her own age, or the ages of her children, the woman who works at home full time is increasingly less likely to find other women in her neighborhood similarly situated.

In a number of ways this increase in the rate of women's participation in the paid labor force is like the classic demographic shift from rural to urban living. Both are due to a shift in the organization of labor (from agricultural to industrial, from industrial to service), and both have meant changes in people's nonwork lives also. As economic factors continue to pull people into the new way of life, attention is drawn to the social problems of the "migrants," whether employed women or the new urban dwellers. There is concern about the problems they are thought to cause for the rest of society and also about the difficulties they themselves experience in attempting to adjust to the demands placed on them. Despite these problems, both urbanization and rising female labor force participation are seen as progress. The shift in both cases is perceived as a move from a traditional to a more modern form of social organization, perhaps because both are tied to increasing industrialization. Moreover, industrial discipline is thought to transform the "migrants" over the long run into new, more "modern" personalities, with different values and psychology. Those excluded from this process are viewed as "backward."[1] This idea of cultural transition implies a subjective revaluation of the "traditional" sphere.

Although social concern is first drawn to those who are the movers and innovators, that is, those who move to the cities or those women doing waged work, there can be little doubt that the lives of those who stay behind are also objectively changed. This is widely recognized in the case of urbanization. Rural areas, no longer able to provide significant employment, were progressively drained of their most energetic and ambitious people. The simple social density of the area declined and with it the informal networks in which personal interactions could occur. Community-based institutions and activities which depended on some critical mass of participants were also undermined. The sense in which one could say there was an autonomous rural culture with a significant impact on the national culture clearly was diminished. Farm work, in an industrial society, is quite different from farm work in an agricultural society.

The analogy of the rural-urban shift with the declining participation of women in full-time housework suggests that the nature of housework as an occupation is also being subtly transformed by the increase in women's paid employment. Housework alone, compared to the combination with paid employment, may not seem challenging or rewarding enough to engage the talents of the best and the brightest. The social density available in most neighborhoods during the daytime has dropped dramatically. For a houseworker to see another adult in the course of a day may increasingly require conscious effort and advance planning, and the vagaries of child care may make this difficult. Whatever daytime community institutions or housework-based culture there may have been to support and sustain individuals may be collapsing for lack of a critical mass. "Women's sphere" may soon no longer constitute an alternative culture able to project its value effectively into social and political life beyond the home, and full-time houseworkers, like farmers, may have to struggle to defend whatever autonomy they have left.

The impact of these changes in the social meaning of housework may be greatest for full-time housewives. The psychological reality of *being* a housewife, rather than merely *doing* housework, is relevant primarily for those women who are "just" housewives. Although all women may have the ultimate responsibility for certain tasks, and most women may have to perform the vast majority of these tasks themselves, it is increasingly a minority of women for whom housework is the salient occupational role throughout their lives. Participation in the paid labor force provides not only extra work to be done but also an alternate social identity, and one which may be more desirable to the woman herself as the cultural value placed on housework declines. Especially as housework becomes a more isolated and culturally marginal activity, the life of a full-time houseworker may actually be becoming less intrinsically rewarding. Not only are the actual work conditions likely to be more isolated and thus less satisfactory, the perception of housework as "typically" done in conjunction with paid employment may make full-time housework seem to be leisure or laziness and contribute to a lower evaluation of the status and importance of housewives. In this context, paid employment may be seen as desirable not only for the economic advantage it brings to the family but also as a way to establish contact with other adults and to obtain other psychological satisfactions (e.g., a sense of contribution to society), which are increasingly scarce or unobtainable in full-time housework.

THE INDIVIDUAL CONTEXT

The extent to which housework meets the social and psychological needs of any given person may vary with individual setting. For women who are well integrated into a community of "coworkers" in and around the home, the experience of full-time housework may well be fully satisfactory, while other women who are deprived of such contact may be slowly "going crazy" at home. Paid employment may provide an alternative source for these basic personal gratifications without reflecting or developing any particular career aspirations. Careers, or career aspirations, may also be relevant. Women who have held paid jobs are more likely to find housework frustrating (Ferree, 1976b). This may simply reflect the likelihood of employment serving to sever social ties that women may have had at home. It may also be a comparison-level effect since, for women who have been employed, housework seems to have less prestige and importance (Bose, this volume). In both these respects, the experience of paid employment, regardless of status of the job, appears to make full-time housework less desirable.

Financial need also forms an important part of the individual context. The notion of paid work as a source of psychic satisfaction has often been contrasted with the economic realities that dictate that most women work for money which they and their families really need. Financial pressure is thought to make psychological motivation irrelevant for women, even though it has long been recognized that both are extremely important for male workers (Kahn, 1972; Caplow, 1954). The need for alternative sources of personal satisfaction outside housework is usually presumed to be felt primarily or exclusively by well-educated, middle-class women seeking the special rewards of a "career" rather than a mere job. Yet the relative importance or unimportance individuals attach to the psychological experience of paid work can in large measure be seen as a function of the extent to which employment provides necessary psychic and social rewards not available elsewhere, just as the financial importance of work depends on it meeting economic needs which would otherwise go unfilled. The relevant contrast, therefore, would be between the psychological rewards of paid work and of housework, not between the psychological and financial aspects of the job. There is certainly no reason to assume that, for women, psychological and financial motivations are opposite ends of a single continuum.

SATISFACTION WITH HOUSEWORK: THREE MODELS

What are the social and psychological rewards of housework and how satisfying do full-time houseworkers find their jobs? This basic problem has been approached over the years in a number of different ways and with certain implicit goals in mind. Although changes in the collective context in which housework is done have largely been ignored, the differences between individuals have been the object of considerable speculation and some empirical research. For the most part, until very recently, attention has focused on satisfaction in general with the global occupational role, an approach which facilitates comparison to satisfaction with other available occupations, but which does not identify the aspects of the job which may be rewarding or unrewarding (e.g., Weiss and Samuelson, 1958). Additionally, the levels of expressed satisfaction with housework have been taken at face value as indicating a generally satisfying occupation rather than taking into consideration the extent to which social norms demand that women find housework gratifying (e.g., Wright, 1978). In both these respects, studies of satisfaction with housework have lagged behind studies of workers' satisfaction in other jobs (see Sheppard and Herrick, 1972).

Nonetheless, satisfaction with housework has generally been studied in ways which are implicitly modeled on studies of occupational satisfaction. The approaches taken have varied and have reflected very different fundamental concerns. These basic theoretical reasons for being interested in housewives' satisfaction have included a concern with productivity, an interest in their political potential, and a desire to describe the specific social-psychological consequences of occupational structure. Each of these concerns has deeply influenced the way satisfaction is conceptualized, the nature of the research questions that are raised, and the conclusions that are ultimately drawn. Before turning to any further inquiry into contextual differences in satisfaction with housework, it behooves us to examine the nature and consequences of the various theoretical perspectives employed.

CONCERN WITH PRODUCTIVITY: THE MORALE MODEL

The earliest theoretical approach to satisfaction in the context of housework as a full-time occupation is also the most traditional approach to occupational satisfaction in general—namely, a concern with worker productivity. Employee satisfaction and morale have long been recognized by employers as significant predictors of productivity. Employers' desire to see continued high productivity has at times mandated job enrichment programs or other changes in the organization of the occupation—especially when sociologists have identified particular problems of boredom or interpersonal conflict as interfering with the quantity or quality of work being done (Whyte, 1948).

Some of the studies of housewives' satisfaction in the 1950s and 1960s can also be seen to fall into this pattern. In these studies, the primary concern is with the adequacy of child rearing or the extent of marital adjustment viewed as products (Orden and Bradburn, 1969; Hoffman and Nye, 1963; Gurin et al., 1960). Conservatives held not only that the wife bears the primary responsibility for each of these outcomes but that women's employment in the paid labor market will interfere with their productivity in these other jobs. While not questioning the wife's responsibility for child rearing or marital adjustment, these early studies attempted to rebut the conservative argument by showing that employment outside the home could, under some circumstances, increase the wife's satisfaction. Increased satisfaction in turn would either improve the "quality of time" she spent with her children or minimize domestic conflict. The studies emphasized that the high quality of these "products" required women's satisfaction with their work rather than their full-time dedication to housework. Thus, women who were happily employed or happily at home full time were equally likely to be good mothers and wives; it was the women who were unhappy at their work, rather than those who were employed, who created difficulties for their families.

Like industrial productivity studies, this research had a decidedly reformist bent. Employment outside the home, a growing phenomenon among married women, needed legitimation. It received this legitimation by being portrayed as a variety of job enrichment programs for those homeworkers who were frustrated or bored. The unspoken condition for this legitimation, however, was that women's productivity at home remain undiminished or even improved, thus vindicating only the "supermom." The woman whose need for self-fulfillment in paid employment led her to cheerfully take on the responsibility for two jobs was seen as making a genuine contribution to her family. Her productivity was acknowledged as being greater than it would have been were she a depressed or frustrated housewife. Those husbands whose wives desired to work were implicitly encouraged to "allow" them to do so by the suggestion that this would improve the husband's domestic life.

The woman who worked only for reasons of financial necessity continued to be seen as a social problem. Because her productivity in the home was not suffering to begin with, employment could not be expected to increase it. Her need to work meant that her overall happiness and her productivity in the home were expected to decline. This may have contributed to legitimizing demands for "help" with the housework, but only as a way of coping with a generally stressful and undesirable situation. Because of the assumption that financial and personal motivations for employment are opposite ends of a continuum, working-class women were thought to generally find themselves in this latter position. In the absence of a free—that is, financially unconstrained—choice to seek paid employment, full-time housework was viewed as the rewarding alternative.

CONCERN WITH POLITICS: SOCIALIZATION OR SOCIAL COMPARISON?

A quite different reason for being concerned with the satisfaction of housewives is an indication of the political possibilities inherent in the occupational role. This type of concern also has its parallel in the industrial sphere among those who are on the one side concerned about "labor unrest," or on the other side interested in the development of worker solidarity and/or class consciousness (e.g., Helmer, 1974; Hamilton, 1972). Those who have posed the question of housewives' satisfaction in this context have for the most part adopted the "labor" rather than the "management" perspective. In this approach, women's present satisfaction with "traditional" sex roles is assumed to be the major factor limiting the potential for sex role change, and full-time housework tends to be seen as the expression of this traditional role.

In this approach, housework is generally seen as inherently exploitative in some fashion, although there is no clear consensus on what makes it so. In addition, houseworkers are generally seen as satisfied with their lot. Where theorists differ most sharply is in their description of the causes of women's satisfaction. The two most common explanations attribute the lack of (appropriate) dissatisfaction either to a sort of false consciousness induced by sex role socialization or to a lack of realistic alternatives. The former explanation stresses general cultural processes which express and perpetuate gender differences in power (e.g., Bem and Bem, 1970). The fact that approximately half of all adult women in the United States are full-time housewives is seen as prima facie evidence that traditional sex roles impede personal fulfillment. Sex role socialization, however, prevents women in general from recognizing their situation for what it is. The second explanation of satisfaction with housework is based on relative deprivation rather than socialization. If, as this approach suggests, housework is the best of an extremely limited set of alternatives, satisfaction would be the appropriate response. Such interpersonal comparison is expected to lead to class-specific differences in the ways in which the occupation is perceived. Middle-class women find housework intrinsically more oppressive, whether or not they have the economic and psychological alternatives that make it possible for them to recognize their exploitation as such. Consequently there is thought to be more awareness of gender stratification, and so more political potential, among middle-class than among working-class women (Friedan, 1963; Rossi, 1973; Dizard, 1972; Freeman, 1975).

Considering this second approach first, it is important to note that the differences in middle-class and working-class women's perceptions of housework are seen as being subjective differences in reactions to objectively similar work. Housework itself is perceived as a single, non-class-specific occupation. It is argued that working-class women, unlike middle-class women, can be satisfied with such work. The reasons advanced for this presumed satisfaction are largely comparative in nature. Some have argued that working-class women have not received the educational or professional training that would overqualify them for menial labor (Friedan, 1963). As a consequence, their aspirations are low (e.g., they do not expect a "career") and can be met as well in housework as in any other unskilled occupation. Alternatively, some have focused on the limited range of employment opportunities in itself as keeping working-class women satisfied at home. Since the paid jobs that are open to working-class women are just as menial and monotonous as housework, the extra time and effort required to work outside the home are not thought to return any intrinsic psychic reward (Carden, 1974; Rossi, 1973). Moreover, the occupational prestige of housework is as high as or higher than most paid occupations open to women so status gains are also ruled out (Bose, this volume; Nilson, 1978). As a result, paid employment is thought to mean incurring a cost without obtaining any benefit other than income. It is therefore assumed that working-class women would prefer to be "freed from the necessity of having to work" and are relatively satisfied as housewives (Dizard, 1972). Finally, some have argued that the relevant social comparison is between husbands and wives. Middle-class wives are thought to envy their husbands' challenging and creative careers, while wives of blue-collar workers are presumed to compare their work at home to that of their husbands. Since the husband's job is equally menial but even more demanding and alienating, the blue-collar wife is assumed to find housework relatively attractive (Freeman, 1975).[2]

Because all three relative deprivation models predict the same class differences in women's satisfaction, they support the same assessment of differential political potential. For all three, the predicted positive view of housework in the working class is a political problem. The women's movement is seen as incapable of presenting any alternatives to full-time housework which would be attractive to working-class women. It is concluded either that the movement is irrelevant to working-class women or that it should attempt to meet their needs within the context of their self-definition as housewives. These needs are essentially seen as financial: The movement should attempt to free women from the economic necessity of having to work outside the home. This effort could take the form of directly providing pay for housework (see Leghorn and Warrior, 1975; Liskov, 1977; Lopate, 1974); indeed, the struggle to find an objective basis for revolutionary potential in housework (Dalla Costa, 1972) is based on the assumption that the majority of women are irrevocably self-defined as housewives. Alternatively the attempt could be indirect: Women would be freed from working by successfully addressing those class issues which make the jobs of blue-collar men unstable or poorly paid (see Rossi, 1973; Seifer, 1973). As in the productivity-oriented model, there is some tendency here to consider the woman who works for reasons of economic necessity to be deserving of sympathy, which implicitly suggests that women, unlike men, have an inherent right to forego paid employment if they so desire.

When the socialization, rather than relative deprivation, model is applied to the issue of the political potential in class differences in satisfaction, the tendency is to invoke working-class acceptance of "traditional values" as an ex post facto explanation. The belief in working-class "traditionality" in terms of sex roles appears to be similar in some respects to the classic construct of working-class authoritarianism (Lipset, 1959). Both are thought to be induced in the work lives and political activities "typical" of each class. Conservative traditions (e.g., religion) are stressed, while more egalitarian traditions (e.g., the tendency for mothers as well as fathers to be major contributors to family subsistence) are slighted.

If there are class differences, then, the socialization model locates them in the different temperament or personality which is thought to be typical of each class. However, socialization need not create systematic class differences. Sex role socialization is said to ignore potential innate differences in liking for housework in favor of allocating roles by gender alone. The basic problem is seen as overdetermination; even those who are manifestly unsuited to housework are constrained by society to take it on, simply by virtue of being female. Unhappiness naturally results, but socialization and continuing social pressure make it difficult for individuals to recognize or acknowledge it. If there were a class difference, then, it would be simply in the ability of individuals to recognize and respond to their unhappiness.

This model is sharply opposed to the morale model in its definition of the meaning of perceived choice. In the morale model, perceived choice is crucial for the woman's satisfaction and so for the outcomes "produced" for the rest of the family and society as a whole. Women should be freely "allowed" to work outside the home or remain full-time housewives as they choose. For the socialization model, distinctions between those who say they have freely chosen housework and those who do not are primarily seen as differences in the efficacy of socialization. Their perceived choice is illusory and their self-reported satisfaction is therefore viewed as misleading.

Note, too, how different this model is from that applied in most sociological studies of the workplace. In industrial and occupational sociology, job satisfaction is not explained by reference to whether or not the auto worker or clerk-typist chose his or her employment freely. It is taken for granted that he or she did not, and their personal perceptions of choice are considered moot. The notion of doing away with any system of socialization in favor of the "the values of individuality and self-fulfillment" as Bem and Bem (1970: 91) suggest with regard to housework is alien to most studies of occupations. Instead, the issue is whether or not the work itself objectively violates certain conditions which are conceived of as essential for human fulfillment or, on the other hand, offers psychic rewards above and beyond those available in most other jobs. The social-structural conditions of employment are thought to be reflected in variations in reported satisfaction.

CONCERN WITH SPECIFIC CONTENT: THE SITUATIONAL MODEL

The third major approach to the problem of housewives' satisfaction tends to deal with it in terms of the occupational conditions conducive to greater or lesser satisfaction. Satisfaction is an outcome most closely related to the characteristics of housework as an occupation rather than to differences among individuals in their reaction to it. Lopata (1971), for example, attempted to show that housewives as workers could find specific opportunities for self-fulfillment and self-development on the job. Her presentation is similar in some respects to those studies of blue-collar, low-status workers which endeavor to show how the qualities of personal strength, intelligence, and creativity in the individual worker are not extinguished in even the most demeaning work (Howe, 1977; Garson, 1975). This approach makes a valuable distinction between the nature of the job and that of the worker. In this model, satisfaction with the job is not a comment on the political acquiescence of the worker nor a nearly inevitable consequence of socialization but an accomplishment of human struggle in wringing personal meaning out of even the most unpromising material. The satisfaction of housewives, as Lopata depicts it, is the vindication of their humanity; housework may be dehumanizing, but housewives are not subhuman. Although distinguishing between the job and the worker, this sort of presentation tends to romanticize the worker, seeing him or her as the "hero" who remains unscathed by oppression and rises above the objective circumstances of his or her job (Warner et al., 1973).

A more realistic application of the situational model to the issue of satisfaction with housework would call for an examination of the particular features of the job *and* the workers's response to them. This approach was first taken by Oakley (1974b) in her now classic study of British housewives. A number of valuable contributions to this model have been made by Berheide et al. (1976), particularly in looking at emotional reactions to particular tasks. This sort of model proceeds on the assumption that housework is an internally differentiated occupation and that satisfaction or dissatisfaction is not endemic but is characteristic of certain identifiable features of the job. These particular job characteristics may be variable from workplace to workplace or class to class. They may also be changing in some specific ways because of changes in technology and/or in the organization of labor in the society as a whole.

In this approach, individual variation in satisfaction is a key to understanding the importance of particular social-structural differences in the nature of the job itself, rather than being a reflection of subjective variation in response to essentially invariant occupational characteristics. Differences in satisfaction between rural and urban or working-class and middle-class women would not be approached on an individual level as a matter of personality or social comparison but would call for an investigation into how the job might itself be different in each of these settings. The model does not exclude the possibility of differences in personality or expectations being relevant to satisfaction with the role, but tends to see such differences as less important empirically and theoretically than the differences in satisfaction which reflect the features of the job.

With this model, as with the previous two, the reasons for being interested in housewives' satisfaction in the first place have had a significant impact on the way that the problem has been conceptualized. For these researchers there has been a particular concern with women's invisibility within the social sciences. Women's lives have not received the "loving empiricism" of intensive study and description; traditional analytic concepts have rarely been applied in sex-neutral fashion and to some extent cannot be, because they have been developed with the experience of men alone as normative (Berk and Berk, 1978; Bose, this volume; Millman and Kanter, 1975). The basic assumption of this third model is that housework is a far more complex and differentiated occupation than male-based (and biased) sociology has recognized. As long as men were defined as being the central actors, it was of little concern to sociology to know what women actually did with their time, so long as they remained out of the labor force and out of competition for "men's" jobs. As a consequence, the structure of housework as a job, like the amount of effort expended on it and its contribution to the economy as a whole, is largely invisible to male sociology. For those researchers attempting to correct this biased view, the question of housewives' satisfaction is secondary to the question of the nature of housework as a whole.

The nature of housework as an occupation may or may not vary by class. Oakley (1974b) suggests that working-class housewives have fewer conveniences afforded them by technology, but that such technological conditions have little impact on work satisfaction. While the status of the job may be relatively higher, and thus less problematic, for working-class women the actual conditions in which they work are worse in several nontechnological ways. Working-class women, for example, have more children and child rearing may make housework a more fragmented and demanding job than it would otherwise be (Berheide et al., 1976). This, as well as the actual increase in workload children cause, may result in less satisfaction with full-time housework. Children may also cause more isolation, but whether this effect is greater for working-class women—who would be less likely to have the convenience of a car—or middle-class women—who are more likely to suffer the isolating effects of suburbanization and geographic mobility—is not clear. Many studies of working-class families and neighborhoods suggest that the women are still for the most part embedded in supportive sex-segregated social networks (McCourt, 1977; Rubin, 1976), which would make isolation less problematic for working-class women. The sex segregation of spheres of influence may be greater in working-class than in middle-class "companionate" marriages; if so, working-class women might be expected to benefit from the autonomy such a sharp division of labor affords.

CLASS AND SATISFACTION

Each of the models considered above has offered some plausible reason why working-class women might be expected to be more satisfied and some explanation of the nature of the difference expected. The morale model implicitly assumes that those women who have to work for financial reasons are less happy—and consequently less productive wives and mothers—than those who have freely chosen employment for self-fulfillment. The women who are stuck at home against their will are generally assumed to be middle-class women with career aspirations. The socialization model often posits more patriarchal attitudes or a more submissive personality among working-class women to account for their greater acquiescence to "traditional" wife and mother roles, while the social comparison model considers greater working-class satisfaction with traditional roles a consequence of the more unappealing alternatives they see. Finally, the structural model offers the hypothesis that the typically larger working-class family size—and consequently greater likelihood of having a young child at home—may make a significant difference in work conditions. Moreover, the sex segregation of activities may be greater in the working class, which might also contribute to better work conditions, such as less isolation or more autonomy. Thus all three models concur in seeing class as an important part of the social context of housework, having significant psychological consequences for those involved in this occupation.

Despite the plausibility of the assumption that class affects satisfaction with housework in some or all of these ways, there is actually very little empirical evidence about either the extent or the nature of class differences. What evidence there is suggests that working-class women may not be happier as full-time housewives than when they are employed (Ferree, 1976a, 1976b) and, moreover, working-class women may not be any more satisfied as housewives than middle-class women are (Wright, 1978). Although there is some evidence that the social status of housework may be less problematic for working-class women (Komarovsky, 1962; Oakley, 1974b; Gavron, 1966; Bose, this volume; Nilson, 1978) the job itself may present many of the same problems and frustrations to working-class and middle-class housewives (Gavron, 1966; Oakley, 1974b; Wright, 1978).

In the following sections, some questions are raised about the importance of class as a determinant of satisfaction with housework. Class, as it has traditionally been understood, may be only weakly related to the actual variation in life contingencies women face. Women without economic resources of their own, such as full-time housewives, may find their happiness more dependent on the distribution of resources *within* the household than on the position of the male "head" relative to other workers. The factors affecting this internal stratification process may be relatively independent of class. Although the reasons that have been advanced for expecting a class difference might be supported when the evidence is in, there are also reasons that could be advanced for expecting no such differences. For the most part, these reasons are compatible with the models of satisfaction that have already been examined. The next section considers some of the unresolved questions about the significance of class, and the following section provides an illustration of how these arguments could be considered empirically.

THE NATURE OF CLASS DIFFERENCES

One issue raised by the morale model of satisfaction is that of freedom of choice. Although the socialization model rightly points out that occupational choice is never really free, actual freedom of choice may be less important for satisfaction than perceived choice. Variation in perceived choice might be due to class if it largely reflects the influence of financial necessity, but it could also be due to the relative control or authoritarianism of the husband, which might or might not vary by class. The presence of children and the absence of affordable child care might also constitute greater necessities for working-class women, but these constraints would tend to tie them to the home against their will. Although working-class women may be more likely to see paid employment as required rather than chosen, they may be more likely to see full-time housework as a matter of obligation or necessity as well.

The legitimacy of housework as an occupation ascribed on the basis of gender makes the issue of perceived choice more important than it is for most other occupations in contemporary society. Our culture does not approve of a father insisting that his son follow in his footsteps even though the father's occupation is indubitably important in shaping his son's "choice" of work; our culture does still condone the legitimacy of a husband insisting that his wife accept the occupation of full-time housework. It is not clear that this legitimacy varies by class. Many middle-class and professional men seem to want to take credit for their wives' occupations as evidence of their own liberality, implying that they feel they had a right to interfere. Whether their wives share this opinion is another matter. For many women freedom may be found not in the absence of financial necessity, but in the delicate balance between the legitimacy of economic need and of their husband's demands. Working-class husbands, who may be less able to meet the family's economic needs singlehandedly, may be less able to demand that their wives stay home and devote themselves to the housework. Working-class wives, on the other hand, may also be less able to resist such demands if they are made. The socialization model, for example, suggested that working-class women have accepted the values of partriarchy more than middle-class women have. While there is little evidence of any great class difference in sex role attitudes, education does make some difference (Huber et al., 1978; Mason and Bumpass, 1975). More traditional attitudes may mean greater acceptance of housework as an obligation, however, without necessarily increasing the satisfaction experienced in the work.

Without further investigation of the actual nature of the job, it is difficult to predict how class would affect it. Rather than family income, it is family outgo—expenditure on household-related expenses—that would be expected to have the largest impact on work conditions, but obviously the two are related. Insofar as money makes a difference to the ease or extent of work involved in the job, working-class women would be expected to be at a disadvantage. However, insofar as the relative deprivation argument is true, working-class women would be comparing the less-attractive paid jobs available to them to the less-attractive conditions of housework they face, and thus may not end up any more satisfied than middle-class women. On the other hand, if income does not matter, then it is hard to see what situational advantages, other than smaller family size, middle-class women would be expected to have. Smaller family size, of course, might be a significant advantage, but then that, rather than class, should be described as the cause of satisfaction.

AN EMPIRICAL ILLUSTRATION

Although a definitive investigation of the importance of class for satisfaction with housework is beyond the scope of this chapter, it may be useful to look at the type of empirical questions that these theoretical considerations raise. As an illustration, some data are drawn from the 1971 Quality of American Life Survey.[3] Although somewhat dated, this study is the only representative national survey now available for secondary analysis that has questions specifically dealing with satisfaction with housework and some of the job conditions that might affect satisfaction. In the present analysis, the dependent measure is satisfaction with housework ("Overall, how satisfied are you will being a homemaker—I don't mean your family life—but with your housework?") and the independent measures are age of children (a child under age six or not), isolation ("Do you get much chance to see other people during the day?"), and career aspirations ("Have you ever wanted a career?"). Since most of these questions were only asked of full-time housewives, no comparisons with employed women are possible. The present analysis is restricted to white, married women who were full-time housewives at the time of the survey. The sample is divided into working class and middle class on the basis of whether the respondent's husband was employed in a blue-collar or a white-collar job.[4]

In this analysis, career aspirations are the only indication of personality type. The person who has never wanted a career could be said to be initially predisposed toward housework as a permanent full-time occupation and would seem to be a different "type" from the person who had some ambitions at some point for some sort of a career. Isolation, on the other hand, is a situational factor. Rather than reflecting the predispositions or preferences a woman might bring to the job, isolation is a characteristic of the job itself. Women who want a career and women who are isolated during the day might both be expected to find housework a less rewarding occupation. Moreover, working-class women would usually be expected to be less likely to either want a career or to be isolated from other people. It is not clear whether having small children at home should relate to greater satisfaction (because of the fragmented and exhausting work involved), but it would certainly be expected to relate to greater isolation (Myrdal and Klein, 1956; Oakley, 1974b). Working-class women might be expected to be more satisfied with housework than middle-class women, but not necessarily net of the effects of these hypothetically intervening variables.

In fact, however, only some of these expectations are borne out in the data. There is no significant difference between working-class and middle-class women in satisfaction with housework, and age of children also does not make a significant difference in satisfaction for women for either class (see Table 1). Working-class women with young children are more isolated than any of the other three groups. It appears likely that the restricted day-to-day mobility that a mother with young children faces is exacerbated by the typically lower incomes of blue-collar families without being balanced by more extensive or closer neighborhood contacts. Isolation itself is significantly related to dissatisfaction with housework, but only for those women whose children are under six years old. This relationship holds regardless of class. Although there is no concrete evidence to explain this interaction, one might venture to hypothesize that social isolation is voluntary for women whose children are in school and involuntary for those who still have children at home.

Table 1   Isolation, Aspirations, and Satisfaction with
Housework by Class and Ages of Children for Full-Time Housewives

	Middle Class		Working Class	
	Children under 6		Children under 6	
	Yes	No	Yes	No
	(n=62)	(n=124)	(n=84)	(n=84)
Percent Isolated	37%	34%	46%	32%
Percent Aspiring	35%	32%	36%	27%
[a]Mean Satisfaction with Housework	2.14	2.12	2.09	2.07
Correlation of Isolation and Satisfaction	-.38*	.07	-.24*	.00
Correlation of Aspiration and Satisfaction	-.19	-.30*	-.13	-.36*

* = p ≤ .01

[a]Higher values indicate greater dissatisfaction; isolation and aspirations were coded 1 = yes; 2 = no.

Despite the common assumption that working-class women would be less likely to desire a career, in these data there is no significant difference in aspirations between middle-class and working-class women. Of course, the fact that working-class women are just as likely to desire a career as middle-class women are does not indicate that the type of work they had in mind was similar, but it does suggest that they may have equal reason to find full-time housework a disappointment. The relationship between aspirations and dissatisfaction with housework is only significant for those women whose children are at least school age. Again, class differences are minimal or nonexistent. Thus, there is no evidence that working-class women are more traditional either by being less likely to aspire to a career or by being less dissatisfied when their aspirations are not met. The difference by age of children might again represent the extent to which perceived choice plays a role: The presence of young children in the home appears to justify the sacrifice of a career, but when the children are older frustrated aspirations relate to discontent. Perhaps children are perceived as a freely chosen constraint, while husband's opposition, for example, is not; in the absence of any direct evidence on perceived choice, this interpretation is admittedly speculative.

In general, it appears that both personality and situational factors relate to satisfaction with housework, but at different stages of a woman's life. While this life-cycle effect was unanticipated, it might reflect differences in the unmeasured variable of perceived choice. Thus, several of the models discussed earlier receive some support. Socialization may affect values such as career aspirations, which relate to dissatisfaction; isolation is an occupational hazard which also may create unhappiness; perceived choice may be more relevant for satisfaction with housework than for other occupations. Class itself, however, appears to make much less of a difference than any of the models predicted. Not only does class not relate to satisfaction with housework, it is also not related to either isolation or aspirations, and, with the exception of the relationship between age of children and isolation, does not specify the relationships found in any significant way.

As this brief analysis illustrates, the various models of satisfaction with housework that have been discussed above may be more useful when treated as complementary rather than competing. The variety of concerns which have led researchers to formulate theoretical models of satisfaction have produced a plethora of hypotheses. Only with extensive empirical work will we be able to distinguish the relative validity of these hypotheses and, consequently, of the models on which they are based. This sample analysis suggests, however, that no one model is likely to emerge from this testing process unscathed and unchanged. If the models discussed above cannot be integrated in some way, perhaps some entirely new approach will have to be developed.

SUMMARY AND CONCLUSION

The social context of housework has both a collective and an individual dimension. The position of housework as an occupation vis-à-vis other occupations determines the collective meaning of housework and establishes the outlines of the social relationships housework entails. Within this collective context there is individual variation in the values the person brings to the job, the actual conditions under which the work is performed, and the value the job has relative to the alternatives available. Both this macro- and microsocial context are relevant to the satisfaction the occupation offers, and both have been dramatically changed by the rapid expansion of women's labor force participation from World War II to the present.

As more women have come to hold paid employment, the numbers of women available at home to maintain daytime social networks and sustain an independent housework-based subculture have necessarily declined, perhaps to the point at which housework can no longer be a self-contained and self-sustaining way of life. This decline in social density around the home, comparable to the rural-urban shift in population, has also left individual houseworkers potentially more isolated. Since most women are not full-time housewives, those women who are at home full time may find it increasingly difficult to build and maintain social contacts with other adults. This isolation in individual households has been repeatedly suggested as a structural source of dissatisfaction with full-time housework. Insofar as it is in fact increasing, housework may be becoming a job in which it would be more difficult for anyone to be satisfied.

The increase in women's labor force participation may also be affecting the meaning housework carries. As housework becomes more likely to be a second job rather than a full-time occupation, the full-time housewife is more likely to be seen as not making her full contribution to society or to her individual family. This endemic devaluation of housework may make it a less psychologically rewarding job and women at all status levels may increasingly need to seek a paid job to meet essential psychological as well as financial needs. As full-time housework becomes less likely to be a lifetime career, women's aspirations may change to reflect this. Not only do overall expectations of the probability of employment rise, but more women have work experience, and these women are more likely to expect a career than those who have never worked. Individually, women who have ever worked for pay may be less likely to find full-time housework adequately rewarding. Even for those women whose jobs are neither well paid nor glamorous, the economic rewards and sense of contribution available in paid work may be difficult to forego. With individual aspirations rising, full-time housework may seem less desirable and the inevitable frustrations of the job less and less endurable.

Not all the frustrations of housework are necessarily inevitable, however. The idea of providing pay for housework, for example, is intended in part as a way of raising the status of housework by providing concrete recognition that housework is real, productive labor (Dalla Costa, 1972; Liscov, 1977). Pay for housework would in this respect be a way of increasing satisfaction with the job by changing a critical aspect of the work conditions. The scheme has a great number of practical drawbacks (Lopate, 1974), but it may be an effective way of increasing consciousness about the value of housework to family and national economics. Whether it would be equally effective in raising individual houseworker satisfaction with the job is more questionable. In fact, any remuneration for housework might increase the pressure that constrains some women to be housewives in the face of a personal preference for other work. Insofar as it reduces the financial pressure that pulls some women into the labor force despite a preference for housework, it might be a good thing, but this would also necessarily reduce the role financial need could play in counterbalancing the other pressures that hold women at home. If freeing women from the necessity of having to be housewives is a social policy goal, then pay for housework is an unlikely route to its realization.

Although it is important to consider the ways in which women could be freed from the necessity of having to do full-time housework, including increasing opportunities for paid employment and the availability of day care and decreasing the legitimacy of the ascription of housework exclusively to women, the fact remains that many women will have to work at home full time for the foreseeable future. In light of this, some concern should also be given to ways of making full-time housework a more satisfying job. One feature of the job that might be readily modified is its extreme isolation. Particularly if, the trend toward increasing labor force participation by women continues, the problems arising from isolation may be creating a crisis for full time housewives regardless of class. If individuals are finding it ever more difficult to see other people during the day, social arrangements could be created that would facilitate such social contact. Housewives' clubs or support groups might make the job more satisfying by providing "coworkers" with whom to share it; this might be especially important for mothers of young children. The declining proportion of women at home makes it increasingly necessary for women to reach beyond the neighborhood or family for such interpersonal support, and working-class women may be more likely to need help in making and sustaining these contacts. Increased public transportation is only part of the solution; it is also important to increase the legitimacy of full-time housewives making use of day care facilities, if only for an hour or two a day. Given the expense and inconvenience of obtaining quality child care today, working-class housewives may need material assistance as well as legitimation and encouragement if they are to be freed from the burden of acute isolation that small children so often create.

If more attention were paid overall to the social context of satisfaction with housework, the job need not remain one which is exceptionally hard to find satisfying. While it may be true that some people are temperamentally more suited to housework than others, no human being is naturally inclined toward enforced hard labor in solitary confinement. While people's options may be so limited that they can be reconciled to such an unpleasant alternative, such an accommodation can only be achieved at great personal and social cost. In the long run it may be far less costly to change the conditions of housework. At present, a fair number of both working-class and middle-class women do find full-time housework satisfying. Rather than considering them either sub- or superhuman individuals, we might do well to investigate the particular conditions under which they work. If such conditions could be furthered for all houseworkers, satisfaction with housework might be increased. The identification of housework with women makes this an important feminist goal. Housework has already become a key issue in the feminist reconstruction of the social sciences; it is time now for the reconstruction of housework to become a key issue for feminist social science.

NOTES

1. The denigration of housewives and housework can thus be seen as part of the glorification of industry and science. Home economics was an attempt to remedy this by bringing industrial discipline and scientific methods into the home (Ehrenreich and English, 1975). This denigration persists, however, and is now often popularly attributed to feminism. While this is for the most part an instance of blaming the messenger for the message, the women's movement has at times also capitalized on the devaluation of women's traditional roles.

2. Though social comparison processes are thus widely viewed as important for satisfaction with housework there is no consensus on what sort of social comparison is actually taking place. Each of these relative deprivation approaches describes a particular type of social comparison—whether between expected and achieved goals, between employed women and housewives, or between husbands and wives—as an essentially universal process. There is no consideration of structural factors which would facilitate one sort of social comparison or another.

3. The study was conducted by the University of Michigan Survey Research Center and information about the sample, the range of topics covered in the questionnaire, and the exact question wording and coding are available in the codebook distributed through the Survey Research Center, Ann Arbor, Michigan.

4. While this definition of class does not entirely capture the class distinction, the lack of consensus in sociological theory on how the class position of women is determined makes any measure endlessly debatable. The simple dichotomy at least has the advantage of not being confounded with age, as education is, or with the number of family members employed, as income is. A serious consideration of the role of class in satisfaction with housework would also have to take these other factors into account.

REFERENCES

BEM, S. and D. BEM (1970) "Case study of a nonconscious ideology," pp. 89-99 in D. Bem (ed.) Beliefs, Attitudes and Human Affairs. Belmont, CA: Wadsworth.
BERHEIDE, C., S. BERK, and R. BERK (1976) "Household work in the suburbs: the job and its participants." Pacific Sociological Review 19: 491-517.

BERK, R. A. and S. F. BERK (1978) "A simultaneous equation model for the division of household labor." Sociological Methods and Research 6: 431-468.

BIRNBAUM, J. (1975) "Life patterns and self esteem in gifted family oriented and career oriented women," pp. 396-418 in M. Mednick, et al. (eds.) Women and Achievement. New York: John Wiley.

BOSE, C. (1978) "Technology and changes in the division of labor in the American home." Presented at the annual meeting of the American Sociological Association.

BOTT, E. (1957) Family and Social Network. London: Tavistock.

CAPLOW, T. (1954) The Sociology of Work. Minneapolis: University of Minnesota Press.

CARDEN, M. L. (1974) The New Feminist Movement. New York: Russell Sage.

DALLA COSTA, M. (1972) "Women and the subversion of the community." Radical America 6 (January/February): 67-102.

DIZARD, J. (1972) "The price of success," pp. 192-201 in L. K. Howe (ed.) The Future of the Family. New York: Simon & Schuster.

EHRENREICH, B. and D. ENGLISH (1975) "The manufacture of housework." Socialist Revolution 5, 4: 5-40.

FERREE, M. M. (1976a) "Working class jobs: paid work and housework as sources of satisfaction." Social Problems 23: 431-441.

––– (1976b) "The emerging constituency: feminism, employment, and the working class." Ph.D. dissertation, Harvard University.

FREEMAN, J. (1975) The Politics of Women's Liberation. New York: David McKay.

FRIEDAN, B. (1963) The Feminine Mystique. New York: Dell.

GARSON, B. (1975) All the Livelong Day. New York: Penguin.

GAUGER, W. (1973) "Household work: can we add it to the GNP?" Journal of Home Economics 65: 12-15.

GAVRON, H. (1966) The Captive Wife. London: Routledge & Kegan Paul.

GLAZER, N. (1976) "Housework." Signs 1: 905-922.

GURIN, G., J. VEROFF, and S. FELD (1960) Americans View Their Mental Health. New York: Basic Books.

HAMILTON, R. (1972) Class and Politics in the United States. New York: John Wiley.

HELMER, J. (1974) The Deadly Simple Mechanics of Society. New York: Seabury.

HOFFMAN, L. and I. NYE (1963) The Employed Mother in America. Chicago: Rand McNally.

HOWE, L. K. (1977) Pink Collar Workers. New York: Putnam.

HUBER, J., C. REXROAT, and G. SPITZE (1978) "A crucible of opinion on women's status: the ERA in Illinois." Social Forces 57: 549-565.

KAHN, R. (1972) "The meaning of work: interpretations and proposals for measurement," pp. 159-204 in A. Campbell and P. Converse (eds.) The Human Meaning of Social Change. New York: Russell Sage.

KOMAROVSKY, M. (1962) Blue Collar Marriage. New York: Vintage.

LEGHORN, L. and B. WARRIOR (1975) Houseworker's Handbook. Cambridge, MA: The Women's Center.

LIPSET, S. M. (1959) "Working class authoritarianism," chapter 5 in Political Man. Garden City: Doubleday.

LISCOV, A. (1977) "The valuation of housework: a problem of conceptualization and measurement." Presented at the annual meeting of the American Sociological Association.

LOPATA, H. (1971) Occupation: Housewife. New York: Oxford University Press.
LOPATE, C. (1974) "Pay for housework?" Social Policy (September/October): 27-31.
MASON, K. O. and L. BUMPASS (1975) "U.S. women's sex role ideology, 1970." American Journal of Sociology 80: 1212-1219.
MASON, K. O., J. CZAJKA, and S. ARBER (1976) "Change in U.S. women's sex role ideology, 1964-1974." American Sociological Review 41: 573-597.
McCOURT, K. (1977) Working Class Women and Grass Roots Politics. Bloomington: Indiana University Press.
MILLMAN, M. and R. KANTER (1975) Another Voice. Garden City, NY: Doubleday.
MORGAN, J., I. SIRAGELDIN, and N. BAERWALDT (1966) Productive Americans. Ann Arbor, MI: Institute for Social Research.
MYRDAL, A. and V. KLEIN (1956) Women's Two Roles: Home and Work. London: Routledge & Kegan Paul.
NILSON, L. (1978) "The social standing of a housewife." Journal of Marriage and Family 40: 541-548.
OAKLEY, A. (1974a) Woman's Work: The Housewife Past and Present. New York: Pantheon.
——— (1974b) The Sociology of Housework. New York: Pantheon.
ORDEN, S. R. and N. BRADBURN (1969) "Working wives and marital happiness." American Journal of Sociology 74: 392-407.
OPPENHEIMER, V. K. (1973) "Demographic influence on female employment and the status of women," pp. 184-199 in J. Huber (ed.) Changing Women in a Changing Society. Chicago: University of Chicago Press.
ROSSI, A. (1964) "Equality between the sexes: an immodest proposal." Daedalus 93: 607-652.
——— (1973) "Women in the seventies: problems and possibilities," pp. 314-399 in C. Stimpson (ed.) Discrimination Against Women. New York: Bowker.
RUBIN, L. (1976) Worlds of Pain. New York: Basic Books.
SEIFER, N. (1973) Absent from the Majority. New York: American Jewish Committee, Project on Ethnic America.
SHEPPARD, H. L. and N. HERRICK (1972) Where Have All the Robots Gone? New York: Free Press.
SWEET, J. (1973) Women in the Labor Force. New York: Seminar.
U.S. Department of Labor (1975) Handbook on Women Workers. Washington, DC: Bureau of Labor Statistics.
——— (1978) "Employment in perspective: working women." Washington, DC: Bureau of Labor Statistics.
VANEK, J. (1978) "Housewives as workers," pp. 392-414 in A. Stromberg and S. Harkness (eds.) Women Working. Palo Alto: Mayfield.
WARNER, R. S., D. WELLMAN, and L. WEITZMAN (1973) "The hero, the sambo and the operator." Urban Life and Culture 2: 53-83.
WEISS, R. and N. SAMUELSON (1958) "Social roles of American women: their contribution to a sense of usefulness and importance." Marriage and Family Living 20: 358-366.
WHYTE, W. F. (1948) "The social structure of the restaurant." American Journal of Sociology 54: 302-315.
WRIGHT, J. (1978) "Are working women *really* more satisfied? evidence from several national surveys." Journal of Marriage and Family 40: 301-313.
ZWEIG, F. (1952) Women's Life and Labour. London: Gollancz.

5

THE NEW HOME ECONOMICS:
AN AGENDA FOR SOCIOLOGICAL RESEARCH

RICHARD A. BERK

The difference between economics and sociology is very simple.
Economics is all about how people make choices. Sociology is all
about why they don't have choices to make.

                                                        —Dusenberry (1960)

One only has to sample the recent economics literature to observe extensive poaching in traditional sociological preserves. Two recent anthologies,
for example (Amacher et al., 1976; Phillips and Votey, 1977), consider the
causes and consequences of crime, notions of equality, bureaucratic decision making, voting behavior, and the role of higher education. Similarly,
Hirshleifer's (1976) excellent introductory microeconomics text cites illustrative material including the giving of charity, the price of brides among
the Sebri of Uganda, and preferences for male or female children. Whatever the intent of these incursions, they pose provocative alternatives to
the usual sociological perspectives. Yet, as MacRae (1978: 1224) observes,
"Sociologists have too often ignored these developments, which might
constitute both a challenge and a source of fruitful innovations."

Perhaps nowhere have the economic alternatives been more visible than
in studies of family life and particularly the "productive" activities undertaken in households. What Marc Nerlove (1974: 529) has christened the

AUTHOR'S NOTE: I am indebted to Sarah Fenstermaker Berk for critical comments
on the Marxist theory of household production and admonitions to "remember the
ladies." Thanks also go to C. J. LaCivita for a careful review of the exposition on the
New Home Economics. Trina Marks Miller, Cheryl Goluch, and Leslie Wilson gave
conscientious attention to preparation of the final manuscript.

113

"Chicago School" of the "New Home Economics" has addressed such topics as the decision to marry (Becker, 1974b), extramarital affairs (Fair, 1978), marital instability (Becker et al., 1977), leisure and labor force participation (Gronau, 1977), fertility behavior (Willis, 1974), and schooling decisions (Rosenzweig, 1977). While many aspects of such work have been criticized by sociologists (e.g., Duncan, 1974, Berk and Berk, 1978) and economists (e.g., Nerlove, 1974, Griliches, 1974; Pollak and Wachter, 1975), the New Home Economics has become a viable social science enterprise speaking to important sociological concerns.

Unfortunately, few sociologists have covered themselves with glory in the relatively rare instances when the New Home Economics is addressed.[1] William J. Goode (1974: 346), for example, considers Becker's (1974b) theory of marriage, claims to find "many" (but unspecified) tautologies, and then concludes that "often" the mathematical formulas provide "a beautiful flight but ... not reliable ... transportation." While part of Goode's critique rests on legitimate empirical contradictions of some of Becker's hypotheses, Goode makes the error of asserting that Becker's formulation necessarily rests entirely on "monetary variables." In fact, Becker's economic actors are maximizing utility (i.e., "satisfactions"), not profit (or income), and the real issues involve tradeoffs between various opportunity costs.[2] Perhaps Goode has strapped on his parachute prematurely.

In an effort to improve the quality of dialogue between sociologists and economists, this chapter will provide an overview of the New Home Economics and then consider a set of instances in which fundamental sociological questions are raised. The goal is neither to categorically refute nor to confirm economic models of household behavior, but to suggest mutual areas of concern that might benefit from an interdisciplinary research effort.

AN OVERVIEW OF THE NEW HOME ECONOMICS

Traditional microeconomic theory clearly distinguishes between the actions of firms and the actions of consumers. Firms, motivated by a search for maximum profits, produce consumer goods (and capital goods). Consumers, motivated by a search for maximum utility, purchase these outputs with the wages earned while selling their labor power to firms. Firms and consumers are therefore functionally linked on one hand by the exchange of income for goods and on the other hand by the exchange of labor power for wages. In a competitive market, these transactions are equitable in the sense that labor power and goods are exchanged at their market values, with money the measure of value. While a range of alternative formulations certainly exists (see, for example, Dobb, 1973) in which the assertion of equity is fundamentally challenged, this "neoclassical" approach has informed mainstream economic perspectives on the distinct activities of firms and consumers.

Beginning most visibly with the work of Becker (1976) and Lancaster (1966) over a decade ago, the notion that households "only" consume was dramatically challenged.

> In broad outline, this [new] approach views as the primary objects of consumer choice various entities, called commodities, from which utility is directly obtained. These commodities are produced by the consumer unit itself through the productive activity of combining purchased market goods and services with some of the household's own time. In this framework, all market goods are inputs used in production processes of the nonmarket sector. The consumer's demand for these market goods is a derived demand analogous to the derived demand by a firm for any factor of production [Michael and Becker, 1976: 134].

Elsewhere, Becker notes

> The integration of production and consumption is at odds with the tendency of economists to separate them sharply, production occurring in firms and consumption in households. It should be pointed out, however, that in recent years economists increasingly recognize that a household is truly a "small factory": It combines capital goods, raw material and labor to clean, feed, procreate and otherwise produce useful commodities [Becker, 1976: 92].

Figure 1, taken in a simplified form from a discussion paper by Oli Hawrylyshyn (1976), illustrates the difference between the traditional and new approaches Michael and Becker describe. In essence, the traditional view treats households as a black box; market goods come in one side and somehow utility comes out the other. The activities of household members by which market goods are made to yield utility (i.e., satisfactions) are totally neglected, and the "real" work is assumed to occur only in the market. In contrast, the new framework fully acknowledges the existence and legitimacy of household production in which time and market goods are combined to produce household commodities that in turn are the immediate sources of utility.[3] Note also that these household commodities can take a variety of forms: a made bed, a cooked meal, a disciplined child, watching a soap opera, and the like.[4] Finally, it is important to

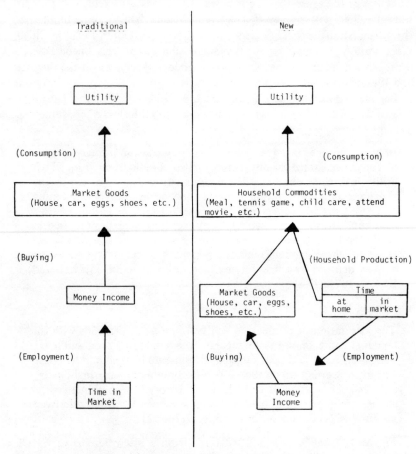

Figure 1   Schematic Comparison of Traditional and New
Theories of Household Behavior

stress that as a "small factory," the household is treated as the decision-making unit,[5] and it is the *family's* utility that is at issue. In a slightly different context, Mahoney (1961: 12-13) notes:

> We start with the concept of the spending unit defined as a household of persons who pool their resources to make joint decisions concerning the expenditure of those resources. . . . The welfare of the entire spending unit is assumed to be the criterion for decision making.

With some groundwork on the New Home Economics now in place, we are ready to turn to a more detailed discussion. In principle, there are a number of somewhat different formal expositions on which we would have drawn (Becker, 1974b, 1976; Gronau, 1974; Willis, 1974; Rosenzweig, 1977), but the model derived in Michael and Becker (1976) is perhaps the most useful for our purposes. While it predates some recent advances (Gronau, 1977; Wales and Woodland, 1977), its formal properties are more easily explained. Moreover, most of the essential ideas from the New Home Economics can be seen at work.

A MODEL OF HOUSEHOLD PRODUCTION

Becker's model of household production begins with the premise that household commodities (not market goods) are the immediate sources of utility. In addition, it is assumed that households will attempt to achieve the highest level of well-being (i.e., maximize their utility) within the resources available to them. This means not just that a superior "quality of life" is preferred, but that households will act to maximize their quality of life subject to practical constraints on their ability to do so. Hence the problem: What combination of household commodities should be produced within existing constraints in order to yield maximum utility? Should the household routinely eat Sunday dinners out, for example, or should such meals be prepared and eaten at home? Is it wise to make special efforts to keep an especially clean house, even if it means that less time will be available for child care? Is the time saved by a microwave oven worth the purchase price? Intuitively, it should be apparent that such decisions involve tradeoffs (i.e., opportunity costs—an hour spent on household work, for example, means that there is one less hour available for child care).[6] Becker's model of household production (as do all models within the New Home Economics) attempts to formally represent these dilemmas within the neoclassical framework and show how households balance a range of tradeoffs within the constraint of resources available so that a maximum level of well-being is achieved.

More formally, Becker begins by postulating the existence of a utility function which is nothing more than a mathematical formulation of the process by which household commodities are combined (e.g., added together) to yield utility. Typically, the utility function is represented in a very general form; utility is seen simply as some function of a set of household commodities, and presumably some combinations of commodities produce more utility than others. The amount of utility may be represented by U, the commodities by Z_i (the subscript indicating the particular commodity) and the function by u. Thus:

$$U = u(Z_1, Z_2, \ldots, Z_n). \qquad [1]$$

Once the source of utility is stated, the next problem is to express the manner in which household commodities are produced, how market goods and time are combined to yield the sources of satisfaction. Looking back at Figure 1, it should be apparent that we are moving from top to bottom in the right-hand column.

The relationship between the inputs of time and market goods on the one hand and household commodities on the other is represented in a household production function that is rather general in at least two senses. First, it is to be understood that there are in principle different production functions for different commodities although in some concrete applications the production functions are assumed to have certain properties in common (e.g., Becker, 1974b: 302) permitting aggregation across all household commodities.[7] That is, "the" household production function is actually a set of production functions. Second, much as in the case of the utility function, the precise functional form is typically left unspecified (for an exception see Becker, 1974: 305).[8] Given the usual purposes of such models this presents no special problems.

If Z_i is a particular household commodity, z_i its production function, x_i a set (vector) of market goods inputs, t_i a set (vector) of time inputs, and E a set (vector) of " 'environmental variables' reflecting the state of the art of production, or the level of technology of the production process" (Michael and Becker, 1976: 135), then the household production function can be represented as follows:

$$Z_i = z_i(x_i, t_i, E). \qquad [2]$$

Since the Z_i are the sources of utility, and it is assumed that as households attempt to maximize utility, households should also attempt to maximize the output of household commodities. However, there are limitations because the household's resources are finite. This leads Becker to formulate two kinds of constraints on the production of household commodities. First, there is a time constraint; whatever the time interval in question (a day, a week, a month, and so on) the total number of hours available for household production is limited. Letting T represent this limit, t_w the amount of time spent in the market (i.e., at "work"), and t_i the amount of time used in the production of a given (i-th) household commodity, the time constraint is[9]

$$T = t_w + \sum_{i=1}^{n} t_i. \qquad [3]$$

The second constraint is the more usual budget constraint on the amount of income (i.e., money) available to the household. Letting I represent the income constraint and p_i the price of market inputs (e.g., hamburger meat, a broiler) for a given (i-th) household commodity:

$$I = \sum_{i=1}^{n} p_i x_i. \qquad [4]$$

In other words, the income constraint equals the total input of market goods into the production of household commodities. Then it turns out that one can combine the time and income constraints into a single resources constraint representing the household's full income (see Becker, 1976, for details and justifications):

$$S = wT + V = \sum_i (wt_i + p_i x_i). \qquad [5]$$

If w is the household's wage rate (assumed to be constant),[10] and V is the household's nonwage income (e.g., interest on a savings account), equation 5 indicates that the full income of a household is the sum of the money taken in through work and through other sources. In addition, the full income is necessarily equal to the amount of money spent on market inputs (p_i times x_i) and the wages *foregone* when time is allocated to the production of household commodities (w times t_i), assuming that all available income is spent on achieving the household's well-being.[11] Put in other terms, full income defines a household's total earnings if time is allocated to maximize wealth rather than utility.

At this point, all of the components are in place, and it is appropriate to address the fundamental question of how households allocate their resources to achieve the greatest possible well-being. Recall that to gain maximum utility, households must produce the optimal configuration of household commodities subject to available resources. As a first step, the maximization problem is expressed in a Lagrangian form which includes the fact that utility depends on both the configuration of commodities and the full income constraint. In other words, a mathematical expression is developed that presumably captures the allocation problem that households attempt to solve.

Letting L represent the expression and lambda a parameter reflecting the "importance" of the constraint,[12]

$$L = u(Z_1, Z_2, \ldots, Z_n) - \lambda(\sum_i (wt_i + p_i x_i) - S). \qquad [6]$$

With the use of some differential calculus[13] to achieve a representation of the optimal allocation process, a variety of interesting results surface. Note, however, that these results hold *only* for the configuration of inputs yielding maximum utility. That is, they hold only "at the margin."

To begin, maximization with respect to the *commodities* implies

$$\frac{MU_i}{MU_j} = \frac{w \dfrac{dt_i}{dZ_i} + p_i \dfrac{dx_i}{dZ_i}}{w \dfrac{dt_j}{dZ_j} + p_j \dfrac{dx_j}{dZ_j}} \equiv \frac{\pi_i}{\pi_j}. \qquad [7]$$

MU_i is the marginal utility provided by commodity i, and MU_j is the marginal utility provided by commodity j. By marginal utility one roughly means the change in utility per unit change in the amount of the commodity in question (much like a regression coefficient in linear regression). For example, if one could measure utility in a cardinal fashion, one might find that each ironed shirt yielded 5 units of utility.[14] The d's in equation 7 refer to the derivatives which, again like regression coefficients, indicate (roughly) the change in the variable in the numerator for a unit change in the variable in the denominator. For example, dt_i/dZ_i indicates how much time is used in the production of one additional unit of commodity Z_i. The π's represent marginal costs which in turn are determined by the prices of market and time inputs. As such, they are called shadow prices to indicate that they are not directly observed through market transactions. In other words, since household commodities are not placed on the market, there is no observed price; the prices must be inferred from the market and time inputs.

Equation 7 reflects the usual results of maximization problems in economics. In this instance, the ratio of the marginal utilities of two household commodities equals the ratio of their marginal costs. In other words, the ratio of one's marginal "benefit" equals the ratio of one's marginal "costs." Hence, if at the margin one obtains twice as much utility from commodity i (e.g., a cooked meal) than from commodity j (e.g., an ironed shirt), the shadow price of commodity i must be twice as large as the shadow price of commodity j. Should this ratio not hold, it might be possible to trade (produce) some of commodity i for some of commodity j and be better off; one would not have allocated one's resources to maximize the output of commodities (and, hence, utility). In short, equation 7 shows the relationship between pairs of marginal utilities and pairs of prices to attain the configuration of household commodities with the largest utility.

It is also possible to differentiate equation 6 with respect to the *factors of production* in order to determine their optimal use. Thus:

$$\frac{\dfrac{\partial U}{\partial Z_i}\dfrac{\partial Z_i}{\partial f_{ik}}}{\dfrac{\partial U}{\partial Z_j}\dfrac{\partial Z_j}{\partial f_{j\ell}}} \equiv \frac{MU_i\,MP_{ik}}{MU_j\,MP_{j\ell}} = \frac{p_{fik}}{p_{fj\ell}}. \qquad\qquad [8]$$

MP_{ik} is the marginal productivity of factor k in the production of commodity i. $MP_{j\ell}$ is the marginal productivity of factor ℓ in the production of commodity j. By marginal productivity one means (roughly) the number of units of a commodity produced by adding one more unit of input from the factor in question. Analogously, f_{ik} is the factor k used in the production of Z_i and $f_{j\ell}$ is the factor ℓ used in producing Z_j. These factors can be either goods or time. When the same commodity is involved ($Z_i = Z_j$), equation 8 indicates that the ratio of the marginal products of the two factors equals the ratio of the factor prices ($p_{fik}/p_{fj\ell}$). This is similar to the results from equation 7; the ratio of marginal "benefits" equals the ratio of marginal "costs." Should this equality not hold, the household is allocating factors in such a manner that maximum output is not being achieved. Some factor is being overutilized and some factor is being underutilized in the production of the given commodity. In other words, the mix of inputs does not yield optimal productivity.

Equation 8 also indicates that if the *same factor* is involved in the production of more than one commodity ($k = \ell$), then the factor will be allocated across the commodities so that the utility values of the factor's marginal products are identical. That is, the given factor is neither underutilized nor overutilized across different household commodities. In short, equation 8 indicates how the "small factory" should allocate its resources to achieve the maximum output of household commodities and, thus, the maximum utility; the maximation problem is solved.

With these results in hand, a large number of empirical consequences are forthcoming. Michael and Becker (1976: 139) describe some of these as follows:

> By incorporating production concepts into the theory of consumption, the household production function approach implies that households respond to the changes in the prices and productivities of factors, to changes in the relative shadow prices of commodities and to changes in their full real income as they attempt to minimize their costs of production and to maximize their utility. A reduction in the price of some factor of production will shift the production process toward techniques that are more intensive in the use of that factor

and toward commodities that use the factor relatively intensely. The theory of derived demand implies, for example, that the relative increase in the use of the factor will be larger the greater the elasticities of substitution in production and in consumption.[15]

Likewise, if factor prices remain constant, an increase in the marginal productivity of some input induces several responses. To minimize costs of production, the factor's relative use in the production process will increase. Since the relative price of the commodity using this factor most intensively is reduced, the relative consumption of this commodity will increase. Since the rise in productivity raises full real income, the demand for all "normal" commodities (those with positive income elasticities) will increase. The absolute demand for the factor whose productivity rose will rise (or fall) if the combined effects of substitution in production and consumption and of expansion through the change in income outweigh (or are outweighed by) the productivity effect itself.

Many of the relationships that Michael and Becker describe can be easily represented in the usual graphic framework popular in microeconomics, and it may prove instructive to go through a brief example.

Figure 2 depicts optimization results for an imaginary two-commodity household (for three commodities the graphs are messy and for more than three, virtually impossible).[16] Suppose commodity Z_1 is the number of rugs vacuumed over the course of a month and Z_2 is the number of loads of clothes washed in the family clothes washer over the same period. In Figure 2, the number of rugs vacuumed is represented along the horizontal axis while the number of loads of clothes is represented along the vertical axis.

Recall that households are attempting to maximize their well-being (utility). In Figure 2, different levels of well-being are represented by the three convex curves I_1, I_2, and I_3 (i.e., the curves bowed toward the lower left-hand corner). I_1 provides the greatest utility, I_3 provides the least utility, and I_2 falls in between. In fact, these are only three possibilities, and, in principle, the entire space between the two axes may be filled with curves for different levels of utility. The Is are formal representations of a household's utility function and are typically called indifference curves (hence the use of "I"). By "indifference curve" one denotes that at any place on a *given* I, the household derives equal utility. Consequently, the household is "indifferent" to its location on that curve. For example, on I_3 a household might choose a combination of Z_1 and Z_2 placing it at either point A or point B. In the case of point A, far more of Z_2 is produced than Z_1. At point B the reverse is true. But, since both combinations fall on I_3, the household is indifferent between these two combinations.

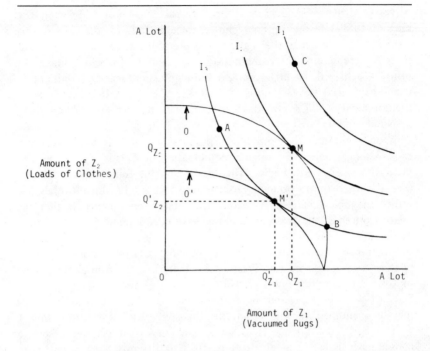

Figure 2   Optimization for a Two-Commodity Household

However, households cannot maximize their well-being in the absence of a consideration of their full income constraint. Put in other terms, the full income constraint provides the upper boundary of opportunities available to the household. Figure 2 shows two such opportunity boundaries, 0 and 0'.

Now suppose that the full income constraint sets the opportunity boundary at 0. This means that the household can select only combinations of Z_1 and Z_2 that fall on the boundary or below it (i.e., in a southwesterly direction). Point C, for example, which falls on I_1, is certainly desirable, but is beyond the household's resources. What about points A and B? They are both possible selections and as mentioned earlier, the household is indifferent between them. Note, however, that point A does not take advantage of the household's production potential since point A falls below the boundary. Consequently, the household can (and is assumed to) do better. Point B uses up the full potential, but is not the optimal mix of Z_1 and Z_2. The problem is that point B falls on I_3, and there are other combinations of Z_1 and Z_2 that fall on higher indifference curves (and hence yield more utility). In particular, point M (where 0 is tangent to I_2) is the optimal choice since it falls on the opportunity boundary and touches the highest possible indifference curve. Point M, therefore, represents the combination of Z_1 and Z_2 for which maximum utility is achieved. At this point the household produces Q_{z1} units of Z_1 (vacuumed rugs) and Q_{z2} units of Z_2 (loads of clothes). In short, these are the combinations of commodities that yield the highest level of well-being.

Now suppose that the price of water is increased. One important consequence is that the household's purchasing power declines because it can no longer obtain the original combination of Z_1 and Z_2 at the same price; the price is now higher. This means that the full income constraint (i.e., the opportunity boundary) shifts to a location in which, overall, less utility may be achieved. A second important consequence is that the relative prices of the two commodities have been altered. Since water is a factor in the production of washed clothes but not a factor in the production of vacuumed rugs, a load of clothes is now more expensive relative to a vacuumed rug. Presumably, therefore, the household will be motivated to produce fewer loads of clothes (e.g., sheets may be kept on beds a few extra days) and more vacuumed rugs (e.g., the living room rug may be vacuumed once a week rather than only just before entertaining).

The first consequence is called an income effect while the second consequence is called a substitution effect. Both impact the opportunity boundary; income effects shift the boundary without changing its slope, substitution effects alter the slope alone. In Figure 2 both effects are captured in 0', which represents the new full income constraint.

Note the results. To begin, a new optimal configuration surfaces at M', and this new point of maximum utility falls on a lower indifference curve. Hence, overall, the household is less well off. In addition, fewer loads of laundry and fewer vacuumed rugs are produced.[17] The price increase of water reduces production of both Z_1 and Z_2. Finally, the reduction in the number of loads of laundry is larger than the reduction in the number of vacuumed rugs. (Compare the change from Q_{z1} to Q'_{z1} with the change from Q_{z2} to Q'_{z2}.)

It is also worth observing that the ratios derived earlier have implications for Figure 2. For example, since the slope of any opportunity boundary tangent to an indifference curve (e.g., at M and M') is the same as the slope of the indifference curve itself, the ratio of marginal utilities equals the ratio of shadow prices.[18] In other words, Figure 2 conforms to the mathematics presented above.[19]

Through reasoning much like that just discussed, even Becker's relatively simple models yield a number of important results. In his analysis of marriage (1974b), for example, the labor input of one spouse is distinguished from the labor input of the other spouse. That is, the two labor inputs are defined as separate factors in the production of household commodities. Then, if the wage of one partner exceeds the wage of the other, and the partner with the lower wage is at least as efficient in the production of household commodities when the time inputs of the two are equal,[20] the low-wage partner will allocate less time to the market sector and more time to household production (Becker, 1974b: 303). In other words, if the balance of potential contributions suggests that one partner spend relatively more time in household production and relatively less in the market, Becker argues that households allocate their resources accordingly. Note that sex roles, norms, and other causal variables of sociological concern are irrelevant; all that counts is one's ability to contribute to overall household welfare. While there is some evidence supporting this general view (e.g., Gronau, 1974, 1977; Berk and Berk, 1978), it is also true that a number of anomalies surface. In particular, when both spouses are employed full time, even at relatively equal wages, women carry far more of the household burdens than do men (see, for example, Walker and Woods, 1976; Robinson, 1977; Berk and Berk, 1978).

The typical finding that wives do most of the household work despite full-time employment raises a number of important issues about the marriage "bargain" and the distribution of the fruits of household production. Presumably, women who are employed full time and who also invest a great deal of time in household work have little time for leisure. Becker's model is relevant here because he argues that a couple will not choose to marry unless (a) the woman's commodity "income" when married is equal to or greater than her commodity "income" when single, and (b) the man's commodity "income" when married is equal to or greater than his commodity "income" when single. That is, marriage cannot make either partner worse off. However, *both* are likely to be better off to the degree that the time inputs for each are "not perfect substitutes for each other or for goods and services supplied by market firms or households" (1974b: 304). And this raises the question of how the "surplus" is distributed. Becker's (1974b: 322-326) answer is that the commodities are distributed in part to reflect the marginal productivities of household members and variables such as the sex ratio in the "marriage market." If, for example, there are more eligible women than men, the latter's negotiating strength is increased, presumably leading to a larger share of the household spoils.[21]

Whatever the merits of Becker's theory of marriage, the many citations listed in the initial pages of this chapter indicate that the New Home Economics has been applied to a number of additional issues reflecting activities inside and outside the home: fertility, labor force participation, education, and marital dissolution. Yet even researchers broadly sympathetic to economic approaches to household production are often uneasy with one or another aspect of existing formulations.

First, the New Home Economics as currently applied does not allow for more than one household commodity to result from a single production process. In particular, this rules out psychic rewards derived during production. The output of preparing a meal is only a meal, for example, and whatever satisfaction (frustration, boredom, or fatique) that may be experienced is not considered. Gronau (1974: 460, 1977: 1122) among others has fully acknowledged this "sin," and common sense suggests that for such activities as child care, psychic consequences are critical. Yet Pollak and Wachter (1975) have proved that if psychic rewards and costs are formally introduced into the model, the model cannot be identified. That is, unique expressions for various parameters cannot be obtained. At this juncture, about all that can be said in rejoinder is that economic models of work in the market sector suffer from the same difficulty, and yet much useful research exists.

Second, there is considerable uneasiness with the premise that the household is the decision-making unit. The assumption of a single household utility function appears to require a one-for-all-and-all-for-one ethic which Nerlove (1974: 530-533) characterizes, somewhat derisively, as the "John Donne effect." Though not in direct response, Becker (1976) has more recently allowed household members to incorporate the welfare of others into their own utility function. Yet this creates new complications. For example, the theoretical work on marriage and divorce is premised on narrow self-interest, and it is not clear whether Becker and his colleagues can have it both ways. At what point does a suitor, for instance, drop narrow self-interest as the sole imperative and incorporate the welfare of others into his/her decision making? Even more fundamentally, until a great deal more work is done to operatioanlize such "altruism," Becker may simply be defining the problem away.

Third, as Gronau (1977) points out, the usual models of household production muddy the distinction between commonsense notions of "leisure" and household commodity production (see also Wales and Woodland, 1977). More specifically,

> From a theoretical point of view, the justification for aggregating leisure and work at home into one entity, nonmarket time (or home time), can rest on two assumptions: (a) the two elements react similarly to changes in the socioeconomic environment and therefore nothing is gained by studying them separately; and (b) the two

elements satisfy the conditions of a composite input, that is, their relative price is constant and there is no interest in investigating the composition of the aggregate since it has no bearing on production and the price of the output. Both assumptions are suspect. Recent time-budget findings have established that work at home and leisure are not affected in the same way by changes in socioeconomic variables, and this paper shows that the composition of the aggregate affects many facets of household behavior, such as labor supply, specialization in the household, and demand for children [Gronau, 1977: 1100].

Gronau's (1977: 1104) solution goes as follows:

An intuitive distinction between work at home (i.e., home production time) and leisure (i.e., home consumption time) is that work at home (like work in the market) is something one would rather have somebody else do for one (if the cost were low enough), while it would be almost impossible to enjoy leisure through a surrogate. Thus, one regards work at home as time use that generates services which have a close substitute in the market, while leisure has only poor market substitutes.

Gronau then proceeds to develop a model of household production that separates time inputs into market activities, household production, and leisure. And while such distinctions are apparently rather useful in explaining empirical patterns in time-budget studies, Gronau reintroduces a distinction between "work" and "leisure" that in effect makes them mutually exclusive. This smacks of just the unnecessarily rigid dichotomy that Becker attacked in his early work. Perhaps more important, Gronau's definition of leisure underscores the need to consider psychic rewards in *all* human activities (at home and in the market) since by the "surrogate-impossibility" criterion, there are leisure components in virtually any human endeavor. Yet this raises the spectre of joint production under which the formal maximization model self-destructs. Finally, there is good reason to be uneasy with distinctions between different sorts of activities derived either from states of mind and/or market availability. In the first instance, social phenomena are translated solely into psychological terms; psychological reductionism is the result. In the second instance, neglect of the *social relations* in which employment, household work, and leisure are necessarily embedded seems to trivialize the very distinctions of interest. One is left with an almost Orwellian typology in which production and consumption can take on meaning only in market terms. Marx's fetishism of commodities is resurrected in spades.

Fourth, there have been hellish problems in operationalizing many of the critical variables in the household production function. Estimating the shadow price of time for household members, for example, has received a great deal of attention, but to date existing solutions are unsatisfactory (Gronau, 1974). Even more troubling is how to operationalize and measure marginal productivity in household production. In particular, it is often unclear what the units of output are and how these units may be compared across different kinds of commodities. Such difficulties are further complicated by ambiguities in the proper level of aggregation. Is the output of preparing dinner, for instance, the entire meal or each of the dishes? (See, for example, Berk and Berk, 1979.)

Finally, it is all too easy to take the proposed model of the empirical world and treat it as *prescriptive*. And it is at this point that the underlying premises of the New Home Economics become absolutely critical. The traditional household division of labor, for example, is "justified" through the optimal production of household commodities with inequality and exploitation defined away. If husbands happen to do little household work, this may be explained by their relatively lower marginal productivity and/or their higher wages. Equally important, because the New Home Economics is essentially astructural (from the perspective of a sociologist), the household is viewed primarily as reacting to its "neutral" environment. More will be said about this shortly.

Given these and other difficulties, an overall assessment of the New Home Economics is probably premature. Perhaps the major ambiguity is that any evaluation depends fundamentally on the use to which the New Home Economics will be put. As a pointer to important phenomena that have been seriously neglected in the past, a major contribution has already been made. The significance of the simple observation that productive activities are undertaken in households cannot be overestimated. As a set of "sensitizing concepts," much of the conceptual structure has genuine merit. The importance of opportunity costs, for example, appears critical in any understanding of household activities. As a description of the ways in which households allocate their resources, however, many objections might well be raised. Nethertheless, households are in fact faced with the classic economic problem of scarce resources, and utility maximization probably plays some role.[22] Finally, as a predictive theory, the New Home Economics has experienced a mix of successes and failures about which even its advocates have expressed some concern. Yet at this point the empirical work is so complicated by data and measurement problems that it is difficult to specify where the important flaws might lie.

A SOCIOLOGICAL RESEARCH AGENDA

Whatever one's ultimate feelings about the New Home Economics, it would seem impossible to deny that a large number of important sociological questions are raised. At the very least, then, the New Home Economics underscores a sociological neglect of the productive activities undertaken in households. With this impact in mind, we turn to a discussion of a sociological research agenda implied by the New Home Economics.

WHAT IS A HOUSEHOLD COMMODITY?

The New Home Economics has employed a number of definitions of household commodities. In Reid's (1934) work, for example, household commodities are narrowly defined in terms of the goods and services for which market equivalents are likely to exist. In marked contrast, Becker (1976) is prepared to define almost anything produced by a household's nonwage labor as a household commodity as long as the commodity provides utility. Gronau (1977) apparently wants it both ways: He accepts Becker's definition but then works with two kinds of household commodities. On one hand, there are household commodities with market equivalents and, on the other hand, there are household commodities without market equivalents.[23]

What all these definitions share, however, is a common foundation in utility theory. For an output to be a household commodity, it must yield utility; it must have psychic consequences when consumed. That is, household commodities rest fundamentally on a *psychology of consumption.*

Yet, while this seems to imply that virtually nothing produced by the nonwage labor of household members can be excluded, there are actually nontrivial ambiguities. For example, it is not at all clear how one should view intermediate products in the production process. For example, clean sheets are not themselves a source of utility until they become part of a made bed. There is also an analogy to capital goods. It is common, for example, to find households purchasing simple household appliances that must be assembled at home. These appliances are not a source of utility (unless the psychic consequences of the assembling process are included), but are essential in the production of household commodities that do yield utility. Finally, many outputs of household activities are essentially informational. Employed adults, for instance, might leave behind a list of after-school chores for their children to complete. Should this information be treated as a factor of production, an intermediate product, or what? The more general point is that much of the "output" from the nonwage labor of household members apparently seems to fall outside Becker's umbrella definition.

The use of additional information about the existence of market equivalents does not really solve such problems. One difficulty is that the availability of market equivalents cross-cuts the kinds of products described above and does not eliminate whole classes of them. For example, one can send sheets out to be washed or do them at home. Yet clean sheets are still perhaps best viewed as an intermediate product and not a direct source of utility. A second and more fundamental difficulty is that market-based definitions are subject to the well-known Marxist criticism that by ignoring the social relations surrounding the production process, the essential attributes of commodities are lost (e.g., Marx, 1976a: 24-40).

In short, the definition of household commodities used in the New Home Economics may be unsatisfying on a number of grounds. The psychological underpinnings smack of psychological reductionism while the use of information about market equivalents is vulnerable to legitimate challenges from the intellectual left. And even if the standard definitions are taken on face value, there are many household "outputs" defying easy classification.

Given those objections, one might think that a more instructive definition could be extracted from Marxist literature on household work. As will soon become apparent, however, the Marxist perspectives are rather different in emphasis and not without serious conceptual problems of their own.

Recall that within the neoclassical framework, labor inputs from household members are viewed as "just" another factor in the production of household commodities. That is, labor and market goods possess equal conceptual importance, and both can be fully evaluated in terms of their relative marginal productivities and opportunity costs. Households mix and match labor and market inputs at will (under their full income constraint) in order to maximize their well-being. In contrast, Marxist approaches begin by making domestic labor by itself a topic of special concern whose role depends fundamentally on the given historical period and how the society as a whole organizes the production of goods and services (e.g., under capitalism). Market inputs to household production come up almost in passing as fruits of wages earned in the market sector; they are necessary for household production, but reveal little of what is really going on in households. This emphasis on labor recapitulates, not surprisingly, one of the major debates between neoclassical and Marxist theory and is one of the reasons why Marxists dismiss the New Home Economics as "bourgeois" (see Himmelweit and Mohun, 1977: 19).[24]

With this as background the following quotation from Himmelweit and Mohun (1977: 15) captures the flavor of the more structural approach to domestic labor.

> The direct products of domestic labour are not commodities; such products as clean clothes and cooked meals are not produced for the market by domestic labour and are not exchanged. Rather, they are produced for the direct satisfaction, without further transformation, of the needs of the producer and her family. In this sense domestic labour is private production. But it is not only distinguished by its location in noncommodity production; it is also private production in another sense. No division of labour exists within its realm. All housewives perform very similar tasks, and they perform them in isolation, unless aided by other members of their families. Neither of the types of division of labour that Marx described as operating within commodity production—the a priori division of labour between workers employed by an individual capital through the organizing control and authority of the capitalist, and the a posteriori social division of labour between workers employed by different capitals which, through the market, operates via the coercive force of competition—neither of these divisions of labour touches domestic labour. The only division of labour to which domestic labour is subject is that it is divided from commodity production. Indeed, this division comprises the specific form that the sexual division of labour, in its broadest sense, takes in capitalist society.

What then are the "outputs" of this labor? Again from Himmelweit and Mohun (1977: 16):

> While domestic labour does not produce commodities, it does produce many different use-values, which form a substantial component of the individual consumption of all the members of the family. This individual consumption is precisely what is necessary for the production of labour-power.... Labour-power, or the ability to work, is something that must continually be produced. It is used up (consumed) or wasted every day, and ceases to exist without the replenishment of individual consumption. For this reason, Marx, and other writers since, talked of the production and reproduction of labour-power. But there is another sense in which labour-power must be reproduced. Labour-power exists only as the ability to work of a particular person, the labourer. But labourers grow old and die, and society's stock of labour-power cannot then be replenished without the birth of potential new labourers. Thus while the birth of children

(reproduction of the species) is not in itself the reproduction of labour-power, it is necessary for labour-power to be reproduced that the labourer himself is reproduced. From the point of view of capital, housework is concerned with the reproduction of labour-power both on a daily and on a generational basis.

Housework, in the broadest sense, also plays an important reproductive role with respect to ideology. For the family has a crucial stabilising function through the allocation of sexually defined roles, both in the conditioning of children and in the maintenance of a docile, disciplined and divided working class. The family is one of the most important units for the socialization of individuals in capitalist society (Mitchell, 1971). Authoritarian relationships in social production (capitalist to worker) are facilitated through their previous observation and acceptance in the home (parents to children and husband to wife). But the ideological role of domestic labour, while important in reinforcing and stabilising capitalist society, cannot, ultimately, be determinant. Our task is rather to examine how domestic labour as production is crucial to capitalism, and which aspects are capable of change.

One might be sympathetic to the Marxist approach and still observe that a new kind of black box has been produced. Recall that traditional consumer theory was criticized by Becker for a failure to address the mechanisms by which consumer goods were transformed into utility. Becker filled that black box with the household production function through which household commodities were produced. Marxist views on domestic labor focus primarily on the production of labor power, the reproduction of labor power, and the enhancement of prevailing ideologies. However, the routine processes and social relations *within* households *responsible* for these outcomes are virtually ignored. This is particularly ironic given Marxist concern with precisely these issues in the *market sector*. While the reasons for such neglect are a subject of considerable debate (Hamilton, 1978), it is apparent that to date Marxist approaches to domestic labor have little to say about the ways in which labor and market goods are actually combined by households on a routine basis in service to the larger system. This theme will recur throughout the rest of the chapter.

Where does this leave us? It is perhaps fair to say that the concept of use-values plays roughly the same role within the Marxist framework as the concept of household commodities plays within the neoclassical framework.[25] Yet, with the broad notion of use-values in hand, Marxists quickly jump to more macro issues, leaving the day-to-day nature of household production unexamined (see Zaretsky, 1976; Gardiner, 1976). The result is a major empirical and conceptual hole in our understanding of domestic labor, and little insight on the nature of household commodities or use-values.

WHAT IS THE VALUE OF A HOUSEHOLD COMMODITY?

Debates on the nature of value stand out in both their longevity and their rancor (Marx, 1967: 71-83, 1976b; Robinson, 1964; Samuelson, 1971; Morishima, 1973; Morishima and Catephores, 1978; Sen, 1978). At the risk of grievous oversimplification, the basic question is what accounts for the rate at which market commodities are exchanged (their exchange-value)? Why, for example, is a jar of peanut butter "worth" the equivalent of two loaves of bread? Phrased in this way, the problem seems tame enough, but virtually any answer comes heavily laden with ideological trappings. Indeed, in some circles one's position on the nature of value is the litmus test for loyalty. An answer phrased primarily in market terms implies allegiance to bourgeois economics while an answer phrased primarily in terms of labor inputs places one squarely in the Marxist camp.[26]

As one might expect, debates about the nature of value of market commodities has implications for any consideration of the value of household commodities. While there is not space to consider the issue in great detail, some discussion is clearly warranted.

Within the neoclassical framework, there are two related definitions of value, neither providing an absolute or invariant metric. One definition of value comes in terms of marginal utility which at the margin is proportional to a commodity's price. Price, in turn, is the sum of the market values of the labor and other inputs (Becker, 1976: 91-96). And since equilibrium prices vary as a function of supply and demand, the value of a commodity will also vary. A second definition rests on the comparison between two (or more) commodities. At the margin, the ratio of the marginal utilities of two commodities equals the ratio of the market values of their factor inputs (Michael and Becker, 1976: 134-137. These ratios also respond to market forces.

It is important to understand that within the neoclassical framework, the absence of "true" value is unimportant. The focus is on how households allocate their scarce resources at the margin and, therefore, an absolute standard of value is not essential. What matters is that households are able to evaluate one configuration of commodities relative to some other configuration(s)

Yet, even if one accepts the neoclassical goals and definitions of value, there are significant complications. The difficulties derive from critical differences in the social relations inherent in household production compared to the social relations inherent in market production under capitalism. Marxists and neoclassicists basically agree that in the market sector, the exchange of labor power for wages occurs in a highly impersonal manner. The capitalist does not care if the labor comes from Jones or Smith and the employee does not care if the wages come from ABC Motors or Acme Construction, Ltd. Disembodied labor power is simply exchanged for its market value in wages. In marked contrast, household production is hardly impersonal, and the entities exchanged have symbolic content and situated meaning.

Consider an example of a chocolate cake baked by a member of a household. Within the neoclassical approach, that cake has value proportional to the sum of the market goods and time inputs evaluated at their market prices. Now, take the same cake and assume that it was baked for the birthday of one of the household members. The inputs of market goods and time are precisely the same, but there is good reason to value the cake differently. That is, the chocolate cake produced as a relatively routine dessert may be roughly equivalent in value to an apple pie. But when *defined* as a birthday cake, its value may be significantly enhanced.

The birthday cake example raises at least three problems for the neoclassical definitions of value. First, the "supply" of birthday cakes is *not* fully regulated by impersonal market forces, but requires a consideration of *social definitions of scarcity* (see Levi-Strauss, 1969). Birthdays come once a year by social convention and would lose their meaning if they occurred more frequently. This implies that the value of birthday cakes depends in part on an "artificial" constraint on supply that in turn increases their value. Numerous household commodities have similar properties: "gifts" of various sorts, leisure activities undertaken during "vacations," and commodities consumed in violation of "the rules" (e.g., children sneaking an extra cookie in violation of "proper nutrition").

Second, the birthday cake has *meaning* perhaps affecting its value. The cake communicates to the recipient that someone cares and may also serve to reinforce affective relationships, family loyalty, and a feeling of safety. In other words, the cake has symbolic content. The importance of "transfers" of this kind has been highlighted in the work of "grants economics" (e.g., Boulding, 1973). In the more general case of market exchanges Boulding notes (1973: 16):

> It is not merely commodities that are transferred, but also information, communication or messages. If I pass a store window and see a shirt with a price tag on it that I would like to buy, I have perceived a message from the storekeeper saying "I am willing to give you this shirt, if you will give me this amount of money." When I go to the

store I have to communicate with the storekeeper before he will bring me the shirt out of the window so the transaction can take place. It is almost impossible to think of any relationship among people in which communication does not play some part.

While one might argue whether the communication inherent in market transactions affects the value of the commodities exchanged, there seems little doubt that in a great many instances, the value of household commodities will be in part dependent on their "message."

Third, it is a basic tenet of neoclassical economics that the market price of a commodity does not affect its value; price is only an *indicator* of value. This assumes away such things as conspicuous consumption in which consumers purchase expensive goods simply to be able to say they purchased expensive goods. While this may be a tolerable simplification in the usual market contexts, the impact of price on value in households may be more significant. If, for example, the birthday cake is taken to be a message of affection, greater labor inputs per se may increase its value. Indeed, one could imagine an incompetent household baker turning out a terrible cake that was highly valued precisely *because* it took the baker an inordinate amount of time to bake it. Put in slightly different terms, there is something to the old saw "it's the thought that counts." More formally, for many household commodities an increase in time inputs may have no impact on commodity production (i.e., $dZ_i/dt_i = 0$) but may nevertheless be itself a source of value. Interested readers might find it instructive to review one or more of the neoclassical derivations to see what this does to the resulting models (e.g., Gronau, 1977: 1104-1106).

To summarize, the personal nature of the social relations within households significantly complicates the nature of value for neoclassical theorists. Market production, premised on impersonal social relations, can perhaps ignore the "messages" attached to commodities; indeed there may be few messages at all (although Boulding would vigorously dispute this). For households, expressions of value resting on impersonal market premises may be quite misleading. It should also be apparent that Marxist perspectives on household production (i.e., within households) derived from a labor theory of value would be vulnerable to the same sorts of criticisms. That is, if there were a detailed Marxist model explaining the sources of use-values and exchange-values, a labor theory of value would probably be inadequate. Readers who doubt this conclusion should work through any of the better formal expositions of Marx's approach to value (e.g., Morishima, 1973: 10-45).[27]

HOW IS HOUSEHOLD PRODUCTION ORGANIZED?

One of the ironies of the New Home Economics is that with all the talk about the household production function, scant attention is paid to the actual production processes implied. There is, for example, nothing approaching Adam Smith's famous discussion of the production of pins or Marx's rich descriptions of commodity production under emerging capitalism. Nor is there any use of the input-output formulations developed by Leontief, von Neumann and others (see, for example, Morishima, 1976: 22-53; Pasinetti, 1977: 54-70). The New Home Economics proceeds after simply assuming that households will utilize the most efficient production processes available with the nature of these processes unspecified.

This oversight means that the New Home Economics provides little insight into *how* labor and market goods are combined *over time* to yield household commodities. Production is necessarily a longitudinal process in which a variety of activities must be effectively orchestrated; a meal must be cooked before it can be eaten, for example, and anyone who has ever tried to make all of the dishes come out precisely when household members are ready to eat can testify that a significant organizational effort is involved. In short, the social activity of production is ignored.

A host of issues needs to be addressed with respect to household production processes in order to understand what people actually *do* on a day-to-day basis (see Berk and Berk, 1979). For example, it is apparent that household production must respond to deadlines and time constraints imposed from outside the home. School children must be awakened, dressed, and fed in time to make the opening bell. Shopping must be planned with attention to when stores are open. Dinner must be prepared with an eye to when employed adults return from work. How then do such constraints affect the way in which household commodities are produced? There is some evidence that leisure activities, for instance, are postponed to periods when deadlines are less pressing (Berk and Berk, 1979).

There are also constraints imposed by the production process itself. While it is obvious that dishes must be washed before they can be dried, these and a large number of other imperatives affecting the *feasibility* of different production processes must affect how production is organized. "Doing the laundry," for instance, involves stripping beds, collecting soiled clothes, sorting the clothes and linen (perhaps into "whites" and "darks"), putting the clothes and linen in the washer, transferring them to the dryer, taking the clothes and linen out at the proper time (to prevent wrinkling), folding the clothes and linen, and finally putting the clothes and linen away. Note that the *sequence* is necessarily fixed, and many hours may be spent from start to finish. Moreover, a failure to follow the sequence will likely abort the entire enterprise; another sequence may not be feasible. The point is, however, that much of household production takes on this character and surely affects how time and market goods are allocated over the course of a day (or longer periods).

Beyond feasibility, efficiency is also relevant. To begin, some sequences of activities may yield higher marginal productivities than others. It probably makes sense to dust before vacuuming, for example, in order to avoid having to vacuum twice. The same argument holds for wiping kitchen counters before sweeping or mopping the kitchen floor. It may also be more efficient (i.e., yielding greater marginal productivity) to group complementary activities and separate incompatible ones. While one might iron and watch television at the same time, for example, television and vacuuming probably do not mix well. Similarly, it makes sense to run all of one's errands at once, perhaps on the way home from work.

Finally, household production does not yield known outputs with certainty. The production function specified in the New Home Economics assumes that a given configuration of inputs leads with certainty to some set of household commodities despite the fact that unexpected phone calls, children's temper tantrums, visits from neighbors and salespeople, and a host of other unanticipated interruptions can easily disrupt even the best-planned set of household activities. Consequently, household production must respond to inherent uncertainty that in turn must alter how production is organized. One could easily imagine, for example, households trying to minimize the risks of production failures by trying to finish the most important production process early in the day (leaving time available for later should it be needed).

A far more detailed discussion of these and other issues in the household production process can be found elsewhere (Berk and Berk, 1979). For our purposes the major point is that the New Home Economics leaves such issues unaddressed. Moreover, Marxist perspectives on domestic labor do no better. Neither tradition has bothered to take a good, close look inside households to find out how production is organized on a day-to-day basis. There is no Harry Braverman (1974) of household work.

IS THERE EXPLOITATION WITHIN HOUSEHOLDS?

Controversies surrounding the nature of exploitation are almost as long standing and acrimonious as the controversies surrounding the nature of value (Dobb, 1973). Indeed, the two are inextricably linked since definitions of exploitation rest fundamentally on disparities between value produced and value received (e.g., Morishima, 1976: 74-96; Bharadwaj, 1978; Wolff, 1979). The concept of absolute surplus value, for example (Marx, 1967: 186-198) derives from the difference between the exchange-value of commodities under capitalism and value returned to labor for its efforts (i.e., in the form of wages necessary for the sustenance of the worker and the worker's family).

As long as the competitive market is operating properly, exploitation is largely irrelevant within the neoclassical perspective. At most, exploitation may surface as a temporary aberration having no structural and, hence, no ongoing status. Production factors are paid at their market value and consequently factors are paid what they are worth.[28] Not surprisingly, these views carry over into the New Home Economics. Recall that on one hand, the labor contributions of household members depend on marginal productivity and shadow wages. Thus, the labor allocations are undertaken solely with an eye to maximum production of household commodities, and the division of labor is justified on these grounds. On the other hand, the distribution of household commodities is determined in the marriage bargain as a function of marginal productivity and the sex ratio in the marriage market (among other things). That is, marriage partners negotiate for their share of the spoils based on what they are able to contribute to production relative to what the competition might contribute. To rephrase Marx a bit, from each according to his/her abilities, to each according to his/her abilities.

In short, the New Home Economics essentially defines the problem of exploitation away. Household members contribute labor as they should to maximize production and then get returns commensurate with their nego-tiating strength. Thus, the common observation that wives do most of the household work, even if employed full time, is explained primarily by their much lower wages and far greater marginal household productivity (relative to husbands).

While it may be possible that the vast differences in household work contributions between spouses depend on wage and productivity differen-tials, the existing case is very far from compelling. Likewise it is difficult to understand the unequal distribution of leisure time (Berk and Berk, 1979) within the neoclassical model (leisure being one of the spoils). The disparities are simply too large and too stable in the face of varying household characteristics. This suggests that perhaps households may settle for *less* than the maximum production of commodities if at the same time other ends are being served. That is, the distributions of labor inputs and commodity outputs may not reflect solely some optimal allocation pro-

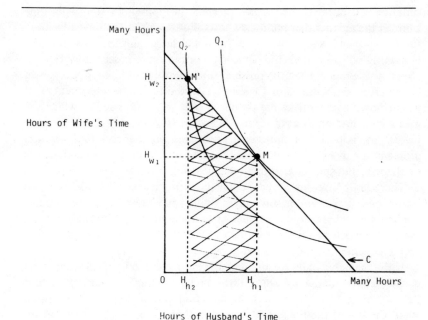

Figure 3   Cost Minimization Subject to a Normative Constraint

cess, but a suboptimal allocation process resulting from a priori constraints on how allocation proceeds.

Becker (1971) himself raises this possibility for market phenomena when he analyzes the impact of "tastes" for discrimination. In essence, racial prejudice subverts the competitive labor market so that suboptimal equilibria result. However, Becker does not apply such models to the household, and in fact they hold some promise.

Consider Figure 3. Suppose there is some given level of commodity production (a quantity) represented by Q_1. To simplify matters, assume that there are only two labor inputs: the labor inputs of the wife and the labor inputs of the husband (in hours). Given Q_1, the household seeks to minimize the costs of production by allocating the labor of the husband and wife in the optimal manner. That is, the household tries to mix the labor of both spouses so that once the shadow prices of their labor are taken into account, the costs of the commodities produced are minimized. This cost minimization curve is represented in Figure 3 by C. Note that C is tangent to Q_1 at point M, and at point M the household allocates H_{h1} hours of the husband's time and H_{w1} hours of the wife's time.[29] Now suppose that normative pressures prevent the household from allocating labor in the manner that minimizes costs. For example, the time allocation for the husband, H_{h1}, may be deemed too large, and the most that the household will tolerate is the reduced contribution represented by H_{h2}. In effect, this eliminates all the possible configurations of labor inputs shown in the cross-hatched area of Figure 3. The result is a new solution at M' at which *fewer* commodities are produced (Q_2 versus Q_1) and at which the wife's contribution is significantly *increased* (H_{w2} versus H_{w1}). In other words, by imposing a *normative* constraint on the cost minimization problem, a new and suboptimal solution results, resting on greater efforts by the wife and smaller efforts by the husband.

There are different ways in which normative constraints could be formulated. For example, one might build a model in which a constraint implied that whatever the number of hours contributed by the husband, the wife contributed more. Or one could build in two constraints so that such inequalities would be tolerated only up to some level.

Unfortunately, while constrained maximization models of this sort hold considerable promise as vehicles for understanding the impact of sex-linked norms, the question of exploitation per se remains unresolved. First, the use of the household as the maximizing unit obscures who wins and who loses when commodities are produced and distributed. Hence, a critical step in addressing exploitation within the constrained maximization framework is the development of models in which the utility of individual household members becomes the fundamental building block. To the author's knowledge, no such models yet exist.

Second, given some a priori definition of equity, a strategic decision must be made as to whether exploitation will be examined in structural terms, ideological terms, or as aberrant patterns within particular households. Absolute surplus value is, of course, an example of a structural approach, resting as it does on relations between antagonistic social classes. Perspectives based on the ideology of patriarchy (e.g., Hamilton, 1978: 50-75) are an example of the second option. "Pathological" relationships among household members, perhaps best exemplified in the recent literature on domestic violence (Gelles, 1974; Steinmetz and Straus, 1974) fall within the third camp. While these three approaches are certainly not mutually exclusive, they should not be confounded with one another. And it should be readily apparent that the approach(es) chosen will focus attention on a particular *kind* of causal explanation at the likely expense of others.

Given the inability to date of neoclassical models to address the possibility of exploitation of one household member by another, one might wonder if Marxist approaches have anything to offer. As noted earlier, however, Marxist perspectives on domestic labor have not looked very closely at relationships within the households and when suggestions of inequities surface, they are given little theoretical attention. In an otherwise instructive piece, Jean Gardiner (1976: 115-116), for example, mentions in passing that "in fact the assumption that the wife consumes as much as the husband is unlikely to hold in part because the wife's unpaid status will tend to keep her consumption down to a minimum." Such observations cry out for explanation.[30] But within the Marxist perspective, none seems to exist.

WHAT IS THE RELATIONSHIP BETWEEN DOMESTIC LABOR AND THE LARGER SOCIETY?

By this point, it should be clear how neoclassical theory links household production to the larger society. To recapitulate, the household serves as a site in which labor and market goods and services are combined to produce household commodities. These commodities are the source of utility and therefore by implication the basis for survival of the household and its members. That is, the household production function provides an important missing link in consumer theory. In addition, the production of household commodities (including leisure) is related to decisions about labor force participation, fertility and education of children (among other things). But here, too, neoclassical models of household production are less involved in fundamentally altering earlier views on these issues and more involved in filling theoretical gaps. One is left then with the broader neoclassical approach virtually intact. Households trade their labor power for wages and their wages for consumer goods. These exchanges are equitable in the sense that exchange-values reflect equilibrium prices; commodities and labor are traded at the market value.

Marxist approaches, of course, find this unsatisfactory. Marxists argue that by focusing on the operation of markets as the primary explanatory mechanism, attention is directed away from the social relations of production through which exploitation of the working class occurs. In this context, households are not just a "small factory" in the larger circulation of value, but a site that plays a fundamental role in supporting capitalist society. This is not to say that there are no counter forces (e.g., in the need for a second wage earner in low-income families), nor to deny a fundamental role for the middle-class family under corporate capitalism (Smith, 1973). However, to date the bulk of Marxist writings have stressed the production and reproduction of labor power in service to the needs of capital.

According to Himmelweit and Mohun (1977), there are basically two competing views on the links between domestic labor and capitalism. One perspective defines domestic labor as "private labour which continues to exist alongside of commodity production" (Himmelweit and Mohun, 1977: 18-19). Some writers within this tradition treat household production much like a vestige from precapitalist forms. Other writers reject such historical explanations and view household production as an entity in its own right operating under its own exigencies. In either case, however, domestic labor is not integrated into the social relations that characterize capitalism. Rather, the exchanges that take place involve exchanges between two rather different production processes each with its own particular set of social relations.

The second perspective defines domestic labor as the "labour that directly maintains and reproduces labour-power" (Himmelweit and Mohun, 1977: 19). Here domestic labor is integrated into the social relations by which capitalism is characterized. Yet there are some fundamental disagreements. In particular, it is not clear whether domestic labor simply transforms market commodities into use-values or whether surplus value is extracted as well.

Any overall assessment of these views is beyond the scope of this chapter. There is a host of definitional issues beneath these debates made all the more difficult by a neglect of the sorts of questions raised in earlier sections of this chapter. Nevertheless, it should be clear that Marxist approaches have staked out a very different territory from the neoclassical perspectives, and in so doing have challenged fundamental neoclassical premises. Yet the recent work by Robinson, Sen, Morishima, and others indicates that—in the market sector at least—a meaningful integration is possible. Perhaps these lessons will be transferred to the study of domestic labor.

CONCLUSIONS

The recent interest in household production is in its infancy and, as such, reflects the growing pains of any new endeavor. All manner of intellectual species have been attracted, characterized by different paradigms, different assumptions, different definitions, and different approaches to data. Among these disparate perspectives, this chapter has focused on New Home Economics as perhaps the most formal, visible, and thoroughly formulated view. Whether or not one agrees with the New Home Economics, it does provide a clear, parsimonious statement of intent that facilitates a consideration of many fundamental questions on the nature of household production.

Beyond the specific issues raised in the preceding pages, there are three more general conclusions worthy of comment. First, it is readily apparent that no single view has a monopoly on our understanding of household production. Perhaps with a full recognition of this reality, the literature on domestic labor can avoid the adolescent quarreling that characterizes the social science enterprise more generally. One could hope that a literature focusing on what is typically a female-dominated activity and which to date relfects the singular contributions of women scholars can become a model of intellectual cooperation.

Second, most of the existing approaches to household production seem to draw far too heavily on formulations developed in ignorance of the special experiences of women. The "small factory" of the New Home Economics, for example, is derived from market production dominated by men and studied primarily by men. In this context it is instructive that the personal nature of the social relations of household production are neglected. This is more than an oversight and drives to the heart of the New Home Economics. Yet, as the old saying goes, "one should not throw out the baby with the bath water unless the baby is very dirty." In the process of developing new perspectives on household labor, it would be a grievous error to dismiss all previous thinking as misogynist.

Finally, there is absolutely no substitute for taking a very long and close look at precisely what activities are undertaken in the process of household production. The New Home Economics is not alone in its failure to examine what is really occurring in households. The production function, for instance, takes an assumed and abstract form with virtually no empirical justification. Perhaps when we thoroughly document the day-to-day activities initiated within the household, many of the existing theoretical disputes will either be easily resolved or with hindsight be interpreted as silly arguments conceived in ignorance.

NOTES

1. In all fairness, however, economists have often caricatured sociological perspectives (e.g., Becker, 1974a: 9).

2. Indeed, in Becker's most programmatic statements (e.g., Michael and Becker, 1976), the idea is to specifically move away from formulations expressed solely in monetary terms.

3. Note that Figure 1 does not show the full set of interdependencies between firms and consumers, but focuses primarily on the role of consumer.

4. Actually, the "new" perspective owes a great deal to the early work of Margaret Reid (1934), who basically staked out the household as an important territory for microeconomics. Unfortunately, her insights went largely unnoticed until quite recently.

5. To quote Nicholson (1972: 180):

A firm is viewed as being run by an entrepreneur who has total dictatorial powers over its operation. Such a view is an obvious oversimplification of decision processes in real world firms. However, since any theory necessarily involves some abstraction, the relevant question is whether the benefits of this holistic approach in terms of greater analytic simplicity exceed its costs. In a wide variety of situations, this has clearly been the case.

6. Dare we say that there is no free lunch?

7. In essence, this allows one to talk about the (weighted) sum of all household commodities rather than particular commodities.

8. A Cobb-Douglas form is cautiously suggested. Basically, this involves a multiplicative relationship among inputs.

9. The sigma means that the time inputs for each household commodity are summed over the total of n household commodities.

10. The assumption of a constant wage is usually not critical and can typically be circumvented (Becker, 1976: 93-95).

11. Of course, households may save and/or invest part of their income, as the chapter by Lehrer and Nerlove in this volume indicates.

12. The use of Lagrangian formulations is fundamental to economic theory, and discussions of its applications and properties can be found in intermediate texts (e.g., Nicholson, 1972). In this context, one can view the terms to the right of the minus sign as constraining the amount of utility that in principle could be achieved.

13. In essence, one differentiates equation 6 with respect to particular parameters of interest, sets these derivatives equal to zero, and then solves the resulting set of equations to obtain the desired expressions.

14. The measurement of utility has a long and controversial history in economics. See Hirshleifer (1976: 54-66) for an introductory discussion.

15. An elasticity is a measure of change, much like a derivative. However, it is standardized to reflect the percentage change in the numerator for each 1 percent of change in the denominator. For example, the elasticity of substituting a wife's time for a husband's time may be -.50. This means that a 1 percent increase in the husband's contribution leads to a .5 percent decrease in the wife's. Or a 100 percent increase in the husband's contribution leads to a 50 percent reduction in the wife's.

16. The mathematical results, however, are relevant regardless of the number of commodities.

17. The reduction in the number of vacuumed rugs is not a general result. With slightly different but equally plausible opportunity boundaries and indifference curves, the number of vacuumed rugs would increase.

18. The slope of the indifference curve is the ratio of the two marginal utilities, and the slope of the opportunity boundary is the ratio of two shadow prices.

19. Through this formal discussion we have assumed that the opportunity boundary and indifference curves are "nicely behaved." This involves a number of issues that we cannot discuss here, and interested readers should consult a good theory text (e.g., Henderson and Quandt, 1971; Nicholson, 1972).

20. In general, economic models of production assume a "diminishing return" form in which marginal productivity depends on how much of a given factor is already being used. Thus, marginal productivities vary depending on the mix of inputs. In this instance, one could well imagine marginal household productivity of either partner declining rapidly as the time input to household production exceeded the "eight-hour day."

21. There are a number of important assumptions here such as the requirement that all household commodities are subject to "negotiation."

22. It is interesting to note that Becker is not wedded to optimization models. In fact, he has argued many useful market results may be obtained with far less demanding approaches (Becker, 1962). Unfortunately, he has never pursued these alternative models.

23. Other sorts of subdivisions exist as well. Gronau (1974), for example, distinguishes between "standard of living" and "child services" (child care). Hawrylyshyn (1976) distinguishes between commodities that produce direct utility and indirect utility. However, these definitions are not essential to our discussion.

24. The comparable argument in the market sector involves the relative conceptual importance of labor and capital. An excellent discussion of these and other issues relevant to the debate can be found in Dobb (1973: 136-165).

25. This is not to say that use-values are the same as household commodities.

26. By labor inputs one basically means the number of units (e.g., hours) of labor required to produce the commodity. This labor comes in two forms: "living" labor power directly used in the production process and "dead" labor power embodied in the capital goods (and raw materials) used in the production process (Marx, 1967: 35-46; Morishima, 1973: 10-20).

27. This conclusion depends, of course, on the use to which the theory of value will be put (Sen, 1978). A labor approach might be useful to isolate and describe some important structural characteristics of household production, even if it had no predictive value. That is, one might learn important things about the relevant social relations while still not being able to derive a formal expression for the value of a household commodity.

28. Exploitation does become a genuine issue through imperfect competition such as under monopoly competition (e.g., Henderson and Quandt, 1971: 206-253). Exploitation can also surface under the guise of "distributional issues" within welfare economics (e.g., Henderson and Quandt, 1971: 254-292).

29. In Figure 3, we have represented a cost minimization problem for a given level of outputs. The "dual" of this process is to maximize outputs subject to the given cost constraint. Thus, one can talk about Figure 3 in either terms. Interested readers should consult any of the microeconomics texts cited earlier (e.g., Hirshleifer, 1976).

30. Ideological explanations have much more to say about such issues. See, for example, Rowbotham (1973), Davidoff (1976), and Bell and Newby (1976).

REFERENCES

AMARCHER, R. C., R. D. TOLLISON, and T. D. WILLET [eds.] (1976) The Economic Approach to Public Policy. Ithaca: Cornell University Press.

BECKER, G. S. (1962) "Irrational behavior and economic theory." Journal of Political Economy 70, 1: 1-16.

——— (1971) The Economics of Discrimination. Chicago: University of Chicago Press.

——— (1974a) "Crime and punishment: an economic approach," in G. S. Becker and W. M. Landes (eds.) Essays in the Economics of Crime and Punishment. New York: Columbia University Press.

——— (1974b) "A theory of marriage," in T. W. Schultz (ed.) Economics of the Family. Chicago: University of Chicago Press.

——— (1976) "A theory of the allocation of time," in G. S. Becker (ed.) The Economic Approach to Human Behavior. Chicago: University of Chicago Press.

——— E. M. LANDES, and R. T. MICHAEL (1977) "An economic analysis of marital instability." Journal of Political Economy 85, 6: 1141-1187.

BERK, R. A. and S. F. BERK (1978) "A simultaneous equation model for the division of household labor." Sociological Methods and Research 6, 4: 431-468.

——— (1979) Labor and Leisure at Home. Beverly Hills: Sage Publications.

BELL, C. and H. NEWBY (1976) "Husbands and wives: the dynamics of the deferential dialectic," in D. L. Barker and S. Allen (eds.) Dependence and Exploitation in Work and Marriage. London: Longman.

BHARADWAJ, K. (1978) "Maurice Dobb's critique of theories of value and distribution." Cambridge Journal of Economics No. 2: 153-174.

BOULDING, K. E. (1973) The Economy of Love and Fear. Belmont, CA: Wadsworth.

BRAVERMAN, H. (1974) Labor and Monopoly Capital. New York: Monthly Review Press.

DAVIDOFF, L. (1976) "The rationalization of housework," in D. L. Barker and S. Allen (eds.) Dependence and Exploitation in Work and Marriage. London: Longman.

DOBB, M. H. (1973) Theories of Value and Distribution since Adam Smith: Ideology and Economic Theory. Cambridge: Cambridge University Press.

DUNCAN, O. D. (1974) "Comment," pp. 430-431 in T. W. Schultz (ed.) Economics of the Family. Chicago: University of Chicago Press.

DUSENBERRY, J. (1960) Demographic and Economic Change in Developed Countries. Princeton: Princeton University Press.

EKEH, P. P. (1974) Social Exchange Theory. Cambridge: Harvard University Press.

FAIR, R. C. (1978) "A theory of extramarital affairs." Journal of Political Economy 86, 1: 45-61.

GARDINER, J. (1976) "Political economy of domestic labor in capitalism," in D. L. Barker and S. Allen (eds.) Dependence and Exploitation in Work and Marriage. London: Longman.

GELLES, R. J. (1974) The Violent Home. Beverly Hills: Sage Publications.

GOODE, W. J. (1974) "Comment: the economics of nonmonetary variables," pp. 345-351 in T. W. Schultz (ed.) Economics of the Family. Chicago: University of Chicago Press.

GRILICHES, Z. (1974) "Comment," pp. 546-548 in T. W. Schultz (ed.) Economics of the Family. Chicago: University of Chicago Press.

GRONAU, R. (1974) "The effect of children on the housewife's value of time," pp. 457-488 in T. W. Schultz (ed.) Economics of the Family. Chicago: University of Chicago Press.

——— (1976) "The allocation of time of Israeli women." Journal of Political Economy 84, 4: S201-S220.

––– (1977) "Leisure, home production, and work: the theory of the allocation of time revisited." Journal of Political Economy 85, 4: 1099-1124.

HAMILTON, R. (1978) The Liberation of Women: A Study of Patriarchy and Capitalism. London: George Allen & Unwin.

HAWRYLYSHYN, O. (1976) "Toward a definition of non-market activities." Institute of Economic Research Discussion Paper 214, Queen's University. Kingston, Ontario, Canada.

HENDERSON, J. M. and R. E. QUANDT (1971) Microeconomic Theory. New York: McGraw-Hill.

HIMMELWEIT, S. and S. MOHUN (1977) "Domestic labour and capital." Cambridge Journal of Economics No. 1: 15-31.

HIRSHLEIFER, J. (1976) Price Theory and Applications. Englewood Cliffs, NJ: Prentice-Hall.

LANCASTER, K. J. (1966) "A new approach to consumer theory." Journal of Political Economy 74, 1: 132-157.

LEVI-STRAUSS, C. (1969) The Elementary Structure of Kinship. Boston: Beacon.

MacRAE, D., Jr. (1978) "Review essay: the sociological economics of Gary S. Becker." American Journal of Sociology 83, 5: 1244-1258.

MAHONEY, T. A. (1961) "Influences on labor-force participation of married women," pp. 11-24 in N. N. Foote (ed.) Household Decision Making. New York: New York University Press.

MARX, K. (1963) Theories of Surplus Value. London: Lawrence & Wishart.

––– (1967) Capital. New York: International.

––– (1976a) Wage-Labor and Capital. New York: International.

––– (1976b) Value, Price and Profit. New York: International.

MICHAEL, R. T. and G. S. BECKER (1976) "On the new theory of consumer behavior," in G. S. Becker (ed.) The Economic Approach to Human Behavior. Chicago: University of Chicago Press.

MITCHELL, J. (1971) Women's Estate. Harmondsworth: Penguin.

MORISHIMA, M. (1973) Marx's Economics: A Dual Theory of Value and Growth. Cambridge: Cambridge University Press.

––– (1976) The Economic Theory of Modern Society. Cambridge, England: Cambridge University Press.

––– and G. CATEPHORES (1978) Value Exploitation and Growth. New York: McGraw-Hill.

NERLOVE, M. (1974) "Toward a new theory of population and economic growth," pp. 527-545 in T. W. Schultz (ed.) Economics of the Family. Chicago: University of Chicago Press.

NICHOLSON, W. (1972) Microeconomic Theory: Basic Principles and Extensions. Hinsdale, IL: Dryden.

PASINETTI, L. L. (1977) Lectures on the Theory of Production. New York: Columbia University Press.

PHILLIPS, L. and H. L. VOTEY, Jr. [eds.] (1977) Economic Analysis of Pressing Social Problems. Chicago: Rand McNally.

POLLAK, R. A. and M. L. WACHTER (1975) "The relevance of the household production function and its implications for the allocation of time." Journal of Political Economy 83: 255-277.

REID, M. G. (1934) Economics of Household Production. New York: John Wiley.

ROBINSON, J. (1964) Economic Philosophy. Harmondsworth: Penguin.

––– (1977) How Americans Use Time: A Social-Psychological Analysis. New York: Praeger.

ROSENZWEIG, M. R. (1977) "Farm-family schooling decisions: determinants of quantity and quality of education in agricultural populations." Journal of Human Resources 12, 1: 71-91.

ROWBOTHAM, S. (1973) Women's Consciousness, Man's World. Harmondsworth: Penguin.

SAMUELSON, P. A. (1971) "Understanding the Marxian notion of exploitation: a summary of the so-called transformation problem between Marxian values and competitive prices." Journal of Economic Literature No. 9: 399-431.

SEN, A. (1978) "On the labour theory of value: some methodological issues." Cambridge Journal of Economics No. 2: 175-190.

SMITH, D. (1973) "Women, the family and corporate capitalism," in M. Stephenson (ed.) Women in Canada. Ontario: New Press.

STEINMETZ, S. K. and M. STRAUS (1974) Violence in the Family. New York: Dodd, Mead.

WALES, T. J. and A. D. WOODLAND (1977) "Estimation of the allocation of time for work, leisure and housework." Econometrica 45, 1: 115-132.

WALKER, K. and M. WOODS (1976) Time Use: A Measure of Household Production of Goods and Services. Washington, DC: American Home Economics Association.

WILLIS, R. J. (1974) "Economics theory of fertility behavior," pp. 25-72 in T. W. Schultz (ed.) Economics of the Family. Chicago: University of Chicago Press.

WOLFF, E. N. (1979) "The rate of surplus value, the organic composition, and the general rate of profit in the U.S. economy, 1947-1967." American Economic Review 69: 329-341.

ZARETSKY, E. (1976) Capitalism, the Family and Personal Life. New York: Harper & Row.

6

WOMEN'S LIFE-CYCLE TIME ALLOCATION:
AN ECONOMETRIC ANALYSIS

EVELYN LEHRER and
MARC NERLOVE

This chapter offers a new approach to the analysis of female allocation of time over the life cycle. We present a simple model which divides the life cycle into five basic stages. Within this framework, we derive several hypotheses as to how various factors influence how much time a woman will devote, in each period, to market and nonmarket activities: work outside the home, education, children, and leisure.

Our work builds on a considerable body of literature, which, following Mincer's (1962) pioneering paper, recognizes that the allocation of women's time is a substantially more complex phenomenon than that of men's time. Some representative studies include Cain (1966), Sweet (1973), Heckman (1974), Schultz (1975).

Largely because of deficiencies in the data, most of these studies follow Mincer (1962) and focus on female labor force participation as observed at the time of the survey. In Mincer's words (1962: 68):

In a broad view, the quantity of labor supplied to the market by a wife is the fraction of her married life during which she participates in the labor force. Abstracting from the temporal distribution of labor force activities over a woman's life, this fraction could be

AUTHORS' NOTE: We are indebted to Sarah Fenstermaker Berk for many perceptive and detailed comments on an earlier draft of this chapter. We gratefully acknowledge the support of the Health, Education and Welfare Department, Public Health Service, under Grant HD 12037-02. The opinions expressed herein are those of the authors and should not be construed as representing the opinions or policy of any agency in the U.S. government.

translated into a probability of being in the labor force a given period of time for an individual, hence into a labor force rate for a large group of women.

In this study, we use microeconomic data from the 1973 National Survey of Family Growth. This survey, which was addressed to about 9,800 women living in the United States, contains fertility and female labor supply histories. Further, it provides abundant information on economic and demographic variables. We are thus able to deal with the timing of labor supply and to analyze women's work in several dimensions. As discussed below, this is of particular importance in the analysis of the fertility-female employment association, since the nature of this relationship varies over the life cycle.

The plan of this chapter is as follows: The first section presents an analytical model which provides a framework for our econometric work. The next section discusses the estimated model and empirical findings. Finally, a summary and some concluding remarks are offered.

ANALYTICAL FRAMEWORK

It is useful to envision the life cycle of a typical woman as consisting of five stages: (1) childhood, (2) the interval between the time she reaches school age and the date of her marriage, (3) the period between marriage and the birth of the first child, (4) the child-rearing stage, and (5) a final period which begins when all the children have reached school age and ends when the mother reaches the age of retirement.[1]

The first period is a crucial one. The money and, very importantly, the time, that parents invest in the child at this stage significantly affect the level and quality of human capital with which the child enters the second period. However, we will ignore this first stage in our analysis, since all the important decisions in this interval are made by the parents; our individual plays at most a passive role.

In the second period, the child is able to exercise a greater degree of choice. Aside from leisure, she can allocate her time between (a) acquiring formal education and (b) working in the labor market. An interesting question that arises at this point is: What determines how much time she allocates to (a) as opposed to (b)? One important factor, certainly, is the amount of human capital with which she begins stage two. This is influenced by hereditary factors (e.g., native intelligence and ability), as well as by the quality of attention received earlier in life. This beginning human capital stock determines, to a large extent, how efficient the individual will be at acquiring further human capital. Those who are more able will perform better in school and will, therefore, have an incentive to seek a higher level of educational attainment. Emphasis on this factor alone gives human capital models in the economic literature a deterministic feature. Referring to these models, Lydall (1976: 21-22) remarks:

> The only reason for differences in lifetime earnings is differences in 'ability', which affect both the earnings of those who have no human capital and the rate of return of those who have such capital. Paradoxically, therefore, a theory which purports to be 'economic' rather than 'sociological' leads inexorably to the conclusion that the really significant differences in earnings, i.e., differences in lifetime earnings, are not the result of 'choice' but are entirely a reflection of differences in exogenously given 'abilities'.

Although the element of ability is important, there is also room for personal choice in this matter. Women at this stage have different lifetime plans. Some intend to spend most of the subsequent periods at home, taking care of house and children, and enjoying leisure. Others have career plans and intend to spend a large proportion of their time working in the market. Clearly, these future plans affect the choices made in the second stage. If we compare two women, one who intends to allocate most of her time to the market, and another who plans to devote most of her life to home activities, the former will have a greater incentive to invest in formal education than the latter, because the rewards to be reaped from her investment are much larger.

It is true that investment in education may also make a woman a better mother, in the sense that the time she spends on her children will be more productive than the time a less-educated counterpart devotes to her offspring. But, most likely, the impact of education on market efficiency is substantially larger than its influence on nonmarket productivity.

We have emphasized two major determinants of the level of schooling sought by women: human capital endowment and life-cycle time allocation plans. One must admit also that often other elements, beyond the individual's control, come into play. If capital markets are imperfect, a woman may be unable to pursue her educational goals simply because she is not able to borrow the necessary funds.

A final point with regard to the second stage is that investment in human capital and labor force participation are, in part, competing activities in this period. More time spent on one implies, necessarily, less time on the other, holding leisure constant.

A husband comes into the picture in the third stage. We consider his earnings as exogenous in each period. This may not be a very restrictive assumption, since men usually do work full time and exhibit little responsiveness to changes in their wives' wages (Ashenfelter and Heckman, 1974).[2] Since these "outside" earnings are associated with a pure income effect, we expect that in each stage the husband's income will have a negative impact on female labor supply.

Women still have the option of spending time acquiring further education in the third stage. Most women, however, have completed their schooling by the time they enter this period.

For those women who have finished their education, an important question is: What impact does their human capital stock have on their propensity to work in the market, ceteris paribus? The answer is ambiguous, on a priori grounds. On the one hand, the high wage educated wives can command in the market leads them to supply a large amount of labor. This tendency, however, is opposed by an income effect: Since women with a high level of educational attainment can earn high wages, they can afford to work less for pay. Thus, we conclude that the wife's education will have a positive impact on her market work if, as is likely, the first effect outweighs the second.

In the fourth period, an entirely new dimension appears. Now there are small children present in the household who require a great deal of attention. Again the nature of the impact of the mother's education on her market work is ambiguous. In addition to the effects described earlier, a third influence, which we might call a "child effect," comes into play in this interval. To the extent a more educated mother is more efficient at producing child services, an increase in human capital will induce her to spend more time at home. This influence works in the same direction as the income effect. Thus, we may expect that the impact of the wife's human capital stock on her labor supply will be less positive (or more negative) in this stage than in the previous one.

The level of female labor supply in this period is also affected by the mother's plans for the subsequent stage. If she intends to devote a large fraction of the period to market activity, this will constitute an important incentive for her to participate in the labor force in the child-rearing stage; the woman will want to improve, or at least maintain, her skills and wage level.

A recent paper by Jusenius (1977) suggests that this effect is likely to be most important for highly educated women. As noted by this author, those occupations which require a low skill level offer little reward to experience and little penalty to discontinuous labor force participation. Thus, wages for occupations such as waitress, elevator operator, or sales clerk are likely to be quite insensitive to variations in the employees' experience. On the other hand, those occupations such as university professor, doctor, or lawyer, which demand a high skill level, are likely to require continuous maintenance and updating of knowledge and skills, to reward strongly those enriched by the experience and know-how acquired through on-the-job training and to penalize similarly those whose skills have depreciated or atrophied because of discontinuous labor force participation.

Another consideration which may affect the wife's labor supply in the child-rearing stage is the fact that her net wage is likely to be substantially lower in this period than in the others. This is because, unless relatives are available, if the wife wishes to work, a babysitter or some other form of child care must be hired.

Once the youngest child has reached school age, the fifth period begins. In this interval, children spend a large amount of time at school, thus requiring less attention at home. Given that the mother's time becomes relatively less important at this stage, the "child effect" will be smaller. Thus, we expect to find that the mother's education has a large impact on her labor supply in this period, relative to that in the previous one.

Coupled with the decrease in children's demand for their mother's time is an increase in their demand for market goods (e.g., piano lessons, books, college tuition). Because of these requirements (which are larger the more children there are in the household), mothers who plan large families may also plan to seek market employment in this last stage. Thus, the observed relationship between fertility and labor supply may become positive.

ECONOMETRIC MODEL

The stylized view of a woman's life cycle described above suggests that the impact of economic variables on female labor supply will vary among the various stages, reflecting the changing demands by the household for the wife's home time and contribution to money income. It also suggests that the observed association between fertility and market activity may change in sign across the periods.

Our model implies that the wife's investment in human capital decisions is an endogenous one. She chooses how much education to acquire at the same time that she makes her lifetime fertility and labor supply plans; the more market activity her plans involve, the more education she will acquire, everything else held constant. Unfortunately, because of data limitations, we must take her education level as exogenous in our econometric model. With this restriction, our dependent variables are reduced to fertility and female labor supply in periods two through five.

The literature on models of female labor force participation and fertility ("New Home Economics" models), offers two basic econometric approaches. The first consists of formulating a "structural" model; the dependent variables are treated as jointly determined, and, using simultaneous equations techniques, the direct relationship among them is quantified (see, e.g., DaVanzo, 1972; Hill and Stafford, 1978). As noted by Rosenzweig (1978), this procedure leads to some problems. First, inappropriate restrictions must often be imposed in order to obtain identification. Second, the information the resulting coefficients give us may be uninteresting for policy purposes. For example, if the coefficient of female work in a fertility equation is negative, this does not imply that, say, increasing employment opportunities for women will reduce family size. The negative coefficient may simply reflect the fact that various exogenous variables have influence of opposite signs on each of the dependent variables.

The second approach, used by Rosenzweig (1978) and others, consists of estimating "reduced-form" equations; i.e., each dependent variable is regressed against all the exogenous variables in the system. Behind this procedure lies the notion that the household decision-making process is such that a common set of exogenous variables determines the values assumed by the dependent variables. Thus, what is important is to measure quantitatively the impact of each independent variable on each endogenous variable.

We will follow the latter approach in this chapter. But, in addition, we will examine the correlations among the residuals of the reduced form equations. As explained below, this provides some information on the impact of *unobserved* exogenous variables on the dependent variables of interest.

As a very simple example, consider the following equations:

$$\text{WORK} \quad = \alpha_0 + \alpha_1 X + \alpha_2 Y \qquad [1]$$

$$\text{FERTILITY} = \beta_0 + \beta_1 X + \beta_2 Y \qquad [2]$$

Let WORK represent the level of female labor supply in some given period, and let FERTILITY indicate complete family size. X is a vector of the exogenous variables on which we do have information. For simplicity, assume that there is only one independent variable on which we do not have information. Say it is Y, a dummy which equals 1 if the mother wished to work in the market in the given period but was unable to find an acceptable job, and is 0 otherwise. Thus, $\alpha_2 Y$ is the residual of the work equation, and $\beta_2 Y$ is the residual of the FERTILITY equation. Suppose we compute the correlation coefficient between these residuals and obtain a significantly negative number. This would imply that Y influences WORK and FERTILITY in opposite directions; while Y has a negative influence on WORK, it has a positive impact on FERTILITY.

In reality, the residuals involve not one but many unobserved variables, ranging from preferences (to the extent these are not captured by the variables we do include) to sex and race discrimination in the labor market. The arguments above indicate that an analysis of the correlations among the residuals from the various regressions provides information as to whether these unobserved variables affect the dependent variables in the same or opposite direction, on average.

We present below our criteria for inclusion in the sample and the definitions of the variables; then we discuss the estimated model and empirical results.

SELECTION OF SAMPLE

In our analysis, we have restricted the sample in several ways: We have only considered women who were formally married, with at least one child and in the fifth stage of the life cycle at the time of the survey. Thus, all the respondents in our sample had completed the formation of their families and none of them had children under six years of age. Further, we eliminated all those cases in which the wife had been married more than once, as well as those in which twins or adopted children were reported. Cases in which the wife had raised the children of her husband from a previous marriage were also excluded. The sample size resulting was 1485.

DEFINITIONS OF VARIABLES

Our endogenous variables consist of the level of female labor supply in periods two through five and the household's fertility. Our main independent variables are the husband's income and the wife's education. In addition, we include a number of background and religion variables, as well as some biological and demographic variables. These are intended to serve as proxies for preferences, for the economic opportunities faced by the wife, and for the couple's contraceptive efficiency and physical limitations. A brief definition of each of these variables follows.

Female Labor Supply Variables: L2, L3, L4, and L5. These variables indicate the proportion of time the wife worked in the market in the corresponding period. For example, if period four lasted eight years, and the wife reports that she worked two years in that time interval, L4 would be .25.[3] Unfortunately, the survey contains no information as to whether the woman engaged in part-time or full-time market activity during the years for which she reports employment.

Fertility Variable: NUM. This variable represents the number of children born alive to the household. Abstracting from infant and child mortality considerations, this measure indicates complete family size for the respondents in our sample.

Husband's permanent income: PERMINC. In order to avoid the confounding effect of transitory income components, we use an instrumental-variable estimator as a proxy for the husband's permanent income. This is based on the equation in Table 1.

The endogenous variable is the husband's income as observed at the time of the survey. Some respondents reported an exact figure when asked about their spouse's earnings. Those who did not wish to do so were shown a card containing various income categories and asked to select the most appropriate one. For these latter cases, we follow Schultz (1969), who, instead of using the midpoint as the average income level in each closed income interval, employs the geometric mean, in accordance with the approximately log-normal distribution of income. For the open-end interval ($25,000 or more), we follow Miller's (1963) suggestion by fitting a Pareto curve to the data.[4]

Turning to the exogenous variables, the husband's education variable is measured in terms of years of regular schooling. The median income earned on his occupation is based on figures reported in the U.S. Summary of the 1970 Census (part 1, pp. 1-766). The experience variable is computed by subtracting six and the years of schooling from the husband's age at the survey date. The underlying assumption behind this procedure is that men work continuously after completing their education, valid in most cases. We also control for race and for residence in the South or outside a Standard Metropolitan Statistical Area. All the coefficients have the expected signs.

Following Willis (1973), we use the estimated coefficients to obtain the husband's predicted income at age 40. We divide this by 1,000 to obtain our variable, PERMINC, measured in thousands of dollars.

Wife's education: WEDUC, WED1. Because of the way the questionnaire was designed, we have two variables to represent the wife's education. WEDUC indicates the number of years of regular schooling completed by the wife. WED1 is a dummy variable which equals 1 if the wife had some other training such as technical education.

Background variables: SOUTHC, LIVPAR, SIBL1. SOUTHC is a dummy variable which equals 1 if the respondent lived in one of the southern states most of the time during her childhood and adolescence. LIVPAR is

Table 1   Husband's Income as Observed at the Time
of Survey (standard errors in parentheses)

Constant	-10195.0
	(2425.6)
Husband's Education	1014.0
	(87.239)
Median Income	.68836
Earned in His Occupation	(.10884)
Experience	447.62
	(160.05)
$(Experience)^2$	-6.2312
	(3.1745)
Non-White Race	-2915.9
	(559.51)
Residence in South	-863.75
	(442.36)
Residence Outside	-2116.7
	(468.65)
R^2	.2621
N	1485

a dummy variable which takes the value 1 if at the age of fourteen the respondent was not living with her own father and mother, due to death, separation, divorce, or some other reason. Finally, SIBL1 is the number of siblings in the woman's family plus 1, i.e., the total number of children in her home.

Religion variables: RELED, CATH. RELED is a dummy variable which takes the value 1 to indicate that the wife received at least some of her education in a religious school. CATH equals 1 if she is Catholic.

Biological variables: CONTR, SUBF. CONTR is a dummy variable which equals 1 if the respondent ever used the pill or IUD since the last pregnancy. SUBF equals 1 if the wife reports it would be difficult or impossible for her to have another child, provided she had not reached the age of menopause and had not had an operation for contraceptive purposes.

Figure 1   Relationship Between Wife's Labor
Supply and Husband's Income

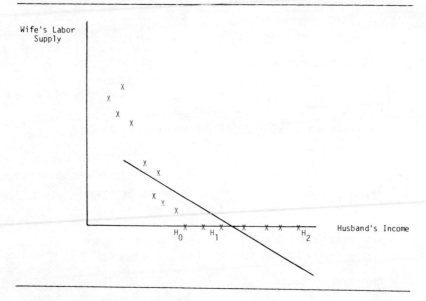

Demographic variables: RACE, AGE. RACE equals 1 to indicate that the respondent is nonwhite. AGE is a continuous variable which controls for the wife's age at the time of the survey.

EMPIRICAL FINDINGS

Reduced form equations. The fertility equation is estimated by ordinary least squares. The labor supply equations require a more special treatment. An examination of the distribution of the L2, L3, L4, and L5 variables reveals that they assume the value zero for many of the respondents in our sample. This corresponds to women who never participated in the market in the corresponding period. Thus, our labor supply variables are truncated at 0, with many observations at that point.

As Tobin (1958) points out, it is inappropriate to use the multiple regression procedure in this situation. This model may lead to predictions for the dependent variable which lie outside the permissible range. Moreover, the concentration of observations at the truncation point is likely to lead to a flat regression line, so that the impact of explanatory variables is underestimated.

The problems involved are illustrated in Figure 1. According to this diagram, women whose husbands have an income of H_0, H_1, or H_2 do not particpate in the labor market. If some exogenous stimulus moved a woman's husband from H_2 to H_0, she would certainly come closer to entering the labor force, but this fact would not be recorded anywhere. This apparent insensitivity of female labor supply to changes in husband's income for $H > H_0$ contaminates the ordinary regression procedure leading to a flat regression line such as the one depicted above, which clearly understates the impact of the husband's income on the wife's labor supply behavior. Further, it can be seen that for large values of H the regression line becomes negative.

Thus, it is more appropriate to use a model which explicitly recognizes that the concentration of female work at zero results because this variable cannot become negative, even if the exogenous variables change in a direction that would tend to discourage participation. We accomplish this by using a maximum-likelihood procedure developed by Tobin, which is known in the literature as the Tobit procedure.

We summarize below the implications of the results shown in Table 2. *(a) Husband's permanent income.* Inspection of the first column of Table 2 indicates that while the husband's income has an insignificant effect on female labor supply prior to the birth of the first child, it has a strong negative impact on the wife's market work in periods four and five. It is interesting to note that, contrary to what one might have expected, the husband's earnings only depress female employment when children are present.

Our results also indicate that the husband's permanent income exerts a significant negative influence on fertility. This finding, which has emerged in a number of other studies, does not imply that children are inferior goods (see Becker and Lewis, 1973).

An important aspect of this phenomenon has been noted in a review article by Birdsall (1977: 76). As she remarks, "High fertility . . . exacerbates the inequality of income distribution among families. . . . To the extent that there are social or economic restrictions on upward mobility, the relatively more rapid increase in numbers of the poor constitutes a drag on any income redistribution effort." A paper by Cramer (1973) using the Panel Study of Income Dynamics, presents some surprising evidence indicating that most low-income families who fall into poverty by having large numbers of children do so voluntarily, not by having accidental births. Although on the surface this would seem to imply that no policy action is therefore required (since what really matters is utility, not income), this argument ignores the welfare of the children who did not

Table 2 Reduced Form Equation for Labor Supply and Fertility (standard errors in parentheses; elasticities in brackets; n = 1485)

	PERMINC	WEDUC	WED1	SOUTHC	LIVPAR	SIBL1	CATH	RCLED	CONTR	SUBF	RACE	AGE	CONST	R²	% of Observations at Limit Point
L2	.0008918 (.001575) [.0784]	.003280 (.002721) [.262]	.009129 (.01414)	-.06053 (.01152)	.01508 (.01164)	-.0005344 (.0007660)	.02907 (.01257)	.001259 (.01409)	-.003037 (.01096)	.01394 (.01172)	.01115 (.01521)	.005822 (.001174)	-.1361 (.05347)		22%
L3	.0005050 (.02409) [.0127]	.1552 (.04213) [3.55]	.7331 (.2102)	-.08840 (.1752)	-.2825 (.1799)	-.01219 (.01242)	.3079 (.1902)	-.0797* (.2120)	.1367 (.1664)	.02703 (.1779)	-.05245 (.2366)	.03319 (.01801)	-.3626 (.8235)		42%
L4	-.01001 (.003530) [-.755]	.02739 (.006173) [1.88]	.07814 (.03151)	.07589 (.02545)	.01786 (.02593)	-.0005727 (.001714)	.02121 (.02865)	.003673 (.03222)	.07125 (.02437)	.06312 (.02617)	.1182 (.03259)	-.009543 (.002595)	.1008 (.1180)		46%
L5	-.01057 (.004725) [-.256]	.02938 (.008133) [.647]	.1084 (.04230)	.07815 (.03421)	-.02262 (.03469)	.001500 (.002166)	.03843 (.03800)	-.0005063 (.04258)	.05328 (.03275)	.03946 (.03505)	.2027 (.04454)	-.01019 (.003480)	.5157 (.1584)		26%
	-.04630 (.01079) [-.190]	-.08658 (.01841) [-.321]	-.1549 (.09733)	-.1952 (.07828)	.01774 (.07950)	.01027 (.005084)	.2661 (.08678)	.1313 (.05748)	.02152 (.07501)	-.1987 (.08025)	.7803 (.1026)	.08072 (.008004)	1.587 (.3611)	.1957	

choose to be born into a large, poor family. Thus, even if further research with other bodies of data were to confirm Cramer's results, a policy issue would remain.

(b) Wife's education. The wife's education variables have insignificant coefficients in the L2 equation, reflecting the fact that in this period, investment in formal education and labor force participation are competing activities. In all the other stages, WEDUC and WED1 have a strong, positive influence on female work. An interesting result is that, as expected, the magnitudes of both coefficients are substantially larger in the period between marriage and first birth than in the subsequent stages.[5] This is consistent with the hypothesis that human capital raises the productivity of the wife's time spent on child services. Further, it can be observed that the coefficients associated with these education variables are somewhat smaller in the child-rearing period than in the final stage. This may be interpreted as weak evidence that the "child effect" associated with changes in the wife's education is stronger in the former period. As noted in the previous section, this effect leads mothers to supply less labor as their human capital rises, because of the resulting increase in nonmarket productivity.

As expected, the wife's education has a significant negative impact on the number of children. Thus, WEDUC and WED1 strongly influence fertility and female labor supply in opposite directions.

(c) A comparison between the elasticities of the husband's income and the wife's education. An examination of columns 1 and 2 in Table 2 reveals that in every equation, the elasticity associated with the wife's education is larger than that associated with the husband's income. To the extent that the former variable is a good proxy for her potential market wage, we may conclude that this is a more potent force than the husband's income in both the fertility and labor supply decisions.

This result must be qualified in two important respects. First, our measure of the husband's income reflects only permanent income. Thus, our estimates do not capture possible female labor supply responses to temporary variations in the husband's income (e.g., an unemployment spell, or an unusually low level of earnings in the third stage, when the husband may be just beginning his career).

Second, holding constant the husband's education, the omission of tastes from our equations leads to a positive and negative bias, respectively, in the coefficients associated with the wife's education in the labor supply and fertility equations (see Nerlove, 1974; Nerlove and Razin, 1978: appdx. B). As noted in these papers, the difference in educational attainment of husband and wife partly reflects the couple's preferences for children. Positive assortative mating by education in the marriage market leads men with very high education to marry women who also have high levels of schooling. Differences in tastes are not likely to be reflected in the educational attainment of men; however, it is very plausible that women with low tastes for market activities and high preferences for children will tend to seek smaller amounts of formal education, whereas those women with opposite preferences will tend to invest more in acquiring human capital. Given positive assortative mating by preferences for children, men with a given educational attainment with high preferences for children will tend to marry women with less schooling than the average associated with the level these men have achieved. If the husband's schooling level is associated primarily with an income effect, while the wife's education is associated mostly with a substitution effect, it follows that the negative impact of her opportunity cost of time on fertility will be exaggerated, holding male educational attainment constant, if tastes are not explicitly included in the statistical analysis. A similar argument holds for the labor supply equations.

(d) Background variables. As expected, SOUTHC has a negative effect on L2, indicating the smaller opportunities for market work in the period before marriage. Curiously, this variable has a significant positive effect on L4 and L5, and a negative impact on NUM.

LIVPAR has a weak, positive coefficient in the L2 equation. This probably reflects the fact that girls who are not brought up by both parents have greater financial needs in the premarriage stage.

SIBL1 has a significant positive effect on NUM: Women who come from large families tend to form large families themselves.

(e) Religion variables. As expected, the coefficients of RELED and CATH have positive signs in the fertility equations. The positive sign of CATH on female work in the pre-first-birth years is a puzzling result.

(f) Biological variables. Disappointingly, CONTR has an insignificant impact on our fertility variable.[6] It has, however a strong positive effect on L4 and a weak positive effect on L5, suggesting that women who have used modern contraceptives tend to work more in the market, perhaps because they have more liberal attitudes toward the role of women.

The subfecundity variable behaves as expected. It has a strong negative impact on fertility. It also has a strong positive effect on labor supply in the child-rearing period, reflecting the indirect impact through the number of children variable.

(g) Demographic variables. RACE has a strong positive impact on both fertility and labor supply in the fourth and fifth periods. Its influence on female work prior to the first birth is insignificant, however.

The age variable displays a puzzling pattern of coefficients. It has a positive influence on L2 and L3, as expected, but a very strong negative impact on L4 and L5. Its effect on fertility is positive.

Timing of female labor supply. The last column of Table 2 reports the percentage of observations on the labor supply variables at the truncation point. These figures can be translated into percentages representing the fraction of women who supplied some positive amount of labor to the market in each stage. These are 78 percent, 58 percent, 54 percent, and 74 percent, for periods two, three, four, and five. The lowest percentage is associated with the child-rearing period; the peak participation rate occurs in the premarriage stage. As we would expect, the percentage is higher in the fifth than in the fourth period.

Another dimension of the timing of labor supply may be obtained by examining some cross section information contained in our data. Each respondent was asked whether or not she had worked in the market in the past twelve months. The answers to this question indicate participation rates of 85 percent, 84 percent, 44 percent, and 64 percent, in the corresponding periods. These statistics are rather different from the former, reflecting in part a cohort effect; however, the qualitative conclusions stated above remain unchanged.

ANALYSIS OF THE RESIDUALS

Table 3 presents the simple correlations of the residuals from the reduced-form equations.

As expected, the correlations among the residuals from the labor supply equations are positive. This suggests that those unobserved variables which influence female work positively in one period, operate in the same way in the other stages. The correlation between the residuals of the L4 and L5 equations is particularly large in magnitude and strong in significance. This is probably due to the fact that many of the women who work in the child-rearing period do so precisely because they intend to engage in market activity in the third period and, therefore, wish to prevent human capital depreciation.

The residual of the fertility regression is negatively correlated with the residual of L2, L3, and L4; the unobserved forces which tend to increase fertility also decrease female work in these periods. This negative sign disappears in the fifth stage; the relationship becomes positive, but insignificant at conventional levels.

Table 3   Correlation Matrix of Residuals from Specified
Equations (p-values in parentheses)[a]

	resL2	resL3	resL4	resL5	resNUM
resL2	1.00	.1997	.0691	.0010	-.0766
		(.001)	(.008)	(.970)	(.003)
resL3		1.00	.0264	.0150	-.0506
			(.308)	(.565)	(.051)
resL4			1.00	.5587	-.0307
				(.001)	(.237)
resL5				1.00	.0233
					(.369)
resNUM					1.00

[a]A p-value indicates the probability of obtaining a sample value as extreme as that
actually observed, assuming the null hypothesis (coefficient = 0) is true. The reported
p-values are based on two-sided tests.

CORRELATIONS AMONG THE DEPENDENT VARIABLES IN THE MODEL

The correlations reported in Table 4 may be interpreted as resulting
from the impact of observed and unobserved exogenous variables on each
of the dependent ones. The results show that, in most cases, labor supply
in one period is positively correlated with that in other periods. The
figures also indicate that while at first the relationship between fertility
and female work is negative, this becomes weakly positive in the final
stage. This lends some additional support to the findings for Quebec
reported in Lehrer (1978), which show that the negative association
between family size and the mother's employment vanishes when the
children reach school age. This result probably reflects the goods intensive-
ness of children in this final period.

Table 4 Correlation Matrix of Dependent Variables
(p-values in parentheses)

	L2	L3	L4	L5	NUM
L2	1.00	.1782	.0444	-.0280	-.0440
		(.001)	(.087)	(.281)	(.090)
L3		1.00	.0567	.0379	-.0324
			(.029)	(.144)	(.213)
L4			1.00	.5901	-.0335
				(.001)	(.197)
L5				1.00	.0338
					(.193)
NUM					1.00

CONCLUSIONS AND DIRECTIONS FOR FURTHER RESEARCH

The model we have estimated in this chapter emphasizes the importance of dividing the family life cycle into various stages for the analysis of female time allocation. Our results show that the influence of exogenous variables on time allocation varies substantially over the life cycle. In addition, the association between family size and female employment changes in sign across the stages; thus, an analysis of the relationship between these variables that does not distinguish among life-cycle stages will result in some average measure which obscures the nature of the underlying process.

An important topic for further research in this area concerns the impact of female life-cycle time allocation decisions on income distribution across families: Do working wives narrow or widen the gap between rich and poor? Some preliminary findings, using the 1973 Family Growth Survey data, show that the employment of wives tends to improve the income distribution by a small amount. Table 5, which displays the income shares accruing to the various groups, offers some evidence in this respect. In each period, the Lorenz curve representing the joint income of husband and wife reflects greater equality than the curve associated with the husband's earnings alone.

Table 5   Distribution of Income by Ordinal Groups

Family Quintiles	Husband's Income		Husband's Income Plus Wife's Income	
	Share of Income	Cumulative Share of Income	Share of Income	Cumulative Share of Income
PERIOD 3:				
0-19%	4.75	4.75	5.87	5.87
20-39%	12.54	17.29	12.69	18.56
40-59%	18.19	35.48	18.41	36.97
60-79%	23.67	59.15	24.46	61.43
80-100%	40.85	100.00	38.57	100.00
PERIOD 4:				
0-19%	5.54	5.54	6.26	6.26
20-39%	12.89	18.43	13.13	19.39
40-59%	17.92	36.35	17.71	37.10
60-79%	23.25	59.60	23.07	60.17
80-100%	40.40	100.00	39.83	100.00
PERIOD 5:				
0-19%	5.49	5.49	6.86	6.86
20-39%	13.07	18.56	13.36	20.22
40-59%	17.48	36.04	17.53	37.75
60-79%	23.16	59.20	23.01	60.76
80-100%	40.80	100.00	39.24	100.00

Sample Sizes: PERIOD 3: N = 1050
PERIOD 4: N = 3177
PERIOD 5: N = 1883

These ideas will be pursued at greater length in a forthcoming paper (Lehrer and Nerlove, 1980). Even if future research lends support to our findings with respect to income inequality, it must be emphasized that the same need not be true of a broader measure of well-being. Wives who are employed must necessarily spend less time on other activities, especially child care. They may also spend less time acquiring formal education, which would lead to lower productivity both at home and in the market.

Thus, although greater female labor force participation may result in closing the income gap, whether this leads to an increase in welfare is an open question. It is hoped that future investigations will provide an answer.

NOTES

1. Our model ignores women who never marry as well as those who divorce their husbands. The fertility and labor supply behavior of this group will be examined in a later paper.

2. We also neglect the possibility that the husband's retirement decision may be endogenous.

3. Since the oldest woman in the survey was only 45 years of age, none of our respondents had completed the fifth period according to our definition. Thus, we use the post-child-rearing stage to date.

4. The Pareto fit was found to be appropriate to our data, according to the criterion indicated in Miller (1963). This procedure led us to use $37,610 as the average income in the open-end interval.

5. We do not compare elasticities *among* periods, because these are influenced by the fact that the average level of labor supply is smaller in periods three and four than in the second and last stages.

6. This may be due to the fact that CONTR, our proxy for contraceptive efficiency, captures two effects. First, women who use more modern contraceptive techniques have fewer children, ceteris paribus, because they have a smaller number of unplanned pregnancies. But, second, it may also happen that those couples who have already had many children may seek better methods to avoid increasing their family size further. The insignificant result we obtained may be a result of the netting out of these two influences.

REFERENCES

ASHENFELTER, O. and J. HECKMAN (1974) "The estimation of income and substitution effects in a model of family labor supply." Econometrica 42: 73-85.

BECKER, G. S. and H. G. LEWIS (1973) "Interactions between quantity and quality of children." Journal of Political Economy 81: 493-517.

BIRDSALL, N. (1977) "Analytical approaches to the relationship of population growth and development." Population and Development Review 3: 63-102.

BOWEN, W. G. and T. A. FINEGAN (1969) The Economics of Labor Force Participation. Princeton: Princeton University Press.

CAIN, G. C. (1966) Married Women in the Labor Force: An Economic Analysis. Chicago: University of Chicago Press.

CRAMER, J. (1973) "Births, expected family size, and poverty," pp. 279-317 in J. N. Morgan (ed.) Five Thousand American Families—Patterns of Economic Progress. Ann Arbor, MI: Institute for Social Research.

DaVANZO, J. (1972) The Determinants of Family Formation in Chile, 1960: An

Econometric Study of Female Labor Force Participation, Marriage and Fertility Decisions. Santa Monica: RAND.

HECKMAN, J. (1974) "Shadow prices, market wages, and labor supply." Econometrica 42: 679-694.

HILL, R. and F. STAFFORD (1978) "Lifetime fertility, child care, and labor supply." (unpublished)

JUSENIUS, C. L. (1977) "The influence of work experience, skill requirement, and occupational segregation on women's earnings." Journal of Economics and Business 29: 107-115.

LEHRER, E. (1978) "Women's allocation of time over the life-cycle: an econometric study." Ph.D. dissertation, Northwestern University.

——— and M. NERLOVE (1980) "The impact of female life-cycle time allocation decisions on income distribution among families." Proceedings of the International Economic Association.

LYDALL, H. F. (1976) "Theories of the distribution of earnings," pp. 15-46 in A. B. Atkinson (ed.) The Personal Distribution of Incomes. London: George Allen & Unwin.

MILLER, H. P. (1963) "Trends in the income of families and persons in the United States, 1947-1960." Technical Paper 8, U.S. Bureau of Census, Washington, D.C.

MINCER, J. (1962) "Labor force participation of married women: a study of labor supply," pp. 63-105 in National Bureau of Economic Research, Aspects of Labor Economics. Princeton: Princeton University Press.

NERLOVE, M. (1974) "Toward a new theory of population and economic growth." Journal of Political Economy 84: S200-S219.

——— and A. RAZIN with assistance of W. JOERDING and E. LEHRER (1978) "Child spacing and numbers: an empirical analysis." Discussion Paper 371, Center for Mathematical Studies in Economics and Management Science, Northwestern University.

——— (1979) "Child spacing and numbers: an empirical analysis," in A. Deaton (ed.) Essays in the Theory and Measurement of Consumer Behavior. Cambridge: Cambridge University Press.

ROSENZWEIG, M. (1978) "The value of children's time, family size and non-household child activities in a developing country: evidence from household data," pp. 331-347 in J. L. Simon (ed.) Research in Population Economics. Greenwich, CT: JAI Press.

SCHULTZ, T. P. (1969) "Secular trends and cyclical behavior of income distribution in the United States: 1944-1965," pp. 75-100 in L. Soltow (ed.) Six Papers on the Size Distribution of Wealth and Income. New York and London: Cambridge and Columbia University Presses.

——— (1975) Estimating Labor Supply Functions for Married Women. Santa Monica: RAND.

SWEET, J. A. (1973) Women in the Labor Force. New York: Seminar.

TOBIN, J. (1958) "Estimation of relationships for limited dependent variables." Econometrica 26: 24-36.

WILLIS, R. (1973) "A new approach to the economic theory of fertility behavior." Journal of Political Economy 81: S14-S64.

7

HOUSEHOLD TIME:
A CROSS-CULTURAL EXAMPLE

LINDA NELSON

Major time allocation studies have been carried out in industrialized communities (Szalai et al., 1972) in which people have been socialized to use watches and clocks as monitors of time.[1] Large numbers of people are not oriented to the separation of work and leisure which seems to accompany industrialization. One estimate indicates that by the year 2000, over half (57 percent) the population of developing countries will not be industrialized (McLaughlin et al., 1979: 178).[2] Attention needs to be given to this sector if comprehensive understanding of the meaning of time is to be achieved.

Household time and activity data have been reported most often as single case descriptions (e.g., Lewis, 1959: Oakley, 1974) or as impersonal aggregates of daily or weekly data from relatively large samples (e.g., Mihovilovic, 1973; Robinson, 1977; Walker and Woods, 1976). The former are rich in human detail, but lack a concise way to compare several individuals or households. The latter combine quantities of clock-measured data reported in percentage of time or in hours and minutes, but they do not reveal the flow of activity as actually carried out in sequence.

Increasing concern by researchers about the meaning of housework has led to reporting interview data on attitudes without corresponding time allocation data (for example, Gavron, 1966; Lopata, 1971). What has seemed elusive is a way to combine impersonal, numerical data with personal perceptions of those doing activities in order to reflect the realism of the way clock time and human activities are experienced in life. Two studies (Chapin, 1974: 103-107; Szalai et al., 1972: 711-771) utilize graphs to illustrate the percentage of time invested in various activities over a 24-hour period. These temporal patterns or daily cycles of activity provide an idea of pattern and sequence. However, much detail about household time is lost since different homemaking activities are not distinguished.[3]

Two views of housework itself which may have enticed researchers into distinct methodological approaches have been deemed task-oriented and time-oriented labor (Berch, 1978: 344-345). Task-oriented labor which does not distinguish between work and other aspects of life is a pattern commonly noted in nonindustrialized societies. Time-oriented labor is common in urban, industrialized, clock-dominated societies.

The economic, time-oriented perception of efficiency rather than the human, task-oriented concern for a flow of time in life events seems to be a blinder from industrialized cultures which orients methodological approaches to household time study. The economic approach is limiting for at least three reasons. First, it isolates people who perform within time by considering time as a separate, manipulable resource rather than as an integrated factor in a culture. This leads to the emphasis on numerical rather than attitudinal data.

Second, the economic perception minimizes the dynamic quality of the passage of time during which an activity takes place. This leads to reporting of aggregate data rather than indicating that certain tasks may actually be accomplished in several separate efforts during a time period.

The third limitation posed by the economic view of time is the possible restriction of opportunities to understand the meaning of time in a variety of cultures. Temporality has been identified by Hall (1959, 1979) as one primary factor in cultural communication. Although Hall has suggested no concrete methods for investigating time concepts and their operation in different cultures, he noted, "There can be no doubt that if you know the temporal relationships between events you know a tremendous amount" (Hall, 1959: 69). When the time view of any one cultural group is considered as the base, cross-cultural comparisons tend to be discriminatory. All cultural views which differ from the base group are prone to be considered unacceptable or even inferior.

Can time be viewed in a way which overcomes these three limitations? Can the functions of time be examined in a way which relates people to time, preserves some of the dynamism of time, and eliminates some of the boundaries caused by cultural variation in the meaning of time? Is there a way to visualize the activities of several homemakers in a time frame which approaches the totality of the human experience more than the reporting of aggregate clock time used in preselected activities?

Any unidimensional approach has limitations for capturing the multiple meanings of time because it distorts the Gestalt of time. One attempt to overcome the limitations mentioned and glean the benefits of several approaches to time allocation studies is reported here. The concept of an activity pattern as it was defined and applied to time allocation data gathered between June 1960 and May 1961 from nineteen rural Costa Rican homemakers will be described. Homemakers were visited on three consecutive days in order to collect three perceptions of activities performed on one actual calendar day. Predictions, observations, and recollections of one day are available from each homemaker. These data are compared to illustrate how multiple sources of data can be used to provide insights about household time and its meaning.

At least until 1959, time studies of homemakers tended to be quantitative—that is, they emphasized amounts of time used and were carried out in the framework of home economics (see Vanek, 1973, for a critique of this school of thought). Studies were usually made using chronological diary records for one or more days. Since diary studies are time consuming and require cooperation from literate homemakers, it was discovered that homemakers with little education, low income, and young children were not adequately represented by the participating homemakers. In the 1930s a method was designed to eliminate the limited representation which occurred in diary studies (Warren, 1940). Selected homemakers were asked to recall their activities for some days prior to the interview. This method is based on the assumption that the homemakers' recall is accurate enough to produce a valid representation of time use in the period recalled. Recall is probably a variable factor, thus raising questions about the validity of the data. Variation in the ability of homemakers to remember, the time between the occurrence of the event and the recall, and the relative importance of the events to the homemaker might operate to make recall time different from clock time use. Perhaps the closer the homemakers are to a time-oriented view of labor, the more accurate their recall might be when compared to clock-measured data. Conversely, task-oriented homemakers might have less cultural orientation to recall time allocation data.

Although the data were usually gathered chronologically, they were grouped for reporting. All events related to some major activity were reported as one total time unit, therefore the events in sequence were masked. One researcher (Weigand, 1954: 14) presented a probable weekly schedule of activities which were not carried out daily along with the conclusion that "there was no evidence of a universal work pattern for a week." Upon inspection of many questionnaires, it appeared that only food preparation and dishwashing were assumed to be activities done more than once daily in homes in the United States.

The recall method is relatively inexpensive and Warren (1957) adapted it for use with Latin American homemakers. An uneasiness about the suitability of this method, which depends to a degree on the concept of time-oriented labor, continued to concern the author, so she searched the literature of other disciplines for alternative ways to study time which might overcome the limitations of the economic, time-oriented approach and be compatible with the task-oriented agricultural settings common in so much of the world.

Sorokin and Merton (1937) have pointed out the practical distinctions between social and public time. Basically this is a distinction between subjective and objective measurements. Social time is experienced by human beings in relation to events which have meaning for them. Public time is measured independently using means such as clocks and calendars to synchronize time for purposes of social action and communication. The authors suggested that the concept of social time must accompany, or perhaps supersede, the concept of astronomical time in research on social dynamics (Sorokin and Merton, 1937: 628).

Sorokin and Berger (1939) pioneered the study of diary time records kept for continuous periods of at least four weeks. Of particular interest is the comparison of activities predicted for certain future days with the subsequent diary records for those days. There was some indication that household activities were among those less accurately predicted and that such activities tended to be underpredicted (Sorokin and Berger, 1939: 166-167).

Since both the diary and recall methods were deemed to have limitations in task-oriented, low-literacy populations, the only additional method which seemed available was observation. In anthropological work, Firth (1929) provided a rationale for observational studies of daily work patterns over a period of a year in order to study the organization of activities and the seasonal distribution of occupations in an indigenous culture. Provinse (1937) recorded major daily activities of several Bornean tribal members during a four-week span; his evaluation was that while hourly units were more reliable, such measurement would probably not be cost effective.

Erasmus (1955) studied the work patterns of an entire Mexican village by noting the activity of each person at the moment of first sighting. A thirteen-hour day was observed over a three-month period. The researchers indicated that the same household followed no identical routine from day to day. Duration data for each activity were calculated proportionally by relating the number of observations of each activity to the total number of hours observed, and therefore these duration data are open to question.

In his study of five urban Mexican families Lewis (1959) made the unique contribution of constant observation of a one-day span. The days were randomly chosen and records of all activities, especially interpersonal relationships, were recorded stenographically. The case studies are presented in readable form, but only a partial order of activities can be determined because the author deleted some data "to avoid repetition and insignificant events" (Lewis, 1959: 6) without specifying the criteria for excising an event.

Duration, order, and importance of events are suggested repeatedly as aspects worthy of study in relation to time. Duration and order of events can be measured objectively using a consistent clock measure. The importance of events is still not directly measurable. The problem of the inadequacy of any one approach to the study of the meaning of household activities in a time framework is still evident. Because of the salience of time in human lives and the variations in cultural interpretations of time, it does not seem feasible to use it as a measure until we understand the meanings attributed to it in a particular context—in this case to household labor in a specific cultural setting.

ACTIVITY PATTERN CONCEPT

Based on such research concerns, the concept of an activity pattern was developed. In order to understand the concept as used in the field study, one must first define the concept of time span. A time span is the period of time between two events which may vary in specificity and is selected by the researcher in relation to the purposes of the research. An activity pattern is that ordering of tasks which is characteristic of a person or group of persons during the specified time span. An activity pattern shows the predominant arrangements of the tasks in sequence within the selected time span and may suggest alternative structures. It should be pointed out that since the events which bound any time span may be marked by the clock time at which they occur, the duration of time allocated to an activity pattern, or any breakdown within it, could be indicated. This, however, is not essential to the concept.

Two different dimensions of data sources for construction of activity patterns were conceptualized: a behavioral source and an ideational source. The behavioral pattern is derived from observations of what people do within a specified time span; when literacy is not a problem, diary data would be a suitable source, but recording should occur as closely as possible to the actual happening. The ideational activity pattern is derived from what people say they or others will do, do regularly, or have done. That is, their predictions and recollections constitute ideational patterns. The ideational pattern is a verbal construct revealed through interviewing or by the completion of a questionnaire. The behavioral data are directly observable; the ideational data are a verbal image of the activities. A comparison of data from these sources can be used to provide insights about the meaning of time to the participants.

Three indices could be applied to the activity data to determine patterning. Within any selected time span, the first index is the presence of activities. The second index is their repetition within a time span. The third index is the sequence in which the activities occur. These three indices could be applied to chronological data obtained by observation or diary to determine the existence of a behavioral activity pattern. The same indices could be applied to a chronological listing of self-reported time allocation data obtained verbally or in writing at some time different from the actual occurrence of the events to determine the existence of ideational activity patterns.

METHODS AND SAMPLING

Prior to investment in research focusing on a cross-cultural comparison, this project was designed to test the efficacy of the activity pattern concept. A rural Costa Rican community which the researcher had visited in 1952-1953 was selected as a suitable place for the trial. All homemakers who lived with their husbands in the community and who were not gainfully employed on a full-time basis outside their homes were considered eligible for inclusion in the study. Homemakers specifically excluded were those who were widowed, those whose husbands lived elsewhere because of employment, and those who were regularly employed as storekeepers, telegraphers, or teachers. Homemakers who worked in the market on Sundays, in seasonal agricultural pursuits such as coffee harvest, or in home industry such as sewing, were considered eligible. According to the list prepared by the school directress from the researcher's criteria, 84 persons were eligible. The names were numbered and a random sample of 19 was drawn. Five of these 19 homemakers indicated that they had worked for pay sometime during the six months preceding the initial interview.

The project was explained to the people as an interest in learning how much time was spent by homemakers in household activities each day. They were told that these would be observed through a series of visits on three consecutive days, one of which would be an "all-day" visit with the observer bringing her own lunch, while the other two would be shorter visits on the days before and after the all-day visit; these latter would be used to ask questions about the families and their activities. No reference was made to the fact that homemakers would be asked to predict and recall household activities. Some of the community members indicated that Sunday would be a poor observation day, since they used that day for going to Mass or visiting, and avoided doing laundry as much as possible. While the researcher realized that she might have broadened her explanation to include all the activities of the women, she also realized that the use of Sundays as work days for herself would be contrary to local custom.

The original plan to do continuous cycles of interviews and observations throughout the week was altered so that all the observations would be made on a Tuesday or a Friday. Therefore, two series of interviews, observations, and interview visits could be completed each week, provided that holidays or refusals did not interrupt the work.

After permission was obtained to include a family in the study, a data collection visit was made on a Monday or a Thursday during the early afternoon when, according to various informants, the woman was likely to have a little time to devote to answering questions. After a general conversation, the woman was asked if the following day would be satisfactory for the all-day visit. If permission were granted, the interviewer proceeded with a questionnaire dealing with general census information, household facilities, family participation in household tasks, and a request for information about the next day's activities. Homemakers were asked about predictions in this way:

> Please tell me the things you are thinking of doing tomorrow. Tell them to me in order, beginning with the hour of getting up. . . . If possible, tell me approximately the time in which you are thinking of beginning each one of the activities you just mentioned. . . . [If this is not possible] Tell me how much time you think each one of the activities will take [Nelson, 1963: 142].

A one-day time span had been selected as reasonable for the observations. The work day was bounded by the homemaker's time of arising and putting the youngest member of the family to bed in the evening.

On the day of the observation, the researcher arrived about 6:00 a.m. to note all of the homemaker's activities. When the homemaker changed her activity, the time of day was noted; what she was doing, the equipment used, and her work procedures were noted in as much detail as possible. The observer remained until about 6:00 p.m. in each home or until the youngest child was put to bed. In several homes all the children joined the adults in talking and singing after this "ritual" close of note-taking. It was assumed that the homemakers altered their activities very little on the observation day because the observer was well known to the families, and the technological facilities which might have permitted variation were not available.

On the following day, the observer returned in the early afternoon to complete the questionnaire concerning the homemaker's attitudes toward household activities and to ask about her recall of the previous day's activities. Recollections were asked for as follows:

> Had you planned anything for yesterday that you could not do? Yes No [If yes] What were you thinking of doing? Why didn't you do it? . . . Did you do anything yesterday that you had not planned? Yes No [If yes] What did you do that you had not planned? Why did you do it? . . . Please tell me what you recall of your activities of yesterday. Tell me them in order beginning with the hour of getting up. . . . If possible, tell me approximately the time in which you began each one of the activities you just mentioned. . . . [If this is not possible] Tell me how much time you think you spent in each one of the activities you just mentioned [Nelson, 1963: 143].

THE FAMILIES

Most of the 19 families were in the expanding stage of the family life cycle. The couples had been married from 6 to 31 years, with a median of 10. The median age for the husbands was 38, while the median for the wives was 30. The families varied in size from four to eleven persons with a median of eight. The number of children per family ranged from two to nine, with a median of six. Only two of the nineteen households included persons outside the nuclear family.

All the households had at least one preschool child. Nearly half the families (nine) had infants under one year of age. Four of the families had only preschool children, younger than seven in Costa Rica, while the remaining fifteen families had both preschool and school age children. Field work was carried out only during the school year, since this activity occupied many children for most of the year and probably affected the homemakers' time use.

The age of the oldest child living at home ranged from 4 to 24, with a median age of 9. Potential help for the mother in carrying out household tasks was likely to come from daughters, rather than sons or husbands, so the age of the oldest daughter was noted. The age of the oldest daughter ranged from 3 to 16 years, with a median of 8 years; two mothers had only male children.

Although the median years of education completed was three for both husbands and wives, the range of education was greater for husbands. Farming, either as owners or day laborers, was the occupation of the majority of family heads. The farms were small in relation to median family size. The major cash crops were coffee and tobacco, although some sugarcane, corn, and beans were also grown.

A brief description of the housing and equipment will indicate the limited technological level of the households. The one-story houses ranged in size from two to six rooms with an average of four. These might be called kitchen, living room, and two bedrooms; no house had an indoor bathroom. The majority of the houses had corrugated metal roofing, wooden walls, and earthen floors. The floors were generally swept with leaves tied to a stick; these leaves were replaced a few times a week and the broom-making task usually was delegated to children.

In the majority of homes, artificial lighting was provided by a wick soaked in kerosene. Only four houses had electricity generated by a motor which usually ran from 5:30 p.m. to 10:00 p.m. and provided weak current suitable for radios and low-wattage lightbulbs.[4] Ten of the families had cold running water available in their house or yard, but in the dry season the village pump usually operated only from 6:00 a.m. to 10:00 a.m. Nine of the families had to carry water from a stream, well, or a neighbor's yard; often the homemaker shared this task with other family members. Laundry was done by hand, and ironing was done with charcoal or flat irons. Most furniture was wooden and cleaned with cold water and lemon rind. Each family had at least one table, a few benches and chairs, wooden shelves and counters, and a few wooden beds all of which did not have mattresses or other covering.

Seventeen of the nineteen homemakers cooked on a native stove, an earth-filled box on legs with an open wood fire constructed on top of the earth. One woman did have a chimney added to her stove, and another cooked on a two-burner kerosene stove. Wood-gathering was usually assigned to husbands and children. There were no refrigerators in private homes in the village, although a few storekeepers had kerosene refrigerators.

HOMEMAKERS' BEHAVIORAL AND
IDEATIONAL ACTIVITY PATTERNS

An attempt was made to group the observed events according to the principal activities carried out by the homemakers. The classification represented the observer's view of the operational units which the home-makers used. The first classification was based on the activities named by the women when they were asked what household tasks they had to perform daily, what they predicted for the following day, and what they recalled of the previous day's activities. To this preliminary classification, the researcher added other activities and events which were observed.

Eight major categories were judged by the researcher to include all the varied activities of the homemakers; these are identified by capital letters in Table 1. These primary activities were subdivided into a total of fifteen activities numbered in Table 1. The observation data were color coded for each of these fifteen activities. The color-coded data were aligned on graph paper with each square representing one minute of clock time. Examination revealed no obvious pattern of activities; that is, there was no common clock time in which all homemakers were carrying out a similarly coded task.

The examination did, however, reveal that an identical sequence of meals was observed for all families, although these meals did not occur at the same hour nor with the same duration. Thus, mealtimes of morning coffee, lunch, midday coffee, and supper appeared usable as independent variables. The first preparation of five or more consecutive minutes for each of these meals was selected as the initiation of the time span. Within the one-day span of the study, five distinct time spans were delineated using mealtimes as indicators.

The first, Time Span I, occurred before the beginning of morning coffee preparations. The second, Time Span II, comprised the time between the beginning of morning coffee preparations and the beginning of lunch preparations. The third, Time Span III, took place between lunch prepara-tions and beginning midday coffee preparations. The fourth, Time Span IV, was between midday coffee and beginning supper preparations. The last period, Time Span V, included the time following the beginning of supper preparations to the end of the observation.[5]

The indices of presence, repetition, and sequence were applied to the data available in each of the time spans. The data on presence of an activity came from a simple observational check on how many of the homemakers actually performed, predicted, or recalled the performing of an activity. Repetitions were determined by noting for each activity in each time span how many of the homemakers performed, predicted, or recalled the activity for a period of five or more consecutive minutes interrupted by some other classification of activity for a period of five or more minutes.

The calculation of presence and repetition did not indicate the chrono-logical order in which the tasks were performed. The number of women

Table 1   Coding of Household Activities

A. Food preservation and service

1. Grinding corn -- often done by persons other than homemaker

2. Making tortillas -- always named as a distinct activity by women

3. Preparing other food, serving, and eating -- women usually ate
        while cooking

B. House care

1. Cleaning kitchen -- included dishwashing

2. Cleaning and arranging house other than kitchen

3. Hauling water -- often done by persons other than homemaker

C. Clothing care

1. Laundering

2. Ironing

3. Sewing

D. Child care

1. Routine or "expected" -- including ironing, mending, and food prepara-
        tion involved in getting children ready for school, as well as bathing,
        dressing, nursing, and putting children to bed

E. Recreation

1. Chosen or "expected" -- mainly conversation

F. Personal care

1. Physical

G. Animal care

1. Cows -- clock time devoted to other animals was less than five
        consecutive minutes and, therefore, coded under H-2

H. Interruptions -- forced or "expected" circumstances

1. Caused by children -- care due to illness, special activity, or
        guidance

2. Other reasons -- variety of miscellaneous short activities as well
        as work stoppage to converse with the observer

Table 2   Observed Daily Activity Pattern[a]

Time Span I	grinding corn
	making tortillas

------------------COFFEE---

	(animal care)
	CLEANING KITCHEN
	(grinding corn)
Time Span II	MAKING TORTILLAS or cleaning kitchen
	CHILD CARE or cleaning kitchen
	CLEANING HOUSE
	child care

-----------------------LUNCH--

	CLEANING KITCHEN
	PREPARING FOOD
Time Span III	CLEANING KITCHEN
	CHILD CARE
	cleaning kitchen
	CLEANING HOUSE
	LAUNDERING
	(personal care)
	(hauling water)
	PREPARING FOOD
	CHILD CARE or laundering

-------------------------------COFFEE---------------------------------------

	RECREATION
	PREPARING FOOD
Time Span IV	preparing food or laundering
	CHILD CARE
	laundering or sewing

Table 2   Observed Daily Activity Pattern[a] (cont'd)

	----------------------------------SUPPER----------------------------
	RECREATION or sewing
	PREPARING FOOD
	preparing food or recreation
Time Span V	(ironing)
	preparing food
	CLEANING KITCHEN
	PREPARING FOOD
	CHILD CARE or preparing food
	recreation or preparing food
	child care
	recreation
	child care

[a]Capital letters indicate activities participated in by at least half of the homemakers; they mark the predominant activity patterns. Small letters indicate activities participated in by fewer than half of the homemakers; they mark possible variations. Parentheses indicate insertions based on probable sequence within the time span in which these activities most commonly were performed.

performing, predicting and recalling each activity first, second, third, and so forth within each time span was determined. The activity first participated in, predicted, or recalled by the largest number of women was chosen as the first activity in the sequence. The second activity was that performed, predicted, or recalled by the second largest number of homemakers. The selection continued in this way provided that a minimum of three women performed, predicted, or recalled the activity.

The data from the three indices were combined to construct the observed daily activity pattern shown in Table 2, the predicted daily activity pattern shown in Table 3, and the recalled daily activity pattern shown in Table 4. Table 2 illustrates the behavioral activity pattern, and Tables 3 and 4 show different facets of the ideational activity pattern. These indicate the efficacy of the activity pattern concept. Each indicates a flow of activity, and each contributes some information to our understanding of household time. However, comparison of these data sources will provide special insights.

Table 3   Predicted Daily Activity Pattern[a]

Time Span I	(personal care)
----------------------------COFFEE--	
	(animal care)
Time Span II	grinding corn
	MAKING TORTILLAS
-------------------------------LUNCH---------------------------------------	
	CLEANING KITCHEN
	CLEANING HOUSE
Time Span III	child care
	LAUNDRY
-------------------------------------COFFEE-------------------------------	
Time Span IV	ironing
--------------------------------------SUPPER-------------------------------	
	(recreation)
	CLEANING KITCHEN
Time Span V	CHILD CARE
	preparing food

[a]Captial letters indicate activities predicted or recalled by at least half of the home-makers; they mark the predominant activity pattern. Small letters indicate activities predicted or recalled by fewer than half of the homemakers. Parentheses indicate insertions based on probable sequence within the time span in which the activities were most frequently predicted or recalled.

COMPARING BEHAVIORAL AND
IDEATIONAL ACTIVITY PATTERNS

Three separate, but related, sets of time-use data from the nineteen Costa Rican rural homemakers for the same calendar day can be com-pared. Table 5 indicates that when the three sources of data are examined together, the observations in the behavioral activity pattern generated greater detail. Furthermore, the ideational patterns bear a clear resem-blance to the behavioral pattern. At least half the homemakers both predicted and recalled the sequence of the meals which was observed. Tortilla making, kitchen cleaning, laundering, later kitchen cleaning (in

Table 4   Recalled Daily Activity Pattern[a]

Time Span I	personal care
	----------------------COFFEE--
	grinding corn or making tortillas
Time Span II	animal care, child care, or cleaning kitchen
	MAKING TORTILLAS
	------------------------LUNCH--
	CLEANING KITCHEN
	LAUNDERING
Time Span III	laundering or cleaning house
	(personal care)
	------------------------------COFFEE----------------------------------
Time Span IV	recreation or sewing
	--------------------------------SUPPER----------------------------
	CLEANING KITCHEN
	PREPARING FOOD or recreation
	(ironing)
Time Span V	CHILD CARE
	preparing food or child care
	child care

[a]Capital letters indicate activities predicted or recalled by at least half of the home-makers; they mark the predominant activity pattern. Small letters indicate activities predicted or recalled by fewer than half of the homemakers. Parentheses indicate insertions based on probable sequence within the time span in which the activities were most frequently predicted or recalled.

Time Span IV) and child care also coincided for all the patterns as can be noted by the correspondence of capital letters designating these activities in the same position in each column.

One conclusion suggested by Table 5 is that the women have an ideal or organizational time goal of nonrepetition of activities. They seem to wish to complete cleaning, clothing care, and food preparation activities before changing to some other type of activity. In the making of tortillas, this apparent goal was achieved. Once the homemakers began this task, they seldom changed activities until all the tortillas for the day were completed.

Table 5 Comparison of Behavioral and Ideational
Activity Patterns[a]

	Behavioral	Ideational	
	Observations	Predictions	Recollections
Time		(personal care)	personal care
Span	grinding corn		
I	making tortillas		
	-------COFFEE-------------------	COFFEE----------------------	COFFEE------------
	(animal care)	(animal care)	
	CLEANING KITCHEN		
	(grinding corn)	grinding corn	grinding corn or making tortillas
Time			animal care, child care,
Span			or cleaning kitchen
II	MAKING TORTILLAS or	MAKING TORTILLAS	MAKING TORTILLAS
	cleaning kitchen		
	CHILD CARE or		
	cleaning kitchen		
	CLEANING HOUSE		
	child care		
	-------LUNCH-------------------	LUNCH----------------------	LUNCH------------
	CLEANING KITCHEN	CLEANING KITCHEN	CLEANING KITCHEN
	PREPARING FOOD		
	CLEANING KITCHEN		
	CHILD CARE		
	cleaning kitchen		
	CLEANING HOUSE	CLEANING HOUSE	
Time		child care	
Span	LAUNDERING	LAUNDERING	LAUNDERING
III			laundering or cleaning house
	(personal care)		(personal care)
	(hauling water)		
	PREPARING FOOD		
	CHILD CARE or		
	laundering		

Table 5 Comparison of Behavioral and Ideational
Activity Patterns[a] (cont'd)

	Behavioral	Ideational	
	Observations	Predictions	Recollections
	--------COFFEE--------------------COFFEE----------------------COFFEE------------		
	RECREATION		recreation or sewing
	PREPARING FOOD		
Time	preparing food or		
Span	laundering		
IV	CHILD CARE		
		ironing	
	laundering or sewing		
	--------SUPPER--------------------SUPPER----------------------SUPPER-------------		
	RECREATION or sewing	(recreation)	
	PREPARING FOOD		
	preparing food or		
Time	recreation		
Span	(ironing)		
V	preparing food		
	CLEANING KITCHEN	CLEANING KITCHEN	CLEANING KITCHEN
	PREPARING FOOD		PREPARING FOOD or
			recreation
			(ironing)
	CHILD CARE or	CHILD CARE	CHILD CARE
	preparing food		
	recreation or	preparing food	preparing food or
	preparing food		child care
	child care		child care
	recreation		
	child care		

[a]Capital letters indicate activities performed, predicted, or recalled by at least half the homemakers; they mark the predominant activity patterns. Small letters indicate activities performed, predicted, or recalled by fewer than half the homemakers. Parentheses indicate insertions based on probable sequence within the time span in which these activities most commonly were performed, predicted, or recalled.

They achieved this continuity by verbally instructing other family members to handle such chores as caring for babies, grinding corn, cutting wood, or hanging laundry to dry. The homemaker remained attentive to what was happening, but did not break her physical attention to the tortilla making.

The same ideational pattern appears for cleaning the kitchen and laundering, for example, but the behavioral pattern indicates that these tasks were repeated in Time Spans II, III, and IV. The homemakers who achieved one continuous laundry period were those who closed their kitchen doors and hauled clothing and children to a water source some distance from home. The homemakers with a close water source divided their laundry tasks although their ideational patterns revealed continuous attention until the activity was completed.

Homemakers attempted to achieve all the food preparation in any single time span in one continuous activity. Successful homemakers did this by sending children on errands, waiting by the fire, and watching the food cook. Many were frustrated in reaching this goal because numerous family members requested attention or the homemakers felt pressure from environmental conditions to get clothing outside to dry before showers fell in the rainy season or before the water supply was exhausted in the dry season. Regardless of the behavioral pattern, the goal of continuous activity to completion revealed through the verbalized ideational patterns is presumably an important one.

Little which was coded as recreational was a part of the activity patterns. Only in Time Spans IV and V were more than half the home-makers observed to engage in such activities and never did more than half the homemakers include recreation in their ideational activity patterns. The homemakers seemed to think they were expected to work all the time. They were very skilled in altering the pace of the work in relation to social pressures which they sensed. If the result of a task, such as sewing a button on a school blouse or cleaning rice before cooking, was needed at a particular moment, the women moved quickly. If the mending or food preparation task was needed for another day, the tempo was slowed and the women often joined a neighbor for conversation while carrying out the task. If their husbands appeared, the work activity increased and the conversation diminished. A subtle social pressure seemed to eliminate purely recreational activities for these homemakers.

The frequency of behavioral child care did not form part of the ideational activity pattern in Time Spans II, III, and IV. This may be an indication that the women did not define child care as similar to other household tasks. One reason why many of the women may not have indicated the repetitive child care activities in their ideational patterns is that they often delegated parts of the physical care to others and may not have realized how much time they themselves invested in such care. The congruence of child care activities in all patterns in Time Span V may only reflect the fact that putting the youngest child to bed had been specified as the "close" of the work day by the observer.

Ideationally, or mentally, these homemakers were well organized and repeated few tasks. Behaviorally, more repetition was evident. Readers from disciplines other than home economics may derive many other insights from the comparison of data in Table 5. Certainly Table 5 gives some visual idea of how time and activities interrelate in a sequential sense.

CONCLUSIONS AND IMPLICATIONS

Observational data, homemakers' predictions, and recollections from nineteen randomly selected rural Costa Rican households were obtained in relation to one calendar day. The concept of an activity pattern was defined; indices of presence, repetition, and sequence were applied to the data to construct behavioral and ideational activity patterns. The comparison of the patterns was used to illustrate inferences about the time goals of these homemakers.

First, it is clear that time-use data gathered at the time of the events and estimations made before and after the events are not equivalent data. If an understanding of how time operates in household settings is to be gained, it is advisable that both behavioral and ideational data continue to be collected and compared. Study of both behavioral and ideational patterns provides a stronger framework for the inference of time-use goals and goal attainment than does the study of either pattern separately.

Second, it seems probable that neither the duration of activities nor the aggregate clock time devoted to the activities within a daily time span is the most meaningful way to study household problems in which time plays a part. Study of the ordering of activities within a time span may provide clues to cultural differences in household time use. Mealtimes may be a universal independent variable which can be used to mark the boundaries of time spans within a daily time dimension, but there are certainly not four mealtimes in all cultures.

Third, classification or coding of activities is a more serious problem than had been indicated in the early time studies. Especially when studies are made within cultures unfamiliar to the researcher, it cannot be assumed that what the researcher views as congruent activities or single units of activity will be so identified by the homemakers. Some attention needs to be paid to the determination of activities which the participants consider to be related. The technique of asking people what they are doing while they are working should provide the necessary clues for formation of meaningful categories prior to formal research.

Fourth, there are three types of activity pattern research which would seem valuable for examining the function of time in households: longitudinal, cross-cultural, and simultaneous studies in nonhomogeneous families. A series of studies needs to be made to determine activity patterns for time spans longer than a day. It seems logical that longitudinal studies would reveal more of the dynamism or flow of time than studies limited to a one-day time span. The application of the indices of presence, repetition, and sequence to activity data within time spans of varying lengths should reveal rhythms of activity.

It is possible that alterations in activity patterns for any one family will be associated with days of the week, seasons of the year, crisis periods, ages of the family members, family standards, or other variables. Simultaneous study of the activity patterns of families of different sizes, of different age composition, of different occupations and social class, and possessing different technological facilities may reveal variations in activity patterns. Formal education, amount of discretionary income, caloric intake, and intervals between pay periods likewise may be associated with activity pattern variations.

In addition, the study of the activity patterns of all family members during the same time span, rather than only those of the homemaker, should provide insights into problems and possible goals with respect to the intermeshing of time patterns of family members. Studies of the duration, order, and content of family interactions may also contribute to understanding the meaning of time in households.

Homemaking occupies the time of a majority of women all over the world. Development plans generally assume increased productive activity of both men and women. Homemaking is seldom classified as a productive activity, yet when it is not completed in some way the quality of life changes. Children learn their attitudes toward time use and activity at home in their formative years. What they are learning may need to be relearned when they become adults if they are to become productive in the work world.

Attention paid to the study and understanding of activity patterns of all who contribute in any way to cause or carry out household work should facilitate our understanding of time as a dynamic factor in human activity. Such understanding should increase our ability to solve practical problems of alternative ways to accomplish household work and orient humans so that ideational and behavioral patterns can be recognized and perhaps more closely synchronized.

NOTES

1. The work by Szalai and colleagues was published several years after the conception and completion of the field work being reported. The volume contains an excellent overview of methods of time study as well as documenting the importance of time studies in the industrialized world.

2. In 1970, 63 percent of the population in developed countries resided in urban areas, and it is predicted that by the year 2000 79 percent will do so. The corresponding figures for developing countries are 26 percent in 1970 and a prediction of 43 percent for 2000 (McLaughlin et al., 1979: 178).

3. Another researcher (Kundak, 1958), in her report of Turkish homemakers' time use, presented data in graphic form. She combined chronological clock time in a figure showing percentages of 44 homemakers who used the hours between 4:30 a.m. and 11:00 p.m. for any of ten major activities, most of which were homemaking activities (Kundak, 1958: 42).

4. A few years after the field work was completed, the national electric company extended service to this village, although not many families connected to the lines at that time. During a visit in February 1979, the author noted an increase in television sets in the community (two were there in 1961, but not in homes in the sample). It would be useful to study what impact this technological change may have had on activity patterns.

5. In addition to preparing the four meals, several homemakers were observed to have one other food preparation activity. In the evening nearly three-fourths of them either prepared a beverage before bedtime or cooked corn or beans for use at unspecified future meals. It is possible that if the observations had continued later in the evening, the pre-bedtime beverage preparation might have appeared as a universal event, indicating Time Span VI.

REFERENCES

BERCH, B. (1978) "The development of housework." International Journal of Women's Studies 1, 4: 336-348.

CHAPIN, F. S., Jr. (1974) Human Activity Patterns in the City: Things People Do in Time and Space. New York: John Wiley.

ERASMUS, C. J. (1955) "Work patterns in a Mayo village." American Anthropologist 57: 322-333.

FIRTH, R. (1929) Primitive Economics of the New Zealand Maori. New York: E. P. Dutton.

GAVRON, H. (1966) The Captive Wife: Conflicts of Housebound Mothers. London: Routledge & Kegan Paul.

HALL, E. T. (1959) The Silent Language. Garden City, NY: Doubleday.

——— (1979) "Learning the Arabs' silent language: Edward T. Hall interviewed by Kenneth Friedman." Psychology Today 13, 3: 44-54.

KUNDAK, S. S. (1958) "Factors related to use of time in homemaking activities by selected Turkish housewives." M.S. thesis, Purdue University.

LEWIS, O. (1959) Five Families. New York: Basic Books.

LOPATA, H. Z. (1971) Occupation: Housewife. London: Oxford University.

McLAUGHLIN, M. M. and the Staff of the Overseas Development Council (1979) The United States and World Development: Agenda 1979. New York: Praeger.

MIHOVILOVIC, M. (1973) "An analysis of some factors influencing the time-budget of employed and unemployed women in Yogoslavia." International Journal of Sociology of the Family 3, 1: 70-85.

NELSON, L. J. (1963) "Daily activity patterns of peasant homemakers." Ph.D. dissertation, Michigan State University.

OAKLEY, A. (1974) Woman's Work: The Housewife, Past and Present. New York: Vintage.

PROVINSE, J. H. (1937) "Cooperative ricefield cultivation among the Siang Dyaks of Central Borneo." American Anthropologist 39: 77-102.

ROBINSON, J. P. (1977) How Americans Use Time: A Social-Psychological Analysis of Everyday Behavior. New York: Praeger.

SOROKIN, P. A. and C. A. BERGER (1939) Time-Budgets of Human Behavior. Cambridge: Harvard University.

SOROKIN, P. A. and R. MERTON (1937) "Social time: a methodological and functional analysis." American Journal of Sociology 42: 615-629.

SZALAI, A. et al. (1972) The Use of Time: Daily Activities of Urban and Suburban Populations in Twelve Countries. The Hague: Mouton.

VANEK, J. (1973) "Keeping busy: time spent in housework, United States, 1920-1970." Ph.D. dissertation, University of Michigan.

WALKER, K. E. and M. E. WOODS (1976) Time Use: A Measure of Household Production of Family Goods and Services. Washington, DC: Center for the Family of the American Home Economics Association.

WARREN, J. (1940) "Use of time in its relation to home management." Bulletin 734, Agricultural Experiment Station, New York.

——— (1957) "Use of time by homemakers in Uruguay, 1957." (unpublished)

WIEGAND, E. (1954) "Use of time by full-time and part-time homemakers in relation to home management." Memoir 330, Agricultural Experiment Station, New York.

8

CONTRIBUTIONS TO HOUSEHOLD LABOR:

COMPARING WIVES' AND HUSBANDS' REPORTS

SARAH FENSTERMAKER BERK and ANTHONY SHIH

In the last decade of family research, little has contradicted the statement that family sociology is "wives' family sociology" (Safilios-Rothschild, 1969). One important exception has been research which compares spousal accounts of family activities and attitudes. When researchers brave the inclusion of reports from *both* wives and husbands, they often find considerable disagreement between spouses on family matters of all varieties.

Disparities in the reports of husbands and wives have been routinely noted by those studying family decision-making, power, and authority (e.g., Heer, 1962; Ballweg, 1969; Olson, 1969; Granbois and Willett, 1970; Turk and Bell, 1972; Van Es and Shingi, 1972; Niemi, 1974; Douglas and Wind, 1978) and those interested in spousal estimates of family income (e.g., Ferber, 1955; Haberman and Elinson, 1967; Ballweg, 1969). Others have combined measures of decision making or reports on the exercise of family influence with accounts of the accomplishment of selected household tasks (e.g., Brown and Rutter, 1966; Granbois and Willett, 1970; Centers et al., 1971; Larson, 1974; Araji, 1977; Craddock, 1977; Booth and Welch, 1978; Douglas and Wind, 1978).

AUTHORS' NOTE: A preliminary version of this chapter ("The 'Rashomon' of Household Labor") was presented at the annual meetings of the American Sociological Association, Sociologists for Women in Society, 1978. Thanks go to Richard A. Berk, Spencer Cahill, Joan Huber, and Thomas Wilson for their helpful comments. Additional thanks go to Cheryl Goluch for typing the manuscript. The research was supported by a grant from the NIMH Center for the Study of Metropolitan Problems (MH 27340-01).

The broad implications of this literature vary depending upon the concerns of its interpretors. When discrepancies in report are defined as a *methodological* problem, debates may center on the degree to which researchers can continue to "safely" interview only one family member (usually the wife) and still conclude that some "objective" family reality has been tapped (e.g., Heer, 1962; Wilkening and Morrison, 1963; Scanzoni, 1965). Advice is sometimes offered for how one might "enhance" spousal agreement through reliance on more detailed survey items (e.g., Granbois and Willett, 1970: Olson and Cromwell, 1975; Jaco and Shepard, 1975), or which spouse one can "trust," depending upon the kind of family activity or decision under scrutiny (e.g., Wilkening and Morrison, 1963). As Larson (1974) has suggested, if a model of underlying consensus-equilibrium is used to interpret family process and relations, then disagreement between spouses will likely be viewed as a function of the inability of researchers to capture the "real" family they wish to describe.

In contrast, for a few others, the issue of spousal discrepancies reflects the multifaceted nature of family realities and perceptions. For example, the recent work of Booth and Welch (1978) strongly suggests that a continued search for a single, underlying (and unmeasured) factor which one might call "spousal consensus" may be fruitless. Rather than bemoan or explain away differences between spousal reports, apparent disparities become data on the way members perceive family life and relations. Such disparities may provide an understanding of how, when members are in dissimilar social positions, they exhibit differential perceptions of family process (e.g., Safilios-Rothschild, 1969; Turk and Bell, 1972). In short, the issue could be transformed from one of *methodological* inconvenience or measurement artifact to one of *substantive* insight. As Larson (1974: 124) argues, "There is no necessary reason for assuming that differential perception is not an aspect of family reality, instrumentation notwithstanding."

While one might study spousal consensus surrounding a great number of household activities or decisions, here the focus will be on reports of the household division of labor. Rather than treating consensus as a methodological concern, we will assume that, at least in part, the fit between different accounts of "who does what" in the household will reveal something of the way the household work site is apprehended by its members. Three general questions will be addressed. First, how much agreement is there between wives' and husbands' reports on household task contributions? Second, what is the nature of the disagreement between spousal reports? Third, to what degree do other factors affect the nature of disagreements? The first question speaks to the degree of spousal consensus surrounding perceptions of household task contribution. The second question addresses the character of spousal disagreement. The third question explores the impact of particular characteristics of households and household work which may alter patterns of disagreement.

The separate and independently gathered responses of married couples to questions about their own and their partners' participation in 45 routine household tasks will be analyzed. Data are presented through an analysis of the percent spousal agreement for reports on wives' *and* husbands' contributions. Further, a regression analysis is employed to explain the nature of spousal report disparities, with primary attention paid to the report of a spouse about his/her partner's contribution as an "explanatory" variable. Finally, selected biographic and task-related inter-action terms are examined for their effects.

REFINING THE PROBLEM

In light of the often contradictory findings from past consensus research, this examination of wives' and husbands' reports on the division of household labor departs from previous efforts in several respects.

First, analysis will be limited to a large number of household work and child care tasks representing a significant subset of routine family activities either directly observed (Berk and Berheide, 1977), or reported by respondents (Berk, 1979; Berk and Berk, 1979). Thus, rather than a potpourri of behaviors which may have little known relationship to each other or to other household activities (e.g., Booth and Welch, 1978), the 45 tasks chosen are, on their face, relatively homogeneous and have some empirical grounding to everyday life.

Second, the present study limits itself to those activities that Booth and Welch (1978) have called "shared events or conditions": The reports of members about each others' behaviors and those behaviors around which they have some observable referents. There is evidence to suggest (e.g., Olson and Rabunsky, 1972; Sudman and Bradburn, 1974; Douglas and Wind, 1978) that the measurement of behavior (as opposed to decision making or attitudes) results in fewer measurement artifacts. Regardless, this analysis promises attention neither to behaviors other than those surrounding the apportionment of routine household tasks nor to decision making about them.

Third, a number of past research efforts (e.g., Scanzoni, 1965; Brown and Rutter, 1966; Granbois and Willett, 1970; Larson, 1974; Douglas and Wind, 1978) have explored the degree of consensus surrounding some household task allocations. However, only a few have given serious attention to the nature of the tasks themselves as possible sources of variation in consensus (e.g., Larson, 1974; Douglas and Wind, 1978). For instance, Larson (1974) has argued that traditional sex role expectations may generate a "pull" effect whereby levels of spousal agreement are greatest in areas of traditional definition and role differentiation. Thus, from both Larson's (1974) and Douglas and Wind's (1978) findings, one must be sensitive to the fact that when trying to explain patterns of spousal agreement in family labor allocations, the *kind of task* in question may be critical. Indeed, since any interest in the division of household labor involves issues surrounding both households *and* labor, it is particularly appropriate that qualities of the tasks themselves are included as possible sources of explanation for revealed variation.

Fourth, previous research has focused on the *degree* of consensus with correlation-related measures as key indicators. Typically, assorted household and biographic characteristics have been applied in zero-order association with spousal accounts. Regardless of whether such "background" factors represent characteristics of a single household member (e.g., Granbois and Willett, 1970), or are used as components of a more general index such as "couple heterogeneity" (e.g., Jaco and Shepard, 1975), all attempt to describe the degree of consensus through correlational (or ordinal) measures of association. What is systematically neglected is a description of the *nature* of the link between spousal reports. In the present analysis, regression provides a model for explicitly positing a *linear* relationship between spousal reports and allows for a consideration of the simultaneous impact of several variables on the nature of spousal reports. Finally, a variety of interaction terms will be examined for their influence on spousal consensus. Here we will address whether the relationship between the accounts of wives and husbands changes when selected biographic and task-related factors are included in the equations.

DATA AND METHODS

The data analyzed here were generated as part of a larger study on household labor from a national probability sample of 748 intact households in moderate to large urban areas in the United States. One component of that study is the immediate source of data for this examination. In separate interviews, married couples were asked to undertake a card-sorting operation. Each card represented 1 of 45 household activities. Respondents initially sorted each card on the frequency with which the activity was undertaken in their household, regardless of who actually accomplished the task.[1] When the sorting procedure was completed, the cards representing tasks which were never accomplished were removed, and respondents were asked to answer the question: "Who generally does this task?" on the back of each of the remaining cards.[2] "Generally" was operationalized for respondents as accomplishment greater than approximately 50 percent "of the time." In addition, respondents were reminded that both a shared contribution (at different times) and a joint contribution (at the same time) could justify a designation that more than one household member "generally" does a task.[3] Finally, respondents were asked to re-sort the cards along a nine-point scale representing the degree of pleasantness and the degree of importance they attached to each task.

The data analyzed here do not include the total sample of 748 households. While 748 wives participated in two interviews with a variety of card-sorting operations, financial constraints dictated that comparable data for husbands be gathered from a random subset of only half the sample households, with approximately 350 husbands participating. For this analysis, concern is with the sorting operations which were undertaken by both wives and husbands and with their *matched* responses to questions about the allocation of household tasks. This subset of matched households, however, does not differ on the average from characteristics of the total sample.

The mean age of husbands and wives is 42 and 39 years, respectively. Approximately 35 percent of the sample families are childless or have no children living at home. Twenty percent of the families have at least one child under the age of three. For this sample, only about 20 percent of the wives are employed full-time, with 16 percent employed part-time. They work primarily in clerical and retail sales jobs, or in lower-level professional and technical occupations. Eighty-two percent of the husbands are employed full-time, with about 30 percent at high-prestige jobs. The mean yearly income for employed husbands and wives is approximately $14,500 and $5,000, respectively. These biographic characteristics are consistent with descriptions of other married households in large urban areas, with the exception of the slightly lower proportion of wives who are employed full time. This may have resulted from a sampling bias where employed women were more likely to refuse the rather lengthy interview procedures required.

Table 1 lists the household activities, sorted by wives and husbands, which form the basis for the construction of the dependent variables used here. Based largely on direct observation and interviews in a pilot study of household labor (see Berheide et al., 1976; Berk and Berheide, 1977); the activities sorted by couples were designed to reflect a large subset of tasks

Table 1   Household Activities Sorted by Wives and Husbands

1	Cleaning Bathroom	24	Putting Children to Bed
2	Cleaning Kitchen Sink	25	Putting In and Taking Out Clothes from Washer or Dryer
3	Cleaning Oven		
4	Clearing Food or Dishes from Table	26	Putting Ironed Clothes Away
		27	Putting Washed Clothes Away
5	Cooking	28	Serving Meal
6	Cutting Grass	29	Setting Table
7	Diapering Children	30	Sewing or Mending to Repair Clothes and Household Items
8	Disciplining Children		
9	Disposing of Garbage or Trash	31	Shopping by Mail or by Catalogue
		32	Shoveling Snow
10	Dressing Children	33	Sorting and Folding Clean Clothes After Drying
11	Dusting		
12	Gathering Clothes for Washing	34	Sweeping Floors
13	Going to Gas Station	35	Taking Children to School or Daycare
14	Going to Grocery or Supermarket	36	Talking with Children
15	Household Repair	37	Talking with Door-to-Door Sales-people
16	Ironing		
17	Keeping an Eye on Children	38	Telephoning Local Merchants, Stores or Shops
18	Making Beds	39	Telephoning Repair or Service
19	Paying Bills	40	Vacuuming
20	Pet Care	41	Washing Dishes or Loading Dishwasher
21	Picking Up or Putting Away Toys, Books, Clothes, etc.	42	Washing Floors
22	Plant Care	43	Weeding
23	Playing with Children While Doing Nothing Else	44	Wiping Kitchen Counters or Appliances
		45	Wiping Kitchen or Dining Table

which members routinely undertake. Specific attention was given only to the apportionment of labor on a routine basis; extraordinary household task contribution, while perhaps essential to the ultimate maintenance of the household, were not included in this analysis. Despite this decision, one will note in Table 1 that a variety of household activities are represented (e.g., disciplining children, household repair, pet care, shoveling snow). While the list of 45 tasks is not exhaustive, it is hoped that it represents an improvement over the more limited, more globally defined task lists used in past research (e.g., Blood and Wolfe, 1960; Larson, 1974).

DATA REDUCTION PROCEDURES

The initial question of how wives' and husbands' reports compare for all 45 tasks required reduction of vast amounts of information. To begin, if a respondent said she/he "generally" did a particular task, the response was coded "1." If a respondent did not record themselves a contributor to a particular task, that was coded "0." Similarly for their reports about others. Note, agreement per se was not directly addressed by respondents, but was later calculated from the data.

It is critical at this point to underscore that who is actually reported as a contributor is unimportant. The question posed by this chapter is simpler: How does one spouse's account of who accomplishes a task compare with the other spouse's account? Thus, for this analysis, *what* spouses say is not important; *whether they agree* in what they say is vital.

Unlike past descriptions of consensus, the degree of agreement exhibited by husbands and wives about *all* household members was not included here. If, for example, a wife reports that only she cleans the bathroom and her husband lists both his wife and daughter as "generally" doing the task, this would still constitute agreement between the reports of the *couple* for this task. In short, interest is limited solely to the commentary of spouses about their own and each other's contributions to household labor.

There are a number of reasons why examination is confined to the reports *of* spouses *about* spouses. First, it allowed for the application of more tractable multivariate techniques in the treatment of factors which might explain variation in spousal agreement. The additional burden of examining spousal agreement for all the possible combinations of household contributors for 45 tasks would have seriously complicated the analysis.[4] Second, prior research on the division of household labor (Berk and Berk, 1978) suggests that while children can be important contributors to household labor, their total contribution is much less than that of their parents. Further, the role of other relatives or servants in the accomplishment of routine tasks was found to be negligible. Third, since many of the families have no children (or servants) the inclusion of spousal reports about their task contributions would have severely reduced the data base. Thus, the only "constants" in the sample households are the presence of wives and husbands and their ability to assess the contributions which they and their spouses make.

The initial data manipulation procedure described above produced two sets of cross-tabulations. For each of the 45 tasks, the first showed the relationship between the statements made by wives about their own contributions and statements made by their husbands about them. The second showed the relationship between the statements made by husbands about their own contributions and their wives' statements about them. In short, the first set of cross-tabulations treats agreement surrounding *wives'* household contributions as problematic; the second centers on agreement surrounding *husbands'* contributions.

For the two separate sets of cross-tabulations (contribution of wives, contribution of husbands) a measure of the proportion agreement was constructed. This first required the addition of the instances in which the wives and husbands *agreed* that the spouse in question "generally" did the task, and the instances in which wives and husbands *agreed* that the spouse in question did not "generally" do the task. When this figure was divided by the total N (i.e., the total number of respondents), a proportion agreement "score" resulted. Thus, for the separate commentaries on wives' and husbands' contributions and for each of the 45 tasks, this allowed for comparisons by task and between spousal categories. Yet, even when armed with the proportions showing the couples who agreed on the contributions of husbands and wives to each task, it was difficult to discern the ways in which the *kinds of tasks* undertaken might order patterns of consensus. By examining the ways in which the proportion agreement scores tended to cluster across the array of tasks, some typology of household activities (resting on the level of agreement) might be extracted from the data.

There are a variety of existing cluster procedures (Hartigan, 1975; Van Ryzin, 1977), but to date there is apparently no consensus on which are best under what circumstances (Sokal, 1977). Hence, clustering techniques are perhaps best viewed as descriptive algorithms whose relative strengths and weaknesses depend on substantive application and the kinds of data available. For this analysis, a technique was sought that would group kinds of tasks from information on a single variable (proportion agreement), and that seemed to have the most reasonable statistical justification for the resulting clusters. In this context, Fisher's (1969) "exact optimization" cluster analysis was used, with the goal to group household tasks by their similarities in proportion agreement.

While at each step the arrangement of tasks into clusters is optimal in the sense of minimizing the within-cluster sum of squares, there is no firm rule for how many clusters one should ultimately report as the "best" representation (i.e., typology) of the tasks. At the very least, however, each additional cluster should provide a statistically significant reduction in the error sum of squares. At some point additional clusters fail to make the significance criterion, and no new clusters should be constructed.

However, since significance tests rest on maximum likelihood procedures which require that observations for each spouse be independent of one another, they are not formally appropriate here. For purposes of this analysis, clusters were added until 90 percent or more of the variance was explained, but none was added after that. It was felt that the potential loss of parsimony and the risk of including substantively trivial clusters were reduced in this fashion. However, it may be comforting to note that the F-tests were "significant" by conventional (.05) standards.

PATTERNS OF SPOUSAL AGREEMENT

Informed in part by past research, one can begin by positing three factors which might affect agreement on household labor allocations between husbands and wives. First, spouses might simply observe the allocation of tasks (as "shared events") in their particular households and through this shared knowledge converge in their accounts. In short, wives and husbands may share the same empirical household "reality."

Second, couples might share common expectations about what "wives" and "husbands" in general do in the household. That is, regardless of their specific observations of each other, or the characteristics of their particular household, the perception of one's own household task contributions and those of one's spouse might be informed primarily by normative assumptions about the relationship of men and women to household labor. Indeed, the research by both Granbois and Willett (1970) and Larson (1974) suggested this explanation.

Third, one or both of the first two factors might be important, depending upon some additional "condition." For example, some tasks more than others may generate what Larson (1974) referred to as a "pull" effect, where normative expectations inform spousal perceptions and ultimate accounts. That is, a task like shoveling snow as a "husband's job" per se may foster a different sort of account from one where the contribution to a more normatively "neutral" task like talking with door-to-door salespeople is assessed. Further, tasks that are accomplished more frequently may be more resistant to assumptions about who "should" be doing them and perhaps would more likely depend upon shared experience leading to ultimate convergence in account (Douglas and Wind, 1978). Regardless, the nature of the tasks themselves may intervene to explain spousal report patterns.

It is also possible that biographic characteristics of household members might heighten shared experience and enhance agreement. For instance, one might posit that a couple married for a longer period of time might (in their reports) draw upon a longer history of common experience and more likely share the same perceptions of household labor allocations. Or more highly educated couples could be less vulnerable to the impact of traditional expectations and therefore more likely to agree. Finally, one might explore whether those husbands and wives who share the particular household characteristics of "wife's employment" depend less in their accounts upon normative expectations and traditional role differentiation and more upon shared knowledge of their own and their partner's household labor arrangements. The cluster and regression analyses to follow were designed to explore these possibilities.

CLUSTERING SPOUSAL REPORTS

Table 2 presents the separate cluster analysis of proportion agreement scores for wives and husbands across each of the 45 household tasks. For both the contributions of wives and of husbands, four clusters explained 94 percent of the variance in agreement. In regression terms, this means that three dummy variables (and an intercept) were able to explain well over 90 percent of the variance. For the spousal account of wives' contribution, the F-ratio for the addition of the fourth cluster was over 35.0 and for the spousal report about husbands, the F-ratio for the addition of the fourth cluster was 40.0. The numbers 1-4 under the heading "cluster" indicate the cluster in which each task fell. For each cluster, the "$\overline{X}$" is the mean proportion agreement for the tasks in the cluster. The columns under the "wives" heading describe the tasks and the proportion agreement between spouses about the contributions of wives. The columns under the "husbands" heading describe the tasks and the proportion agreement between spouses for the contributions of husbands.

Viewed in the context of relatively high overall agreement, Table 2 does not reveal any clear boundaries between clusters. For example, no large gaps in proportion agreement scores separate clusters. Thus, the patterns that emerge are similar to other clustering efforts (e.g., Douglas and Wind, 1978) and suggest that empirical attempts to construct a compelling task *typology* for spousal accounts will be frustrated. However, while there are no definitive distinctions between clusters, the analysis is useful for describing *ranges* of agreement and general patterns of agreement by task. For instance, Table 2 does suggest that there is greater overall agreement between spouses about the contribution of wives than of husbands. The overall mean for the proportion agreement on wives' contributions is .88, while for husbands' contributions it is .74. Proportion agreement scores

Table 2   Proportion of Spousal Agreement for Wives' and
Husbands' Contributions to 45 Household Tasks

Wives			Husbands		
Cluster	Task Content	Proportion Agree	Cluster	Task Content	Proportion Agree
1	Diapering children	.98	1	Ironing	.91
1	Gathering clothes for wash	.97	1	Cleaning oven	.88
			1	Household repair	.87
1	Making beds	.97	1	Dusting	.86
1	Putting in/taking out clothes from washer or dryer	.96	1	Putting ironed clothes away	.86
1	Serving meal	.96	1	Cutting grass	.85
1	Sorting/folding clean clothes after wash	.96	1	Washing floors	.85
			1	Sewing or mending to repair household items	.84
1	Cooking	.95			
1	Sewing or mending to repair household items	.95	1	Sorting/folding clean clothes after wash	.84
1	Cleaning kitchen sink	.94	1	Putting in/taking out clothes from washer to dryer	.83
1	Putting away ironed clothes	.94	1	Shoveling snow	.83
			1	Cleaning bathroom	.82
1	Putting away washed clothes	.94	1	Cooking	.82
1	Keeping an eye on children	.93	1	Putting washed clothes away	.82
1	Washing floors	.93	1	Serving meal	.82
Cluster 1 $\overline{X}$ = .95			1	Gathering clothes for wash	.81
2	Cleaning oven	.92	1	Going to gas station	.81
2	Washing dishes or loading dishwasher	.92	1	Taking children to school or daycare	.81
2	Wiping kitchen counters or appliances	.92	1	Vacuuming	.80
2	Cleaning bathroom	.91	Cluster 1 $\overline{X}$ = .84		

Table 2　(continued)

	Wives				Husbands	
Cluster	Task Content	Proportion Agree		Cluster	Task Content	Proportion Agree
2	Dusting	.91		2	Cleaning kitchen sink	.79
2	Going to grocery or supermarket	.91		2	Making beds	.79
2	Wiping kitchen or dining table	.91		2	Paying bills	.77
2	Dressing children	.90		2	Washing dishes or loading dishwasher	.77
2	Plant care	.90		2	Sweeping floors	.76
2	Taking children to school or daycare	.90		2	Wiping kitchen counters or appliances	.76
2	Vacuuming	.90		2	Plant care	.74
2	Clearing food or dishes from table	.89		2	Setting table	.74
2	Disciplining children	.89		2	Putting children to bed	.72
2	Ironing	.89		2	Wiping kitchen or dining table	.72
2	Picking up/ putting away toys, books, clothes, etc.	.89		Cluster 2 $\bar{X}$ = .76		
2	Sweeping floors	.89		3	Going to grocery or super market	.69
2	Talking with children	.89		3	Weeding	.69
2	Putting children to bed	.88		3	Disposing of garbage or trash	.68
2	Talking with door-to-door salespeople	.87		3	Picking up/putting away toys, books, clothes, etc.	.68
2	Cutting grass	.86		3	Clearing food or dishes from table	.67
2	Shopping by mail or catalogue	.86		3	Pet care	.67
Cluster 2 $\bar{X}$ = .90				3	Shopping by mail or catalogue	.66
3	Setting table	.84		3	Disciplining children	.65
3	Household repair	.80		3	Dressing children	.65

Table 2   (continued)

3	Playing with children while doing nothing else	.79
3	Telephoning local merchants, stores, shops, etc.	.78
3	Paying bills	.77

Cluster 3 $\overline{X}$ = .80

4	Pet Care	.74
4	Weeding	.73
4	Going to gas station	.72
4	Telephoning repair or service	.72
4	Shoveling snow	.68
4	Disposing of garbage or trash	.66

Cluster 4 $\overline{X}$ = .71

TSS = .302
ESS = .017
% reduction in error =   94%

3	Telephoning local merchants, stores, shops, etc.	.64

Cluster 3 $\overline{X}$ = .67

4	Playing with children while doing nothing else	.61
4	Diapering	.60
4	Talking with door-to-door salespeople	.60
4	Talking with children	.59
4	Keeping an eye on children	.56
4	Telephoning repair or service	.56

Cluster 4 $\overline{X}$ = .59

TSS = .401
ESS = .025
% reduction in error = 94%

for wives' contributions range from .98 to .66, while for husbands the range is .91 to .56.

Equally important, attention to the patterning of clusters for agreement on wives' contributions indicates that spousal agreement varies substantially by task. With the exception of two child care tasks (diapering children, keeping an eye on children), over half the tasks in the first cluster are those that center on the laundry process, ironing, or making beds. The other tasks that show high agreement in the first cluster focuses on kitchen activities (serving the meal, cooking, cleaning the kitchen sink, washing floors). One could argue that spousal perception concerning wives' contribution to these tasks is affected by traditional expectations about women's household labor; all the tasks constitute what one might call a traditional set of "wives' " household tasks.

The second cluster shows a more varied task list and more variation in spousal agreement. Some of the highest agreement scores are reached by five tasks which describe most of the remaining kitchen activities (cleaning the oven, washing dishes, wiping counters, wiping tables, clearing the table). Embedded within the second cluster are also tasks that might be characterized as "female" chores (going to the grocery, dressing and chauffeuring children, dusting, cleaning bathrooms, care of plants, and vacuuming). All these tasks represent those for which over 90 percent of the couples agreed on the wives' contribution to them. The other tasks in the second cluster which show relatively high agreement in part represent the varied tasks of child care. The strong "pull" toward agreement which operated for the task of diapering children in the first cluster is not as evident here. It is also at the lower bound of this second cluster where the first task attached to the "male" domain of household labor appears: cutting the grass.

The third cluster contains tasks that display somewhat lower levels of agreement on wives' contributions. This cluster can be characterized by tasks that may not be so closely connected to normative notions about "female" jobs, *or* those that are thought to be traditional "male" household chores. Thus, setting the table is a task which, unlike laundry or diapering children, may not carry with it an image of the "housewife's" job. In contrast, household repair and paying bills constitute tasks traditionally thought to be stereotypically "male."

The fourth and final cluster suggests as strikingly as the first that stereotypic tasks assume a coherent pattern and may order spousal agreement. In contrast to the first cluster, the tasks found here (pet care, weeding, going to the gas station, shoveling snow, and disposing of garbage) are all tasks one would be hard pressed to describe other than through their stereotyped features. Just as a vast majority of couples *agreed* on the wives' contribution to the "female" tasks of the household, so too do couples *disagree* on the contribution of wives to the "male" tasks of the household.

These findings suggest that household tasks, in interaction with spousal perceptions, may generate a strong "pull" effect toward agreement. However, depending upon *whose contribution one is discussing,* tasks may also generate a "push" effect. That is, couples may agree on the wives' contribution to tasks which are stereotyped as traditionally "female," but may not agree about their contribution to tasks which are stereotyped as traditionally "male."

Table 2 also presents the clusters describing agreement scores surrounding the contribution of husbands. One notices first that there is much lower overall agreement when spouses are reporting on the contribution of husbands than when they are reporting on the contribution of wives. Indeed, the mean proportion agreement score for the first cluster describing reports on husbands' contributions (.84) is only slightly greater than the *final* cluster describing reports on wives' contributions (.80). In short, the second cluster for the contribution of husbands show proportions often as low as the *lowest* scores for the wives.

Much of the first cluster is dominated by stereotypic "female" tasks (ironing, cleaning the oven, doing the laundry, washing floors, cooking, serving meals, sewing and mending, and the like). Indeed, almost 80 percent of these tasks are found in the first two clusters that describe the highest agreement surrounding the contribution of *wives*. All four of the remaining tasks in the first cluster are those which one could argue are stereotypically defined tasks for husbands: household repair, cutting the grass, shoveling snow, and going to the gas station. Consequently, the pattern of agreement surrounding the contribution of husbands suggests that certain tasks generate a "pull" effect toward agreement for both traditionally defined "female" tasks *and* for "male" tasks. The second cluster contains tasks found primarily in the higher agreement clusters for wives (cleaning the kitchen sink, washing dishes, sweeping floors, and so on) and thus relative to husbands' contribution to other tasks, these more stereotypically female tasks show high levels of agreement.

The last two clusters describing agreement scores for husbands' contributions are distinctive for at least three reasons. First, the proportions are quite low. Indeed, for a few of the tasks, fully *half* the couples surveyed simply do not share the same household reality in their perceptions of husbands' participation in household work. Second, both the third and final clusters are dominated by the presence of child care tasks. Of the nine tasks in the complete list which are obviously and directly connected to children, seven of these are found in the clusters with the lowest agreement on husbands' contribution. Third, a number of the tasks which were assumed to designate stereotypic "husband" activities and which did not reach high agreement when *wives'* contributions were considered are also found in the lowest agreement clusters for husbands. The tasks of weeding, disposing of garbage or trash, pet care, and telephoning repair or service personnel show lower agreement levels for the contributions of both wives *and* husbands.

The results of the cluster analysis suggest that spousal perceptions of the allocation of household labor may be more complex than previously assumed. For the contributions of either wives or husbands, agreement is often high for stereotypic tasks, *regardless of whose contribution is being accounted for.* That is, relatively high agreement was found for the contributions of both partners to some stereotypic "female" tasks surrounding kitchen and laundry activities. Likewise, there was relatively high agreement found for the contributions of both partners to a few stereotypic "male" tasks such as household repair and cutting the grass. It may have been this effect which Larson (1974) was describing when he discussed the "pull" effect of familial sex roles.

In contrast, the findings also suggest that these same normative forces may reveal themselves through a "push" effect away from spousal agreement. For some tasks that could be considered sex role stereotyped, *depending upon whose contribution is being assessed,* agreement may be lower. That is, wives and husbands may agree less about the contribution of their partners to their "own" tasks (i.e., tasks which stereotype their own gender role). Thus, for example, it was found that couples showed the lowest levels of agreement surrounding the participation of wives in such tasks as pet care, weeding, going to the gas station, disposing of garbage or trash, and shoveling snow. Similarly, couples showed the lowest levels of agreement surrounding the participation of husbands in such tasks as diapering, disciplining, dressing, and keeping an eye on children, as well as going to the grocery. This last finding suggests that the tasks of child care may be associated with somewhat different normative assumptions. This distinctive perception surrounding the allocation of child care will be discussed at a later point.

Finally, it is clear that spousal perceptions surrounding the activities of husbands may be considerably more complex than that for wives'. Recall, this was suggested both by the general findings of lower overall agreement on the contribution of husbands and in the specific finding that *some* "male' tasks (i.e., weeding, disposing of garbage or trash, pet care, telephoning repair or service) were associated with the lowest levels of agreement, *regardless of whose contribution was being assessed.* Thus, not only is there lower overall agreement between spouses about what husbands do, but particularly for some tasks which were assumed to be "male" stereotyped, wives and husbands are consistently at odds in their accounts. Here, one can only speculate about these findings. Based on prior evidence (e.g., Berk and Berk, 1978) it is difficult to avoid the conclusion that the household remains de facto a *woman's workplace.* It may be that because of the greater participation of wives in a larger variety of household tasks (norms notwithstanding) they may be forced to override more traditional stereotypes in their accounts of their own and their husbands' participation. In both the general case of lower agreement and the specific case of disagreement surrounding some "male" tasks, wives may be consistently resisting the kinds of normative effects which may inform their husbands' accounts. In short, in their reports on their own participation in some stereotyped "male" tasks and in their accounts of their husbands' participation in household labor more generally, wives may be less vulnerable to normative assumptions and more likely compelled to describe their *actual* work lives.

Thus far, the high overall levels of agreement between wives and husbands surrounding their contributions to household labor suggest a significant "shared" household labor reality. However, the patterns revealed through the cluster analysis are striking in the degree to which agreement seems to vary by task. Household tasks are by no means apprehended in a neutral fashion; the patterns of agreement seem to be ordered by gender-linked expectations. Thus, it may be that the "shared" reality which generates high levels of agreement is based as much on shared *normative* assessments and expectations as on shared experience and observation. However, it is not simply the systematic patterning of agreement by task and contributor that should be explored. What is next needed is an examination of the nature of spousal *disagreements* and whether or not particular characteristics of households or couples affects them.

MODELING SPOUSAL REPORTS

Treating spousal accounts of their own contributions as dependent variables, partners' reports about them will be used as explanatory variables in a regression analysis. In addition, some interaction terms that combine the spousal report with a number of household characteristics will be examined for their impact. Each regression equation may be viewed in the aggregate as describing the probability that an individual spouse will report that she/he is "generally" a contributor to the task in question, *given the report of the other spouse* (a conditional expectation). The slope of the regression line measures the effect on that probability of a unit change (i.e., 0 to 1) in the partner's report.[5]

Prior to presentation of the regression analyses, a diagrammatic example may prove useful. Figure 1 depicts a number of hypothetical relationships between spousal accounts in regression terms. It represents a picture of the kinds of disagreements that are possible and those that are not possible in these data.

In Figure 1 there are six pairs of regression lines.[6] The first three pairs represent theoretically possible outcomes for the data presented (A, B, C) and the second three pairs represent theoretically impossible outcomes (D, E, F). In each, the solid line represents a hypothetical empirical relationship, while the dotted line represents a null hypothesis of "consistent prediction." That is, the dotted line always represents a relationship in which a one-unit change in the dependent variable (reportee) will always be "predicted" by a one unit change in the independent variable (reporter). On the average, changes in the report of one spouse will correspond in a one-to-one manner with the report of the other. (For

Figure 1   Hypothetical Regression Outcomes Between
Spousal Reports on Household Task Contributions

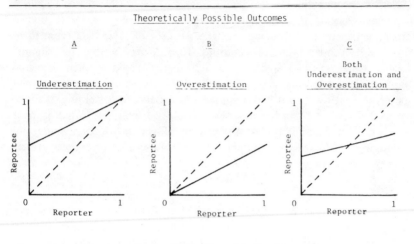

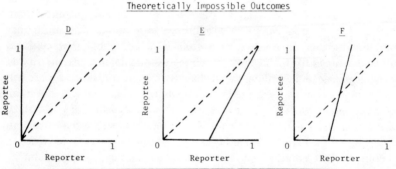

example, husbands' reports about wives will consistently "predict" wives'
reports about themselves.)

Figure 1A represents what one might call "underestimation." Here the
solid line depicts a relationship where the "reporters" will underestimate
the "reportees." For example, if one were using husbands' reports about
their wives' contributions as a predictor, this line would describe that
instance in which husbands tend to report lower levels of contribution for
their wives than wives report for themselves. Note, however, the *degree* of
underestimation is not constant. (It necessarily decreases from left to
right.)

Figure 1B describes the empirical situation of "overestimation." Here,
reporters overestimate contributions of reportees. To continue with the
above example, the solid line shows that husbands would tend to report

greater contributions for their wives than wives report for themselves. Again, however, the degree of overestimation is not constant, decreasing from left to right.

Figure 1C represents the empirical possibility where the two effects are combined. That is, when husbands report no contribution on the part of their wives, they would in fact be underestimating their wives' reports about themselves. In addition, when husbands report a contribution for their wives, they would be overestimating the contribution wives report for themselves.

Figures 1A, 1B, and 1C represent theoretically possible relationships in the data to be examined below. However, for purposes of comparison, it is important to briefly describe those relationships which in principle *cannot* appear. Figures 1D, 1E, and 1F describe theoretically meaningless results for this data set. The solid line in Figure 1D represents a situation wherein the reporter and the reportee agree when there is no contribution, but when the reporter notes a contribution by the partner, the partner reports a contribution greater than 1.0. For example, if a husband reports that the wife contributes to the task, she would have to report a contribution that was somehow greater than "generally" doing it. Clearly, this is an impossibility, since there is no response category greater than 1.0. Similarly, the solid regression line of Figure 1E illustrates the meaningless situation whereby wives and husbands could agree when the reporter says his/her partner contributes to the task, but when the reporter says his/her partner does *not* contribute, the partner would report a contribution less than zero. So, for example, wives would have to report a contribution which is less than simply "not" doing the task. This too is meaningless since there is no response category less than zero. Finally, the solid line of Figure 1F represents the two unreasonable outcomes in combination. These reported upon would cite their own contribution as less than zero and greater than 1.0.

As illustrated by the data to follow, the nature of spousal disagreements can be hypothetically described only by the first three regression outcomes. In fact, the "underestimation" outcome is especially relevant for the present analysis. Given a context in which spousal agreement is high, disagreement is (to varying degrees) of the underestimation variety. Returning to Figure 1A, it is clear that the magnitude of underestimation is solely a function of the intercept. With the variables constructed dichotomously, the highest value is fixed at 1.0. The upper bound of the slope remains constant, and the slope depends therefore on what one spouse says about his/her own contribution when the other spouse reports no such participation. The higher the intercept, the greater the degree of underestimation.

REPORTS OF WIVES' HOUSEHOLD TASK CONTRIBUTIONS

Table 3 lists all the regression equations for the 45 household tasks, with the wives' self-reported contributions as the dependent variables. The tasks are ordered as they were for wives' contributions in Table 2. For the moment, discussion will be limited to the impact of the spousal reports as independent predictors. Since one reasonable expectation is that the interaction effects will be less important to understanding the nature of spousal disagreements, they will be considered last.

The R^2 coefficients are presented in the first column of Table 3 primarily as a convenience and will not be interpreted. With these data, R^2 must be viewed with caution, since it no longer reflects the original data, but the data transformed to correct for heteroscedasticity.[7]

For this analysis, attention to the intercepts is important, since they provide critical information about the *direction of disagreement* embedded in the previous cluster patterns. In the second column of Table 3 the alpha coefficients represent the probabilities attached to the wives' reports that they "generally" contribute to household tasks, under a condition where their husbands say they do not. In short, the intercepts reflect the degree to which underestimation is operating in spousal accounts. The slope coefficients in column 3 (husband report) represent the change in the probability that wives will report themselves as contributors (change in Y) when husbands report a contribution by them (a unit change in X from 0 to 1).

While the significance tests applied to the intercepts are based on the conventional null hypothesis that the intercept is zero (i.e., "consistent prediction"), another null hypothesis was posited when testing for the significance of the husbands' reports about wives' contributions. Since high levels of agreement between spouses had been previously established, a "no correspondence" null hypothesis ($H_0 = 0$) for the slope would not have been as informative as a "consistent prediction" null hypothesis ($H_0 = 1$). Therefore, significance criteria at the .05 level are applied so that when the coefficients for both the intercepts and the slopes reach significance, it means that it is more than a chance *departure* from consistent prediction between spousal accounts.

In the main, the intercept coefficients in Table 3 are strikingly large. This suggests that wives are likely to report contribution to household tasks, even when their husbands say their wives make no contribution. For example, the probability that wives will report themselves as contributors to the task of gathering clothes for wash is .67 when husbands say wives do not contribute. Or, for example, the probability that wives will report

Table 3 Regression Equations for Wives' Reported Household
Task Contributions (metric coefficients)

Task	R^2	α	Husband Report	Husband x Yr. Married	Husband x Hus. Education	Husband x Wife Employment	Husband x Task Frequency
Diapering children		No Variance in Independent Variable					
Gathering clothes for wash	.99	.667[a]	.308[b]	.000	.000	.002	.001
Making beds	.99	.556[a]	.457[b]	−.001[a]	−.000	−.000	−.000
Putting in/taking out clothes from washer or dryer	.99	.600[a]	.422[b]	−.000	−.003	.000	−.002
Serving meal	.99	.818[a]	.163[b]	.000	−.000	−.001	.003
Sorting/folding clean clothes after dryer	.99	.714[a]	.299[b]	.000	−.002	.002	−.006
Cooking	.99	.909[a]	.062[b]	−.000	.000	−.002	.004
Sewing/mending to repair household items	.99	.909[a]	.092[b]	−.000	.001	.000	−.000
Cleaning kitchen sink	.99	.867[a]	.100[b]	−.000	−.002	−.000	.005
Putting away ironed clothes	.98	.714[a]	.335[b]	−.001	−.002	−.005	−.013
Putting away washed clothes	.98	.667[a]	.311[b]	.000	.002	.002	−.003
Keeping an eye on children		No Variance in Dependent Variable					
Washing floors	.99	.429[a]	.539[b]	.000	−.000	−.003	.004
Cleaning oven	.98	.500[a]	.452[b]	.000	.003	−.003	.006
Washing dishes or loading dishwasher	.98	.722[a]	.185[b]	.001	.005	.003	.003
Wiping Kitchen counters or appliances	.98	.944[a]	.095[b]	−.000	−.002	−.003	−.008
Cleaning bathroom	.99	.581[a]	.410[b]	.000	.004	−.007[a]	−.003

Table 3   (continued)

Dusting	.97	$.583^a$	$.342^b$	.000	.001	.004	.005
Going to grocery or supermarket	.98	$.588^a$	$.406^b$	.000	.005	−.002	−.010
Wiping kitchen or dining table	.99	$.913^a$	$.016^b$	.000	.002	.002	.007
Dressing children		No Variance in Dependent Variable					
Plant care	.96	$.667^a$	$.363^b$	.000	−.004	−.002	−.013
Taking children to school or daycare	.99	$.500^a$	$.506^b$	−.000	−.000	−.008	−.001
Vacuuming	.97	$.559^a$	$.399^b$	.001	−.001	.001	.002
Clearing food or dishes from table	.95	$.692^a$	$.228^b$	.002	.003	.002	−.003
Disciplining children	.99	$.727^a$	$.238^b$	.000	−.003	−.003	.005
Ironing	.97	$.818^a$	$.137^b$	−.000	$.012^a$	−.002	$-.017^a$
Picking up/putting away toys, books, clothes, etc.	.96	$.850^a$	$.010^b$	.001	.010	−.000	.004
Sweeping floors	.98	$.778^a$	$.178^b$	.001	.002	.001	.000
Talking with children		No Variance in Dependent Variable					
Putting children to bed	.98	$.823^a$	$.232^b$	−.001	−.009	−.000	−.007
Talking with door-to-door sales-people	.99	$.880^a$	$.137^b$	−.000	−.005	−.002	.001
Cutting grass	.30	$.108^a$	.232	.002	.013	.027	.030
Shopping by mail or catalogue	.98	$.583^a$	$.337^b$	.002	.005	.002	−.019
Setting table	.92	$.622^a$	$.327^b$	−.001	.004	−.002	−.004
Household repair	.41	$.178^a$	$.703^b$	−.005	−.019	.024	−.035
Playing with children while doing nothing else	.99	$.968^a$	$-.049^b$	.001	.003	.003	.004

Table 3   (continued)

Telephoning local merchants, stores, shops, etc.	.95	.788[a]	.050[b]	−.001	.018	−.000	.008
Paying bills	.93	.500[a]	.415[b]	−.001	.002	−.008	.016
Pet care	.93	.481[a]	.541[b]	.005[a]	−.004	.005	−.038[a]
Weeding	.87	.387[a]	.558[b]	−.000	−.013	.015	−.025
Going to gas station	.92	.421[a]	.656[b]	.000	−.025[a]	−.004	−.017
Telephoning repair or service	.92	.591[a]	.346[b]	−.002	−.011	.012	.009
Shoveling snow	.61	.298[a]	.233[b]	.007	−.031	.034	−.028
Disposing of garbage or trash	.70	.446[a]	.413[b]	.000	−.000	−.007	−.007

Summary Statistics: $\overline{R^2}$ = .93

$\overline{\alpha}$ = .651

$\overline{b}$ = .293

[a]coefficient significant at $p < .05$ ($H_o = 0$)
[b]coefficient significant at $p < .05$ ($H_o = 1.0$)

contribution to the task of serving meals is .82, when husbands say there is no such contribution. Probably the most telling example of the overall finding that wives report high contributions for themselves, regardless of what their husbands say, is that three of the tasks (all related to child care) showed virtually no variance in wives' report; almost all wives said they "generally" did these tasks.

The fact that over half the alpha coefficients are at levels greater than .50 suggests also that when there is disagreement between spouses about the contribution of wives, it is the underestimation regression line which results (see Figure 1A). Recall, the larger the alpha coefficient, the more disagreement can be characterized by underestimation. Consequently, in Table 3, all the intercept values depart significantly from the null hypothesis that they will be zero.

It is not surprising to find that with high levels of underestimation, slope coefficients will be relatively low. In fact, the overall mean slope value is only .293. However, while there is a high probability that wives will report a contribution when husbands disagree, it is also the case that if husbands *do* report a contribution by wives, wives will almost certainly agree. For example, the probability is .43 that wives will report a contribution to washing floors when their husbands disagree. However, an additional probability of .54 is added when husbands report that their wives "generally" wash floors.[8]

There is a single exception to this pattern of relatively high intercept values and low slope coefficients. For the tasks of cutting the grass, household repair, paying bills, taking care of pets, weeding, going to the gas station, shoveling snow, and taking out the garbage or trash, wives are less likely to report a contribution when their husbands say wives do not participate. Thus, the level of underestimation is markedly reduced for tasks which were previously categorized as "male" stereotyped. However, the probability that wives will agree *when their husbands report a contribution* for them remains quite high. For instance, the probability that wives will report participation in bill paying when their husbands disagree is only .50 and quite low compared to the intercept values for other tasks. Still, the probability that wives will agree if husbands report them "generally" paying bills is greater than .91. In other words, it is only for these tasks that overestimation may occur, and only at the upper end (see Figure 1C).

Based on the findings from Table 3 it is clear that wives are very likely to report a contribution to household labor tasks, especially for those stereotypic "wives' tasks" surrounding the care of the kitchen, laundry, and children, even when their husbands report no contribution for them. Thus, disagreement around wives' contributions is appropriately characterized by the "flatter" slope of the underestimation line. The single exception to this conclusion emerges when one considers the tasks which are traditionally perceived to be "husbands' chores." For these tasks, while spousal accounts still significantly depart from "consistent prediction," underestimation is of a lesser magnitude and, indeed, overestimation in small doses may surface. However, as with all the tasks, if husbands report contributions by wives, wives will likely agree.

Besides addressing the nature of spousal disagreement, the regression analyses also help explore whether (within the context of high spousal agreement) variation might be explained by particular characteristics of households or spouses. That is, under the influence of selected conditions, the impact of spousal report could change. The choice of interaction variables was primarily informed by past research. In studies concerned with spousal decision making or attitudes, few consistent effects have been found for length of marriage (e.g., Scanzoni, 1965; Van Es and Shingi, 1972), or for the education levels of spouses (e.g., Haberman and Elinson, 1967; Van Es and Shingi, 1972; Jaco and Shepard, 1975). In the hope of resolving some confusion, these variables as well as one for the employment status of the wife were put in interaction with spousal report as an independent predictor of consensus. A suggestion made by Safilios-Roths-child (1969) informed the choice of one final interaction term. She pointed out that perceptual differences might systematically vary, depending upon the information available to household members about the behavior of others. Therefore, the final interaction term combined the effects of spousal report about the partner with a report on the frequency with which the task was said to be accomplished in the household.[9] Thus, for each task, the reports of husbands about their wives were put in interaction with several conditions: (a) year of marriage; (b) level of husband's education (scale from 0 to 9); (c) dummy variable for wife's full-time employment; (d) husband's report on the frequency with which the task is undertaken in the household (regardless of who does it).[10]

It is clear from Table 3 that few of the interaction terms explained any variation in wives' accounts of their own household labor participation. Only seven of the interaction terms reach an appropriate level of significance and given the large number of significance tests, can easily be explained by Type I error. Thus, with considerable confidence, it can be concluded that for a large number of household labor tasks, the prediction of wives' accounts of their own participation is not significantly altered by characteristics of particular households or husbands. Indeed, this suggests that the forces which lead husbands to certain sorts of perceptions about their wives' contributions to the household remain impervious to a variety of social and economic conditions ordinarily assumed salient. What remains as the most critical determinant of the kind of disagreement surrounding wives' contribution is the nature of the task accounted for.

REPORTS OF HUSBANDS' HOUSEHOLD LABOR CONTRIBUTIONS

Table 4 presents the regression equations with husbands' self-reported contributions as the dependent variables. The tasks in Table 4 are ordered as they were for husbands' contributions in Table 2. Wives' reports about their husbands are used as independent variables, along with wives' reports in interaction with year of marriage, wife's education level, whether or not the wife is employed full time, and wife's report on the frequency with which the task is undertaken in the household.

When comparing Tables 3 and 4, one is struck immediately by the differences between the equations which predict wives' and husbands' accounts of their task contributions. The mean intercept values for Tables 3 and 4 are .65 and .34, respectively. Table 4 illustrates in more detail that spousal reports centering on the contribution of husbands are overall less

Table 4   Regression Equations for Husbands' Reported Household
Task Contributions (metric coefficients)

Task	R^2	α	Wife Report	Wife × Yr. Married	Wife × Wife Education	Wife × Wife Employment	Wife × Task Frequency
Ironing	.41	.070[a]	.546	.012	.001	.063[a]	-.088
Cleaning oven	.69	.101[a]	.908	-.010	.057	-.014	-.135
Household repair	.97	.687[a]	.247[b]	.000	-.004	-.001	.018
Dusting	.56	.131[a]	-.079[b]	.003	-.020	.064[a]	.116
Putting away ironed clothes	.57	.128[a]	1.543	-.052[a]	-.388[a]	-.098[a]	.483[a]
Cutting grass	.93	.439[a]	.471[b]	-.000	.008	-.008	.005
Washing floors	.33	.126[a]	.593	.002	-.042	.027	.010
Sewing/mending to repair household items	.13	.119[a]	.459	-.002	-.119[a]	.123	.003
Sorting/folding clean clothes after drying	.46	.152[a]	1.171	.002	-.000	.006	-.114
Putting in/taking out clothes from washer or dryer	.54	.155[a]	.701	.003	.071	.001	-.083
Shoveling snow	.95	.615[a]	.285[b]	.000	.013	-.015[a]	.012
Cleaning bathroom	.56	.173[a]	1.129	-.002	-.108[a]	.003	-.030
Cooking	.37	.158[a]	-.167	-.000	.023	-.000	.099
Putting away washed clothes	.59	.170[a]	1.056	.004	.074	.000	-.177[a]
Serving meal	.28	.122[a]	.707	.004	-.091[a]	-.004	.003
Gathering clothes for wash	.45	.167[a]	.875	.017[a]	-.085	.014	-.085
Going to gas station	.96	.808[a]	.101[b]	.001	.003	-.000	.003
Taking children to school or daycare	.55	.204[a]	.654	-.001	.014	-.015	-.015

Table 4   (continued)

Vacuuming	.71	.204[a]	.613	-.002	.004	.020	.007
Cleaning kitchen sink	.68	.200[a]	.511	.007[a]	-.054	.025[a]	.010
Making beds	.44	.160[a]	.811	.004	.025	.024	-.119[a]
Paying bills	.89	.341[a]	.510[b]	-.002	.004	-.015	.039
Washing dishes or loading dishwasher	.44	.205[a]	.113	.003	-.026	.013	.060
Sweeping floors	.37	.223[a]	.695	.000	-.087	.002	.009
Wiping kitchen counters or appliances	.59	.232[a]	1.747	.000	-.017	-.005	-.183[a]
Plant care	.68	.226[a]	1.467[b]	-.010[a]	-.041	-.004	-.147
Setting table	.38	.235[a]	1.350	-.008	-.064	-.134	-.087
Putting children to bed	.89	.383[a]	.455	.003	.014	.018[a]	-.021
Wiping kitchen or dining table	.35	.266[a]	.553	.001	.000	.005	-.035
Going to grocery or supermarket	.83	.444[a]	.482[b]	.001	.016	-.013	-.020
Weeding	.92	.620[a]	.165[b]	.002	-.016	.005	.053[a]
Disposing of garbage or trash	.90	.640[a]	.484[b]	-.002	-.004	-.010	-.029[a]
Picking up/putting away toys, books, clothes, etc.	.54	.331[a]	.544	.001	-.009	.023	-.027
Clearing food or dishes from table	.49	.322[a]	-.426[b]	.009	-.010	-.001	.093
Pet care	.81	.438[a]	.338[b]	.003	.040[a]	.001	-.032
Shopping by mail or catalogue	.36	.264[a]	.067[b]	.010	.046	-.019	-.068
Disciplining children	.89	.730[a]	.585[b]	-.005[a]	-.049[a]	-.012	-.021
Dressing children	.79	.359[a]	-.084	.009	.057[a]	.012	.014
Telephoning local merchants, stores, shops, etc.	.67	.411[a]	.441[b]	-.002	-.004	.130	-.033

Table 4 (continued)

Playing with children while doing nothing else	.89	.794[a]	.025[b]	.002	-.001	.009	.004
Diapering children	.75	.409[a]	.599	.002	.077[a]	.012	-.108
Talking with door-to-door sales-people	.57	.442[a]	.431[b]	-.003	.001	-.014	-.037
Talking with children	.93	.793[a]	-.023[b]	.001	.009	.019	.003
Keeping an eye on children	.90	.585[a]	.388[b]	-.002	-.000	.024[a]	-.021
Telephoning repair or service	.85	.567[a]	.264[b]	-.002	.005	.018	.018

Summary Statistics: R^2 = .64   [a]coefficient significant at p < .05 (H_0=0)

$\overline{a}$ = .341   [b]coefficient significant at p < .05 (H_0=1.0)

$\overline{b}$ = .575

likely to exhibit the magnitude of underestimation so prevalent in Table 3. This is especially true for tasks previously characterized as stereotypically "female." Intercept levels are uniformly lower for these tasks when husbands comment on their own contributions. Indeed, this finding is consistent with that for wives' contributions; underestimation is decreased when tasks not stereotypically attached to the reportee are accounted for.

Table 4 also details obvious differences in slope values for the reports of wives about husbands. The mean slope value for the wives' report on husbands' contributions is nearly twice the comparable figure found in Table 3 (.57 versus .29). In fact, for the vast majority of the tasks in Table 4, the null hypothesis of "consistent prediction" could not be rejected. In part because husbands are much less likely to report a contribution when their wives say their husbands do not contribute (i.e., lower intercept values), the wives' reports about husbands can have a much greater unit-for-unit "impact," especially for stereotypic "female" tasks. For example, when comparing a single stereotyped task for prediction of *both* wives' and husbands' reports about their own contributions, obvious differences emerge. Turning back to Table 3, one can see that a report from husbands that wives "generally" serve meals increases the probability only .16 that wives will report a contribution for themselves to the task. In contrast, a report from wives that husbands "generally" serve meals increases the probability .71 that husbands will report a contribution for themselves.[11]

In contrast, recall there was evidence to suggest that for "male" tasks, wives were less likely to report high levels of contribution for themselves when their husbands disagreed. That is, underestimation was of a lesser magnitude and thus husbands' reports about wives were closer to a one-to-one correspondence. In Table 4, the mirror image of this effect is revealed. For prediction of husbands' contributions to stereotypic "male" tasks (e.g., cutting grass, shoveling snow, going to the gas station, paying bills, weeding, disposing of garbage or trash), the intercept values are much higher than for other household tasks. This suggests that the regression line of underestimation is the most accurate description of the kind of disparities that emerge between wives' and husbands' accounts, particularly for reports on tasks which are specific to one's own gender role. In any case, the analysis illustrates that while tasks may show high *proportion* agreement, depending upon their sex stereotypic qualities, the *nature* of the *disagreement* can differ markedly.

Finally, a comparison of Tables 3 and 4 reveals a somewhat startling finding for some of the tasks of child care. Recall that when wives' reports about their own contributions were predicted, some child care tasks show virtually no variance. That is, nearly all the wives reported "generally" doing the tasks, regardless of the reports of their husbands. For those child care tasks which did exhibit variation, the intercept values were among the highest (underestimation). However, while the pattern of these tasks when *husbands'* contributions are predicted is not as uniform, it is the case that for *some* tasks of child care, husbands are reporting their own contribution at a relatively high level, even when their wives disagree. In other words, there is often considerable underestimation surrounding husbands' reports about child care. This is a compelling finding, since it suggests that for certain tasks (e.g., disciplining, dressing, playing, talking, keeping an eye on children) *both* wives and husbands are reporting far greater contribution than their partners attribute to them. Such a pattern departs considerably from the consistent findings of underestimation and prediction which emerged in other comparisons between the two regression analyses. Yet this finding may also illustrate even more fully the power of norms as guidelines for accounts of household contributions. For the vast majority of household tasks other than those of child care, clear patterns of sex stereotyping in spousal reports emerge. That is, when accounting for their own and other's contributions, wives and husbands may use normative expectations to order their perceptions. In the case of child care (especially those tasks which do not involve infant children), the "shoulds" of contribution cannot be so easily distinguished by gender. Thus, normative guides to accounting for participation in parenting may not be particularly useful to members. The result is a pronounced misreading by each partner of the others' contribution.

Unlike the null effects found for interaction terms when wives' reports of their own contributions were examined, Table 4 reveals a number of statistically significant interaction effects. In Table 4 one would expect approximately 9 interactions to emerge as significant simply by chance (.05 level). Yet 26 significant effects appear. While this suggests that there may exist a systematic pattern of effects either for certain kinds of tasks or for certain kinds of household characteristics, it is difficult to identify any pattern which approaches parsimony.[12] Despite some suggestion of causal effects, it is probably unwise to interpret such varied results simply because "something may be going on." The only tentative observation one may make is that certain characteristics of wives (e.g., employment, education) seem to produce the greatest *number* of significant effects and that the tasks of child care as well as certain stereotypic "male" tasks may be the most fruitful for further scrutiny.

SUMMARY AND CONCLUSIONS

Past efforts to chronicle spousal consensus patterns have given little attention to one critical subset of family activity: the allocation of household labor tasks. To address the question of whether levels of agreement between married couples might vary by task or by reported contributor, an optimal clustering technique was applied to matched spousal reports from approximatley 350 families, over a range of 45 routine household tasks. It was expected that if significant discrepancies in the accounts of couples were uncovered, the nature of such disagreements might also depend upon which contributor was being assessed, the tasks themselves, or the particular characteristics of households. Two separate regression analyses were employed to "predict" the reports of wives and husbands about their own household labor participation.

An examination of the *amount* of agreement found across 45 tasks revealed three central features of spousal accounts surrounding the division of household labor. First, for the vast majority of the tasks, aggregate-level agreement proportions were high, although overall there was greater agreement surrounding wives' than husbands' contributions.

Second, for both wives' and husbands' contributions, it was found that agreement is often higher on some tasks that were roughly characterized as

sex stereotyped. Further, this high agreement was often sustained, *regardless of which partner's contribution was being assessed.* Couples were more likely to agree on the contribution of both wives and husbands to stereotypic "female" and "male" tasks. Borrowing Larson's (1974) term, we concluded that a normative "pull" effect toward agreement produced this result. However, it should be reiterated that the characterization of sex-stereotyped tasks is far from precise. Consequently, agreement levels surrounding tasks are also likely to vary, *depending upon whose contribution is being assessed.* For some tasks a normative "push" effect away from high agreement was revealed. This was particularly evident for accounts of wives' contributions to stereotypic "male" tasks and for husbands' contributions to some tasks of child care. These findings suggest that spousal perception surrounding the division of household labor is a complex configuration of normative assumptions and specific task-related characteristics deserving considerably more attention.

The regression analysis was designed to address both the nature of spousal disagreement and how variation around it was affected by task and contributor. Further, the question of whether particular characteristics of households or members significantly altered prediction of spousal self-reports was explored. Four central findings emerged from this analysis.

First, it became clear that disagreement between spouses is (to varying degrees) of a single type: the spouse assessing her/his partner's contribution "underestimates" the report of that partner. That is, when wives and husbands disagree, it is because both are attributing greater participation to themselves than is attributed to them.

Second, within the context of disagreement as underestimation, there is considerable variation. Similar to findings for the *amount* of agreement, the kind of task seemed to explain in part the degree of underestimation operating between spouses. Certain tasks seemed to "push" or "pull" couples to greater or lesser levels of underestimation. There was a strong suggestion that couples are pulled" toward underestimation if they are being assessed for contribution to tasks which stereotype their own gender role. Thus, underestimation was at its highest levels when wives' contributions to "female" tasks are reported by couples and husbands' contributions to "male" tasks are reported. In short, depending upon the type of task and gender of the reporter, disagreement centers on the underestimation of contributions to sex stereotypic tasks by the spouse who (normatively speaking), might call such tasks his/her "own." Likewise, the "push" effect away from high levels of underestimation represents the mirror image of the above findings. Underestimation levels for disagreeing couples were found to be lower when wives were assessed for their participation in "male" tasks and husbands for their participation in "female" tasks.

Third, child care tasks may stand apart from the more general effects which other tasks may have on the nature of disagreement. This task group in part seemed to heighten underestimation, regardless of whose contribution was being assessed. Thus, some child care tasks not only engender low levels of agreement between spouses, but are also associated with the kind of disagreement wherein both spouses perceive far greater contribution for themselves than is attributed to them.

Finally, no parsimonious pattern was found in the analysis of the interaction of spousal report with particular individual or household characteristics. For the assessments of wives' contributions, very few significant effects surfaced; for husbands' contributions, no immediately sensible pattern by task or interaction term emerged.

This research carries both methological and substantive implications. From a methodological standpoint, it confirms that future efforts to measure salient features of household labor apportionment among family members must give attention to the myriad tasks which actually constitute household work. The invention of more global (and more convenient) categories such as "housework," "child care," and "chores" may confound the realities of the work itself and the complex perceptions which surround it. Further, the inclusion of the reports of wives *and* husbands (as well as children) in efforts to measure the division of household labor is obviously indicated.

The substantive implications raised by this analysis must be more speculative. The most provocative substantive findings revolved around the nature of spousal disagreements. It was found that both wives and husbands underestimate the report of the other about his/her own contributions to the household. It may be that the household member accounting for his/her own contribution may more thoroughly incorporate his/her "own" task-specific gender expectations. That is, the more thorough incorporation of the "oughts" of household labor may be reflected in the reports of one's own contribution. This may begin to explain the pattern of underestimation where for sex stereotypic tasks linked to the gender role of the spouse being "accounted for," underestimation was high.

Yet the role of these normative guidelines and gender expectations which lead couples to report as they do deserves much more focused research attention. In light of the data presented here we conclude that the nature of spousal disagreement depends upon much more than the so-called objective information available to household members. For example, it is difficult to conceive of any reason why underestimation

should be so strongly associated with stereotypic tasks and the contributor based solely on the fact that couples may not always share the same information or household experiences. This argument becomes even more suspect given that task frequency reports showed no effect in interaction with spousal report.

Thus, further evidence is needed for *how* gender-specific normative assumptions order spousal perception. Perhaps a fruitful area for future examination of this question would be to examine those tasks which do not seem to carry such powerful normative messages and cues for members, thus rendering reported contribution more problematic. Child care emerged as the obvious example in our preliminary analysis, although a more detailed look at the varied household tasks undertaken by members would certainly reveal other areas where the assessment of contribution is not easily facilitated by reference to norms.

Not only is the study of the extent of agreement and the nature of agreement important for an understanding of spousal perceptions, but also important is the study of couples' *own* perceptions of *consensus* and *dissensus* (Scheff, 1967). Little attention has yet been given to the interaction of spousal accounts of household labor allocation (or any family activity) with their perceptions of household consensus surrounding it. In light of the pervasive underestimation which marks spousal disagreement, one must wonder if members become aware of the extent to which their partners often "miss" what they themselves take to be their own and obvious labors. One must further wonder what implications such differences in perception might have on the way household labor is in fact allocated or managed as a family problematic.

It is clear that there are many features of household labor around which couples' accounts converge. It is also clear that particular qualities of the household or its members do little to enhance such convergence. Like the everyday allocation of domestic labor tasks, perceptions surrounding it may be responsive to pervasive assumptions about the "appropriate" roles for men and women. *Both* work realities—who does the work and how the allocation of work is perceived—combine to form the qualitatively different relationships which women and men have to this unique work site.

NOTES

1. Response categories for the measure of task frequency were: "never"; "less than once a month"; "once a month"; "several times a month"; "once a week"; "several times a week"; "once a day"; "several times a day."

2. Response categories for the apportionment of household labor were: "myself"; "spouse"; "daughter"; "son"; "relative"; "friend"; "neighbor"; "servant"; "other." Multiple responses were allowed.

3. Note that this way of measuring household task allocation departs from many earlier efforts. First, the initial sorting by frequency enabled a relevant task set for each particular household to be established. Second, respondents were asked which member (or members) "generally" did each of the tasks listed, which allowed for more accurate assessment of day-to-day and routine participation. Third, the more common five-point scale of task participation was not used (e.g., Blood and Wolfe, 1960; Granbois and Willett, 1970; Douglas and Wind, 1978). While the five-point scale (e.g., 5 = "wife always" to 1 = "husband always") allows for joint participation, it also rests on perhaps an unwarranted assumption that the measures are equal interval.

4. The use of more than two contributors would have required multivariate models for nominal dependent variables with more than two categories. Moreover, the specifications for this chapter require models in which both nominal and interval predictors could be included. While estimation procedures exist for such circumstances (Nerlove and Press, 1973), they are computationally expensive, difficult to interpret, and would have provided few clear benefits to the analysis. Shortly these issues will be considered in greater depth.

5. The reader will note that the usual linear regression model is interpreted somewhat differently when the dependent variable is dichotomous. For example, it is not possible to predict exactly an individual wife's report about her own contribution, by knowing her husband's report about her. Therefore, a more reasonable approach is to predict the *likelihood* of her response, given information from her husband (Pindyck and Rubinfeld, 1976: 238). Further, with this type of data, it is obvious that the assumption of constant error variance is inappropriate. For example, cases where the probability of a wife's report is close to 1.0 (a likely occurrence) will have relatively low variances, while others in the middle ranges will have higher variances. This will lead to inefficiency and biased estimates of the variances of the regression coefficients. Thus, using weighted least-squares (as a special case of generalized least-squares), the appropriate data adjustments for heteroscedasticity were undertaken, resulting in newly estimated error variances (Pindyck and Rubinfeld, 1976: 240-243). In principle, a form of analysis using limited dependent variables could have been employed. This would have eliminated the possibility of obtaining predicted values outside the 0-1 range as well as the other problems with ordinary least-squares. However, besides the complications described earlier, there seemed no compelling reason to worry about anomalous predictions, since predictions per se are of little interest. Moreover, estimation procedures for limited dependent variables typically assume a nonlinear (e.g., logistic) relationship between the independent and dependent variables. There is no reason to force that assumption here, particularly since the argument is not that one spouse's account *causes* the other's, nor need we assume that the impact of the independent variables is greatest in their middle ranges. Such a model does not seem relevant here. In short, by adjusting for heteroscedasticity, the most troublesome problems with the linear probability model were eliminated without having to move to an entirely different mode of analysis with dubious advantages.

6. Here it is the *nature of the relationship* between spousal reports and not the degree of agreement or disagreement that is of concern. The former is reflected in the

regression coefficient, while the latter can be expressed by the R^2 (although for these data the R^2 will be severely attenuated). In other words, one could have a regression coefficient of 1.0 and still have a relatively low R^2. Similarly, one could have a far smaller regression coefficient and a rather high R^2. In this analysis, the regression coefficient, therefore, will be taken as an indicator of *how* the two accounts correspond. The R^2, but more appropriately the proportion agreement measure used earlier, reflects the *amount* of agreement.

7. Since the marginals for the reports about one's own contribution and the contributions of others are often highly skewed (e.g., most wives report that they "generally" do the ironing and most husbands agree), R^2s prior to the transformation for heteroscedasticity were often very small. This resulted from the inability of measures of association to accurately reflect consistency between variables in the face of little variance. Once the dichotomous variables are made into qualitative variables through the transformation, however, the observations are "spread out" and the consistency between the two variables is revealed. (However, this was an unintended consequence of transformation.)

8. This implies that the degree of disagreement decreases with an increase in the probability that the husband says the wife does a particular task. Moreover, for all practical purposes, overestimation rarely occurs.

9. We know that the inclusion of these interaction terms is not based on firm theoretical expectations. Yet given a research tradition which clings to the idea that such "conditions" markedly affect spousal report, we decided to explore any potential role they might play in the mechanisms behind spousal disagreement. In contrast to the null hypothesis applied to the intercept and the hypothesis of "consistent prediction" applied to the slope, the null hypothesis for interaction terms represents a methodological rather than a substantive decision. That is, in the case of the interaction terms, we made the conventional and conservative assumption that they would not generate any additional effects ($H_0 = 0$).

10. Since it is the spousal report about the partner which is used as the primary predictor variable, some of the interaction terms are constructed to reflect characteristics of the *reporter* as the conditions under which the impact of the reporter's perceptions may change. Consequently, when husbands' accounts of wives' contributions are used as predictors, they are placed in interaction with *husband's* education and *husband's* report on task frequency, as well as the year of marriage and whether or not the wife is employed. Similarly, when wives' accounts are used as predictors, the interaction terms include *wife's* education and *wife's* report on task frequency. Finally, the original intention was to include an interaction term which tapped into spousal perceptions of task importance. However, the zero-order correlation between wives' reports on the frequency of task accomplishment and their reports on the importance of the tasks to the household was .96. For husbands' reports, the correlation was .61. Thus, because of the severe problems of multicollinearity, only spousal reports on task frequency were used in interaction terms.

11. While some of the slopes suggest that one may get predicted values greater than 1.0, it should be kept in mind that all the coefficients in any given equation must be considered, and not simply the single coefficient for the wives' statements.

12. For example, all the interaction terms are significant for the task of putting away ironed clothes. However, none emerges for the task of putting away washed clothes. Likewise, one finds that the interaction term "wife report x year of marriage" shows significant impact on the prediction of husbands' reports for the

tasks of putting away ironed clothes, gathering clothes for wash, cleaning kitchen sink, plant care, and disciplining children. Moreover, the signs of many of these effects often show inconsistencies across tasks.

REFERENCES

ARAJI, S. K. (1977) "Husbands' and wives' attitude-behavior congruence on family roles." Journal of Marriage and Family 2 (May): 309-320.

BALLWEG, J. (1969) "Husband-wife response similarities on evaluative and non-evaluative survey questions." Public Opinion Quarterly 33 (Summer): 249-254.

BERHEIDE, C. W., S. F. BERK, and R. A. BERK (1976) "Household work in the suburbs: the job and its participants." Pacific Sociological Review 19 (October): 491-517.

BERK, R. A. and S. F. BERK (1978) "A simultaneous equation model for the division of household labor." Sociological Methods and Research 6 (May): 431-468.

——— (1979) Labor and Leisure at Home: Content and Organization of the Household Day. Beverly Hills, CA: Sage Publications.

BERK, S. F. (1979) "Husbands at home: the organization of the husbands' household day," pp. 125-158 in K. W. Feinstein (ed.) Working Women and Families. Beverly Hills, CA: Sage Publications.

——— and C. W. BERHEIDE (1977) "Going backstage: gaining access to observe household work." Sociology of Work and Occupations 4 (February): 27-48.

BLOOD, R. O. and D. M. WOLFE (1960) Husbands and Wives: The Dynamics of Married Living. New York: Free Press.

BOOTH, A. and S. WELCH (1978) "Spousal consensus and its correlates: a reassessment." Journal of Marriage and Family 40 (February): 23-32.

BROWN, G. W. and M. RUTTER (1966) "The measurement of family activities and relationships." Human Relations 19 (August): 241-263.

CENTERS, R., B. H. RAVEN, and A. RODRIQUES (1971) "Conjugal power structure: a reexamination." American Sociological Review 36 (April): 264-278.

CRADDOCK, A. E. (1977) "Task and emotional behavior in the marital dyad," pp. 239-247 in N. Glazer and H. Y. Waehrer (eds.) Woman in a Man-Made World. Chicago: Rand McNally.

DOUGLAS, S. P. and Y. WIND (1978) "Examining family role and authority patterns: two methodological issues." Journal of Marriage and Family 40 (February): 35-47.

FERBER, R. (1955) "On the reliability of purchase influence studies." Journal of Marketing 19 (January): 225-232.

FISHER, W. D. (1969) Clustering and Aggregation in Economics. Baltimore: John Hopkins Press.

GRANBOIS, D. H. and R. P. WILLETT (1970) "Equivalence of family role measures based on husband and wife data." Journal of Marriage and Family 32 (February): 68-72.

HABERMAN, P. and J. ELINSON (1967) "Family income reported in surveys: husbands versus wives." Journal of Marketing Research 4 (May): 191-194.

HARTIGAN, J. (1975) Clustering Algorithms. New York: John Wiley.

HEER, D. M. (1962) "Husband and wife perceptions of family power structure." Marriage and Family Living 24 (February): 65-67.

JACO, D. and J. SHEPARD (1975) "Demographic homogeniety and spousal consensus: a methodological perspective." Journal of Marriage and Family 37 (February): 161-169.

LARSON, L. E. (1974) "System and subsystem perception of family roles." Journal of Marriage and Family 36 (February): 125-138.

NERLOVE, M. and S. J. PRESS (1973) Univariate and Multivariate Log-Linear and Logistics Models. Santa Monica: RAND.

NIEMI, R. (1974) How Family Members Percieve Each Other. New Haven, CT: Yale University Press.

OLSON, D. H. (1969) "The measurement of family power by self-report and behavioral methods." Journal of Marriage and Family 34 (August): 224-234.

––– and R. E. CROMWELL (1975) "Methodological issues in family power," pp. 131-150 in R. E. Cromwell and D. H. Olson (eds.) Power in Families. New York: Halsted Press (a Sage Publications book).

OLSON, D. H. and C. RABUNSKY (1972) "Validity of four measures of family power." Journal of Marriage and Family 34 (May): 224-235.

PINDYCK, R. S. and D. L. RUBINFELD (1976) Econometric Models and Economic Forecasts. New York: McGraw-Hill.

SAFILIOS-ROTHSCHILD, C. (1969) "Family sociology or wives' family sociology?: a cross-cultural examination of decision-making." Journal of Marriage and Family 31 (May): 290-301.

SCANZONI, J. (1965) "A note on the sufficiency of wife responses in family research." Pacific Sociological Review 8 (Fall): 109-115.

SCHEFF, T. (1967) "Toward a sociological model of consensus." American Sociological Review 32 (February): 32-46.

SOKAL, R. R. (1977) "Clustering and classification: background and current directions," pp. 1-15 in J. Van Ryzin (ed.) Classification and Clustering. New York: Academic.

SUDMAN, S. and N. H. BRADBURN (1974) Response Effects in Surveys. Chicago: Aldine.

TURK, J. L. and N. W. BELL (1972) "Measuring power in families." Journal of Marriage and Family 34 (May): 215-222.

VAN ES, J. and P. SHINGI (1972) "Response consistency of husband and wife for selected attitudinal items." Journal of Marriage and Family 34 (November): 741-749.

VAN RYZIN, J. (1977) Classification and Clustering. New York: Academic.

WILKENING, E. A. and D. E. MORRISON (1963) "A comparison of husband and wife responses concerning who makes farm and home decisions." Marriage and Family Living 25 (August): 349-351.

9

DOMESTIC LABOR AS WORK DISCIPLINE: THE STRUGGLE OVER HOUSEWORK IN FOSTER HOMES

JUDITH G. WITTNER

A significant proportion of housework involves children, who must be fed, clothed, supervised, and trained in some of the social skills they will need in the wider world. From the perspective of parents and other caretakers, children are the cause and focus of much household labor, relying as they do on the goods and services produced in the home to sustain and educate them in the long and often costly period of their dependency. But children are not simply the recipients of household goods and services produced by others. By virtue of their position as dependents, they are connected to the household production process as apprentices and assistants to the housewife or her substitutes (Oakley, 1974). The organization of domestic work which subordinates children to their caretakers' control and demands their obedience is justified on several grounds. First, children are not considered competent to participate equally in household affairs, but instead require direction from adults. Second, children owe caretakers compensation for their material support. Third, the qualities demanded of children in the household division of labor—responsibility for chores and obedience to the orders of caretakers—are orientations which they will need in their adult work roles (see Kohn, 1969).

Most recent studies of household labor look at children from the perspective of their primary caretakers, housewives. In order to reconstruct the housewife's world, they examine the impact of young children on the range and duration of her tasks (Berk, 1979; Vanek, 1978; Walker, 1973) and calculate her worth in households with dependent children compared with her wage-earning capacity (Gronau, 1974, 1976; Mincer and Polacheck, 1974; Liebowitz, 1974). This chapter will attempt to reconstruct some aspects of the child's world of household labor by examining the problems and issues surrounding housework from the perspective of dependent minors. The data on which the study is based were provided by 43 then current and former wards of the state of Illinois in interviews which took place in 1975 and 1976. As early as their first days of life, and some time before reaching the legal age of maturity, these youngsters joined 300,000 or so others in the United States who have been adjudicated "dependent," "neglected," or "in need of supervision," the last status assigned truants, runaways, and other minors "out of control." Under the law, the state becomes the guardian and protector of its wards, seeing to their care, well-being, support, and training. Daily responsibility for these tasks is delegated to foster parents who are reimbursed by the state or by state-subsidized private agencies for child care expenses, and to salaried employees of large and small residential institutions.

Normatively, households in American society are constituted by kin. In practice, the bonds of blood and marriage help to organize the division of labor and the sentiments of the domestic group. State wards reside in households which are not so constituted, and therefore cannot draw on family sentiments as recipes to guide their conduct of affairs with others. This break between domestic life and family ties defines the situation of foster children and helps to make explicit the exchanges of support for control between minors and their caretakers. These exchanges are often the basis of the organization of work that goes on in the household.

To some extent, all children and their caretakers are involved in an exchange whose inequities are legitimized by beliefs surrounding family life and age relations. The need for this exchange originates in the social relations of production which separate children from the means of direct support. This, and not their biological connection or age, beyond their earliest years, creates and maintains their material dependence on others. In this respect, children share their subordinate status with women, especially housewives, whose market position also disadvantages them and locates them in the home as dependents of men (Vanek, 1978; Oakley, 1974). In the household, however, women and minors do not share the same status. There, a division of labor subordinates children to women and puts their interests in opposition. The more control the housewife or caretaker is able to exercise over the household and its schedule of work, the more children in the household lose their control over their daily activities. How much children participate in determining the disposal of their own time, and how much of that control is given over to others, may vary according to the intensity of the struggle between them over the dimensions of the work day in the home. This calls for a more direct focus on the organization of housework by women and children, to supplement studies concerned with arrangements between husbands and wives.

THE WORK OF WOMEN AND CHILDREN

HOUSEWORK

In the abstract, housework involves undertaking the repetitive tasks necessary to maintain living and working spaces in the proper order and to maintain the people who exist within these spaces. Concretely, the daily struggle against the disorder and decay of material objects in the service of personal needs occurs in a social-historical context, and the practical activities and techniques that are part of housekeeping repertoires are specific to their particular time and place. In our own time, housework links an expanding market and a domestic economy increasingly subordinated to it. It is not simply that houseworkers must spend more of their time purchasing as commodities the goods and services which once were produced in the private household, although that is an important element of their situation. Houseworkers are also dominated by housework techniques and schedules which appear as rational and efficient ways to organize work. This in turn is related to the ways in which goods and services are distributed to households, where they will be transformed into items of domestic use. As Weinbaum and Bridges (1967: 92-93) point out:

> Housewives are expected to wait for weeks for installations and repairs, to wait in line, to wait on the phone. Changes in the distribution network and the expansion of services demands physical mobility within this less-than-flexible series of schedules. The increase in the number of services means housewives spend more time travelling between centers than in producing goods and services. The centralization of shopping centers and services may make distribution more efficient, but at the expense of the housewife's time.

Although the home may appear to be the sphere of private life, the household schedule is increasingly determined by needs and schedules originating elsewhere. As the housewife's time becomes increasingly dependent on these external schedules, she must adapt her work in the home as well. Within the household, the housewife works around the less-flexible schedules of businesses, stores, and providers of services by creating timetables and arranging tasks in ways that reflect and reproduce the organization of commodity production itself. As Oakley (1974)

demonstrated in her study of London housewives, when private houseworkers follow an apparently self-imposed regimen, sequencing tasks,
alloting time to each, and executing them in specific ways, they are in fact
reproducing for themselves the conditions of supervised labor that management imposes on wage workers. Fundamentally, the autonomy of the
housewives Oakley studied was a fiction, in which labor discipline
appeared to them as their own self-imposed schedule.

Although the demands Oakley's housewives imposed on themselves were
externally determined and did not arise out of their own needs, they
preferred this arrangement to the direct supervision experienced by wage
workers, where the last vestiges of control over work would be eliminated.
When children are conscripted into the labor of the household, in contrast,
caretakers control their work schedules and supervise them as they undertake their chores. In this way, the antagonism between children and their
caretakers is structured into the organization of housework itself. In
households based on family ties, this domination is rationalized by
parental authority based on cultural traditions and institutionalized
patterns of conduct. In foster homes and institutions for wards of the
state, the organization of housework is not guided by old habits or by
legitimating norms of conduct. Who works, what they work at, and the
conditions of their labor are likely to be called into question and become
matters to be worked out between children and their caretakers. As the
two parties bargain or struggle with each other, they help to fashion the
structure of the households in which they jointly reside.

PAID WORK

If caretakers and children jointly determine the structure of the working day within the household, they do not do so "just as they please."
Family relations are structured in many ways by economic and political
forces beyond the control of individuals. As the economy changes, shaping
new segments of the work force and new relations to wage labor, the
everyday life of working people also changes, including how they repair,
restore, and reproduce themselves within the household. The consistently
lower market value of women's and children's work, when compared with
that of men, has accounted for their domestic dependence on fathers and
husbands, and continues to disadvantage them when they do not have this
support. The poorest households in the United States, for example, are
headed by women with children (Ross and Sawhill, 1975). Historically,
women and children have served as a labor reserve, entering and leaving the
labor force on the crests and troughs of the economic cycle, earning the

lowest wages, suffering the highest unemployment, and commanding the fewest marketable skills (Kalachek, 1969; Bell, 1977). Presently most women and teenagers are employed in low-wage, expanding industries, women predominating in clerical and sales work, and young people sharing the service sector with minorities and the aged, as well as with women. Their similar positions as workers and widely held beliefs about their essential domestic natures were institutionalized in a political-legal system which reinforced their dependent positions. These vicissitudes in labor force participation affected their position and the range of their duties in the household. The glorification of feminine domesticity, and the consignment of women to the home, coincided with their elimination from the work force after World War II to make room for returning veterans (Trey, 1972). Currently an extensive literature explores the consequences of women's expanding labor force participation on family structures and on their position within the home (Hoffman and Nye, 1974).

Less well studied is the concurrently expanding teenage labor force, which has more than doubled since 1964 (Kanter, 1978). A substantial increment to this youthful labor force is the as yet unknown numbers of children, some quite young, who engage in informally organized work in their neighborhoods. Hired by private families and individuals to babysit, mow lawns, move heavy items, clean basements, and perform a wide variety of odd jobs and services, children provide a cheap and available source of assistance to homeowners, mothers of small children, the aged, and others in the community. This is important, but for the most part sociologically invisible labor, much as housework was (and still is) the invisible labor of women.

It would be reasonable to expect the increased labor force participation of young people to affect age relations within the household, because it increases the resources children are able to mobilize on their own and decreases their dependence on other family and household members. In the case of foster children, the state acts as a surrogate employer, providing them with a means of subsistence which affects their dependence on their own families and on the households in which they reside. Hirschhorn (1978: 159) argues that welfare has changed from "a system of social control tied to immediate labor market conditions" to one which "regulate[s] the growth, structure, and development of the 'displaced population'." Among the "displaced population" of foster children, who are disproportionately poor, state support may function like the wage, increasing the independence of these wards from their own families and from the foster homes and residential institutions which are, in the last analysis, intermediaries between children and the child welfare departments and social service agencies which support them. In light of the increasing labor force participation of young workers, the relations that foster children and their caretakers create in the context of this external source of support may be models of developing family relations in general. Before turning to examine the structuring of household relations by foster children and their caretakers, a brief description of the informants and their milieu is necessary.

METHODS AND SAMPLE

The data presented here were gathered as part of a study of the foster care system in Illinois. Two- to three-hour unstructured interviews focusing on the daily lives and long-term careers in care of 43 state wards were conducted in conjunction with a more extensive survey of the children, their parents, caseworkers, and caretakers. Group and individual interviews took place in 1975 and 1976, to extend the portrait of foster care from the perspective of the dependent child. The 43 informants, with the exception of 3 friends or housemates of the original sample, were part of a stratified sample of 370 foster children selected for the wider study on the basis of the household type in which they resided at the time of the interview.

The informants for the study reported here were chosen on the basis of their race, sex, and length of time in foster care. Slightly more than half the sample (23) was male and ranged in age from 14 to 21 years. Their 20 female counterparts were between the ages of 15 and 21 at the time of the interviews. Of the informants, 17 were black, 17 white, 7 Hispanic, and 2 Native American. The 43 wards began their state careers at different ages, ranging from birth to 15 and remained under state care from 2 to 18 years.

Excluding the large population of black children in correctional institutions, which remain the major form of black institutional placement (Billingsley and Giovannoni, 1972), black children are more likely to be placed in foster homes and white children in institutions. Young children and girls are also most often placed in foster homes. The 43 informants lived in many households as state wards. Faulty memories, especially about the early years of long and eventful careers in foster care, and the notorious inadequacies of the case records in this regard, make it difficult to estimate the total number of households in which they lived. An approximate (but probably conservative) figure is 206, an average of nearly 5 placements for each foster child. Included among these were 79 foster or group home assignments, and an additional 23 in the homes of relatives and friends. Correctional institutions, institutionally based treatment programs for the behaviorally disturbed, and mental hospitals accounted for 42 placements. Temporary commitment to Juvenile Hall to await court hearings (which included stays up to one year) initiated or punctuated the careers in 17 instances, and placement in the Chicago Parental Schools for truancy or other school-related offenses occurred at least twice. Three individuals spent some time at the YMCA, and 3 more were on their own, but receiving support from the state child welfare agency under a program providing a monthly income directly to wards.

This chapter will focus on housework in two contrasting residential alternatives for wards of the state: foster homes and residential institutions. An overriding feature of housework in both settings is its conceptualization as an exchange with caretakers for support. This exchange creates the need for consensus on the values of children's work and obedience and on the returns they can expect from their labor. Adherence to this principle of exchange is common to foster homes and institutions, though its details differ in these different settings.

THE PRINCIPLE OF EXCHANGE

The principle of exchange is a central feature of the relations between children and their caretakers and is an axis along which various accommodations to foster care emerge (see Erikson, 1976). Most foster children, no less than their caretakers, accept the premise that children are costly to their parents and caretakers. Caretakers, as strangers who are not obligated by the bonds of kinship to assume this burden, need and deserve compensation for their ministrations. Apart from the regular state subsidy, which they bring with them to their foster homes and institutions, wards of the state can only offer their labor-power and their obedience in return for support. Under these conditions, housework acquires a dual aspect. It is a useful activity which results in a product or service of value to the household or to some of its members. At the same time, it is a process with particular rules and standards of performance. In this latter aspect, it becomes the means of measuring and displaying obedience.

The rate of exchange is as salient an issue in small foster homes resembling "natural" families as in institutions. When a child assumes the legal status of state ward, he or she moves from dependence on kin acting in the name of family obligations and sentimental ties, to dependence on caretakers, who serve under the direction of state welfare departments and private agencies for a wage or fee. It is this aspect of the relations between foster children and their caretakers, not the size and shape of the household, which gives foster care its special identity.

Exchange is the feature which unites the range of apparently diverse households that make up the foster care system. Within this overall unity, however, important differences based on household size, caretaker status, and the permeability of the boundaries between the home and its immediate environment shape work relations in the household. The two sections which follow explore the place of housework in institutions and foster homes, which differ along these dimensions.

DOMESTIC WORK IN INSTITUTIONS

The most explicit evaluation of housework was in residential treatment facilities whose population included many youngsters diverted from juvenile corrections into the reputedly less stigmatizing child welfare system. These youngsters came to the attention of authorities as a result of truancy, shoplifting, sexual conduct (girls), flirtation with gangs (boys), and other petty offenses and minor crimes. Although they escaped the more serious label "delinquent" and its consequences, incarceration in a juvenile corrections institution, they were named "minors in need of supervision" and placed in institutions which would control their behavior and attempt to "re-form" their personalities. In these environments, a popular disciplinary technique has been the highly elaborated system of rewards and punishments known as "behavior modification." This technique makes housework the metric against which behavior is judged and the tool by which it is re-formed.

For example, daily schedules were strictly structured by the housekeeping routine.

> They had so many rules. There was this one way you had to make up your bed, a certain way to throw your clothes at night. You have different chores to do, like sweep, like mopping halls. You'd have to mop a whole hall by yourself and that don't be punishment. That's just ordinary work [seventeen-year-old high school dropout, on his stay in a youth detention center].

Punishment followed unacceptable work.

> If you be working in the kitchen, they'd show you how to set the trays and if you mess that up they don't say too much, but if the dishes don't be too clean, they'd say that they'd do this to you. They'll have you standing on your head for five hours. They'd be exaggerating, but they will have you on your head for at least an hour.

Housekeeping performances could keep wards out of trouble with their caretakers or bring them punishment. Performances could also bring rewards. One institution offered credits for domestic work, which could be exchanged at the rate of "two points a penny." Other media of exchange for the work or obedience of inmates were time and gradations of privilege.

In institutional settings of all kinds, members of both sexes were responsible for the upkeep of their immediate surroundings. When they broke rules or ran away, housework was also a form of punishment for boys and girls alike. This was accomplished by multiplying the chores for which the guilty party would be held responsible or by inflating the assigned work to proportions that distinguished it from everyday activity. For example, runaways in one institution were forced to wash the cottage floors with a toothbrush.

Girls often engaged in bitter struggles over the terms of their work obligations in foster homes. This was not the case in many of the treatment institutions to which older girls were sent. Among girls in this sample, those who were placed in large treatment institutions chose those settings in preference to remaining home. All but one made this choice in order to end ongoing conflicts with parents and relatives over housework or over their confinement to the home. It is no wonder, then, that they found the housekeeping schedules in institutions less onerous than those they left behind. Girls who were placed in the old-style orphanages because of family-related problems such as death, divorce, illness, or the desertion of a parent, rather than as above, as part of a decision in which they participated, and who usually entered the foster care system earlier in their lives than did the first group, found domestic chores and household schedules to be a problem, especially at first. This was because they contrasted their responsibilities in the institution with their typically light or nonexistent duties in their own homes, where their deceased, ill, or runaway mothers had assumed most of the burdens of housework. Occasionally, girls entering institutions for the first time found little difference between their own homes and the new environment, at least in respect to household labor. For example, upon arrival at the county's youth detention center, one girl was told by her floormates, "You have to work just like you do at home."

Girls' household responsibilities were an unremarkable component of their daily lives in institutions. Even if housework was an initial source of difficulty, as the girls became familiar with institutional life and rules it became just another part of the daily routine. New housework problems arose as girls reached the last stages of their tenure with the state and began to plan for their work futures. In the period prior to leaving their institutional homes for good, some girls regretted their lack of experience with the normal range of domestic duties. In these age-segregated environments, for example, there was little informal contact with babies and young children, though potential employers, from mothers seeking baby-sitters to day care centers and nurseries, all preferred or required experienced workers. The lack of opportunity to "get experience with a baby" was one of a range of skills, traditions, and lore concerning housekeeping, child care, household administration, cooking, and other domestic arts and crafts which girls claimed were not taught or were not well taught in institutions. Their concerns stemmed from their desire to marry and keep house for families of their own, though that was not their only ambition. During their last years with the state they became more concerned about readying themselves for the future by identifying and pursuing an appropriate career. Their connection to the child welfare system was a source of information about possible occupations, and they felt uniquely qualified by virtue of their own histories to join their caretakers as probation officers, caseworkers, and child care workers of one kind or another. Again, they felt deprived by institutional life of the wider experiences which would provide them with more information about their opportunities, demonstrate their competence to themselves and others, and help them to choose a suitable line of work.

Housework presented different problems and offered different rewards to institutionalized boys. Girls often found institutions less demanding than home, though they suspected these were possibly unsuitable settings in which to acquire domestic competence. Boys, many of whom came from homes in which all males were exempted from housework, were introduced to a new state of affairs and for the first time in their lives were expected to participate in household upkeep.

> I learned to make my bed, cook, wash. I knew how to cook and wash at home, but I never did it because my grandma and my ma would do it. In a way I enjoyed it, in a way I hated it . . . learning new things, learning different ways.

Required to participate in the feminine world of housework, boys used a masculine language of self-reliance and independence to describe and evaluate it.

> You [can] take care of a house, you [can] cook for yourself. Then you don't have to worry about having a wife, getting a girlfriend, spending your paycheck on dinner in a restaurant [seventeen-year-old resident of a group home, reflecting on his thirteen years in a Catholic orphanage].

It helped me so when I get older, bang, you know, I'll know then I won't have to go to school and study them or anything (fifteen-year-old boy in a group home, on his experiences in the same institution].

Boys believed that housework provided lessons in work discipline and that the possession of this discipline would win them jobs. Caretakers promoted this idea by emphasizing that industriousness, obedience, and responsibility were qualities that would allow the dependent youngster to earn and maintain his independence. The daily schedule of the institution was to help implant these habits of work discipline in the boys.

I learned to take responsibility on my own. You're on your own out here. You don't have your mother and father to tell you what to do. You pick up things on your own, you learn to discipline yourself. At home your mother says 'don't do that.' Here you tell yourself 'don't do that,' that's how you know. That's the way you learn [fifteen-year-old resident of a suburban treatment institution].

Certainly some discipline was required to sustain the monotonous round of low-paid, low-skill work to which these teenage workers had access. In this sense, caretakers were proved right. "Once I get there it's over with," one sixteen-year-old boy said in reference to the difficulties of showing up regularly at his all-night job at a fast food chain near the institution where he lived.

Reliability was not, however, the only quality required of a good worker. A second was the willingness to follow orders. Boys developed this ability as they engaged in their work in the institution, and brought it with them to the world of wage labor.

I was polite. I wasn't mad. I did everything they told me. That's the way I had to act or I wouldn't get a job [eighteen-year-old former resident of a Texas institution].

In summary, housework in institutions was surrounded by a system of rewards and punishment which motivated the work, though it worked differently for boys and for girls. Housework and its products were the measure of obedience and of one's ability to follow orders, resources to be offered in exchange for money, time, or privilege, and a set of practical and social skills that were necessary to future success. To children in institutional care, housework was a means by which they could learn essential skills and, ultimately, earn adult status. In foster homes, by contrast, housework functioned less as the means by which work discipline and occupational goals were pursued and more as the object or goal of disciplined behavior itself.

DOMESTIC WORK IN FOSTER HOMES

The foster home is the traditional arrangement for the provision of small group care, and the likely first placement for young children, for girls, and for blacks, who historically were excluded from large institutions for dependent children (Billingsley and Giovannoni, 1972). Typically, foster parents have been drawn from among the upper stratum of the working class and from the lower-middle class (Costin, 1972: 345). In the foster homes described here, men played minimal roles, and foster parenting was almost exclusively the work of women. Except for the fact that it took place in the home, it resembled many paid service jobs which draw on women's domestic skills (Fanshel, 1970). The management of affairs between foster children and caretakers in foster homes was based on a familial model of parental authority, which gave the foster mother primary responsibility for the supervision and control of her wards on a daily basis. Since control effectively ended at the front door, private households were not preferred placements for children who refused to acknowledge the authority of their caretakers. Many foster mothers attempted to restrict their foster children to the household by requiring that they return home straight from school, by limiting their social activities with friends, and by imposing full and demanding schedules of domestic work.

Struggles between caretakers and foster children over rules and restrictions were common in foster homes. From the point of view of foster parents, the attempt to impose limits on the foster child must have seemed reasonable. Caretakers, as state employees, had responsibility for protecting their foster children, a responsibility they translated into restriction to the household. Caretakers could only fulfill this obligation to control, discipline, and protect their foster children if they kept them as close to the home as possible. In foster homes, to be out of sight was to be out of the range of control—a situation which had its parallel in institutions as well, but in institutions the problems were not necessarily compounded by the dangers and temptations of the streets. Nor did a foster parent have the support available to institutionally based caretakers: authoritative rules and procedures; a regular means of enforcement; and colleagues and superiors to reinforce control. The problem of control is one of the principal reasons why foster parents and caseworkers consider girls and young children to be better foster home placement material than boys and teenagers. Indeed, the few teenage boys in this sample who lived in foster homes had more freedom than did girls and young boys who were more easily restricted to the home. From the point of view of many children who reluctantly spent much of their time in the house, this explains why they had more chores and responsibilities than did their teenage foster brothers.

The foster mother, as the main caretaker, organized the chores and directed the work. In many cases, assigning chores was the first order of business when a foster child arrived at a new home.

> When I first came she showed me around. She told me about the house . . . you know, chores. You get up, you make your bed, wash the floors. We had turns washing dishes. And we sweep up [seventeen-year-old girl, now in a home for girls, with a history of eleven foster home placements].

> As soon as I got through taking off my stuff she came up to me and said, 'Now when you get through here, you have to mop downstairs, clean up the kitchen. You have to mop the dining room, clean the windows.' She had me clean up a whole lot [eighteen-year-old former foster home child placed in five foster homes].

The imposition of heavy domestic schedules on the children made foster homes appear similar to institutions in their restrictiveness and control. A fourteen-year-old youth who had lived in foster homes and institutions believed that these settings were "almost the same," though caretakers in foster homes "worked harder on you." Nevertheless, a different rationale supported and legitimized the labor in these households.

In institutions, housework was the currency of exchange which wards could use to buy freedom from supervision and other privileges. Thus, it was oriented to present and future exchanges. Housework in foster homes, in contrast, was oriented to the past and conceived to be repayment to caretakers of debts incurred by foster children for the cost of their care. While caretakers in institutions supposed that domestic work was necessary to promote discipline, caretakers in foster homes supposed that discipline was necessary to assure that work was done. Foster children generally believed that foster parents deserved compensation for "doing what only parents would do." However, there were differences between caretaker and ward over what constituted a fair compensation. What was the worth of a caretaker's support? What was the value of a foster child's work?

Although foster children did not challenge the caretaker's right to assign domestic work, conflicts often arose over the scope and timing of the required tasks. Children distinguished between chores made necessary by their presence in the household or chores that contributed to the general household maintenance and those which constituted special services to individuals. For example, one girl washed her foster father's socks only for a fee. However, if members of the household did not respect the distinction between obligations to the group and private arrangements, then the accounting between caretakers and wards became more explicit.

> Every morning they'd get up and go to work. They're supposed to come home and the house is supposed to be clean, you know. We didn't mess it up. So why should we clean it up? Everybody's going to say that. So they'd get mad. 'You shouldn't have your ass in here if you wasn't going to clean it up. . . . I said, 'You expect me to go around here and clean up the house when I didn't do nothing, I didn't mess up nothing?'

In addition, some considered their obligations limited by the fact of state support, though the contract between the state and the caretaker was also the source of the caretaker's authority. For example, one foster girl refused to do the bidding of a boarder in her foster mother's household, explaining, "the state don't pay her for keeping me and she's not my guardian."

Some foster children believed that caretakers coveted the money they received for providing them with a home.

> I get so much money a month, and they keep it for themselves, and they help pay the fucking bills with it, and when they want something they go out and buy it, you know. So without the money I don't think they'll be able to survive. . . . 'Cause when my parents get mad they go, 'Well at least she's paying rent.' That's how they see it, as I'm paying rent to them [sixteen-year-old in suburban foster home].

However, many more speculated that they were really valuable to caretakers as a source of free domestic labor.

> There were a lot of things they wouldn't have if not for me. Like I would go to the store for them. I'd take their clothes to the laundromat. I was just like their everything. She didn't want me to realize—she wanted me to always think I don't need you. You're just doing this because they don't give me that much money for you, staying here, so you have to make up for it in some kind of way [eighteen-year-old veteran of four foster homes, on the home in which she spent twelve years].

> For a while it was nice. But then they got really strict. I ended up being their workmaid. I did dishes every night, and just a lot of things. She'd always have me doing things for her. She'd ask me to get the salt and papper and then get the butter and I never got a chance to eat for getting up and running around for all the stuff she

didn't have on the table [seventeen-year-old ward of the state since the age of five, who had moved among foster homes, institutions, and group homes during her career].

Although they believed that "real" families did not engage in such careful accounting, foster children employed a criterion of equivalent exchange to evaluate their foster homes and their caretakers. Wards believed they owed caretakers work in exchange for care, but they also believed that caretakers owed them the resources and autonomy to enable them to construct home and community lives which did not disadvantage them compared with children who lived with their parents. A caretaker who did not exploit the labor of her foster child, who imposed no extraordinary restrictions and demands, and who did not let the financial aspects of the relationship predominate in the everyday work and life of the household was living up to these obligations. Beyond adequate maintenance, a good caretaker also provided valuable resources, such as clear and explicit instructions in household work and in the rules and expectations that surrounded it. In addition, she provided introductions to others able to guide and sponsor the foster child in the community and in the local school. Some caretakers lent or gave money to their children. A few helped their children to find babysitting and other jobs in the neighborhood, either by vouching for their good character or by giving advice about where and how to look.

Caretakers also promoted the idea that they were involved in an exchange with their wards. But while their foster children suspected that their labor might be exploited, caretakers looked at the problems of foster care differently. Based on the children's reports these caretakers found foster parenting costly, and suspected they were not getting fair compensation from their children for this investment.

My foster mother was always talking about how she do this and do that and us foster people never appreciate nothing. So I tell her, 'What are you doing for us that we got to appreciate?' She say, 'Well, I spend some of my money on you' [eighteen-year-old former foster child].

He asked me to do stuff like cook steak, vacuum. I'm supposed to want to or feel guilty. We'd cook, he'd take care of the house bills [eighteen-year-old woman, in a group home when interviewed, on one of two foster home placements].

A lot of times she'd say I only get $90 a month for you and that isn't enough to buy you clothes and all that stuff. Look at all the toys you've got. She bought all of those old fashioned clothes that I couldn't stand [seventeen-year-old girl with multiple placement experience, at the time of the interview caring for her own son in a foster home in Chicago; comments refer to her first foster home].

Thus, one standard against which foster children measured the adequacy of caretakers—their resistance to the financial pressures of their work—was an insistent problem expressed by many caretakers. A second difficulty for foster home children was that skills did not accumulate from one placement to the next. "You learn things in one place, and then the rules change." The way learning took place also changed from one placement to the next. "Staff helped me in some foster homes," said one person who had lived in many, "but in others they say do the best you know." Girls who learned to work according to one routine and set of standards found these counted for little or nothing in a new home. This exacerbated the tension and conflict that lay just beneath the surface of the foster parent-foster child relationship.

> You know, they would tell me to do this and do that and I'd get up and do it. Then like she'd come back to check. 'You didn't do it cause it ain't right.' She sit there and holler and I supposed to know how they want it . . . and I told her what's the matter with it and she showed me and I remopped it.

The conflict between foster children who tried to maintain control and foster mothers who tried to control the children made it likely that one of them would try to terminate the relationship. In this way foster home care promoted movement from household to household, a characteristic feature of many foster children's careers.

Mobility is structured into the foster care system. The vicissitudes of funding, the scarcity of homes, and the changing distribution of people and space puts even a seemingly durable arrangement in a vulnerable position. People who entered the foster care system often arrived already experienced with a life on the move. One girl on aid began her foster career by directing her caseworker to find her a placement away from home and, after a brief sojourn in an institution, took matters once again into her own hands. Others began their careers as runaways, a useful strategy as well as a commonplace identity. But these familiar strategies were reinforced by the structure of foster homes themselves, where, for example, foster parents could eject a child from their household if they wished. These elements combined to produce careers which began with a series of short-term placements until they reached a period of stability. A youngster about to enter his first foster home was well advised by a friend that it would "take five or six moves before you settle down." A girl with numerous foster homes in her past liked "to go from place to place to see how it is."

When wards did not know about the opportunities to be gained by moving around, foster brothers and sisters with more experience were likely to be good teachers. So too were foster parents, who used the threat of expulsion as a means of control. Thus, another career pattern emerged: a long first placement, followed by a series of later moves.

In this way, skills and habits developed which encouraged further mobility, until for many they became ways of life, useful both for avoiding difficulties and seizing opportunities. For one, moving could take care of "placement errors" and was a source of some power and control by foster children, who used the practice to direct the course of their placement careers. This strategy empowered the children only up to a point. Used too often, it limited this control, not only by assuring placement in a setting still more restrictive than the foster home, but also because constant movement isolated the children, and interfered with the progress of their social as well as academic education.

SUMMARY AND CONCLUSIONS

In this chapter I argue that the system of age stratification is part of a structure of production and reproduction supported by the ideology of parent-child relations. This ideology justifies children's subordination to adults as "natural necessity" (Chodorow, 1978). However, the basis of this subordination is social and is rooted in the economic and political position of minors within the wider society. The subsistence needs and legal status of minors situates them in the household and reproduces their dependency in everyday experience. In this way, the division of labor by age structures and perpetuates adult dominance over children in the household, just as the division of labor by sex structures and perpetuates men's dominance over women.

Adults appropriate the time and labor of children and return it to them in the form of training and discipline. Children are expected to carry out tasks and follow rules they have had little or no part in constructing. Indeed, the more the housewife or caretaker exercises control over her own domestic work, the more control must she exercise over the children in her care. The issue of control over work processes and schedules, therefore, is built into the caretaker-child relationship, creating a tension that is inherent in any division of labor such as this, which assigns the planning and the execution of tasks to different individuals (Braverman, 1974). In foster care, these tensions surface in the struggle between caretakers and wards over the organization of work, from which specific household arrangements emerge, with their own rationales and incentives.

Foster homes and institutions presented different concrete problems to those who lived in them, and differing resources and possibilities for their resolution. In large institutions, work was organized according to clear, widely known, and consistently enforced rules. These bureaucratically organized households supported the authority of caretakers by removing the power to allocate the work time of wards to the upper levels of the organization. Children in such households shaped their work roles within parameters already established by their caretakers. For example, institutionalized youngsters might decide not to work for privileges that caretakers bestowed for good conduct.

In institutions, caretakers encouraged boys to value housework as a measure of their maturity and to respect it as an instrument of their reform. They represented housework not as an end in itself, but as a form of training by which boys might develop traits that would promote and protect their future independence as working adults. For girls, housework needed no special justification, though some feared they might be disadvantaged in the job market by their relatively undeveloped domestic skills.

In foster homes, housework raised different issues and was surrounded by different meanings. First, housework was clearly a useful activity in itself and not simply, or even principally, a means to other ends. Second, and related to this, housework was what children owed their foster parents in return for their support and guidance. Third, in the smaller and more familiar environment of the foster home, children had greater opportunities to reestablish some control over their work. This meant that the conflict between caretakers and children in these settings erupted more often into open struggles between them.

The situation of state wards highlights the antagonism embedded in the relations between all dependent children and their caretakers. Children's time belongs to others, to whom they are subordinated in the working household group. This inequality, the basis of the household division of labor, generates discontents which ultimately undermine household organization. In this sense, the conflicts between children and their caretakers are political struggles. Any particular resolution of these conflicts within the confines of their unequal relations is at best a temporary solution to their mutual but contradictory efforts to control the conditions of their life and labor.

REFERENCES

Bell, C. S. (1977) "Women and work: an economic appraisal," pp. 10-28 in A. H. Stromberg and S. Harkess (eds.) Women Working. Palo Alto, CA: Mayfield.

BERK, S. F. (1979) "Husbands at home: organization of the husband's household day," pp. 125-158 in K. W. Feinstein (ed.) Working Women and Families. Beverly Hills, CA: Sage Publications.

BILLINGSLEY, A. and J. GIOVANNONI (1972) Children of the Storm: Black Children and American Child Welfare. New York: Harcout Brace Jovanovich.

BRAVERMAN, H. (1974) Labor and Monopoly Capital: The Degradation of Work in the 20th Century. New York: Monthly Review Press.

CHODOROW, N. (1978) The Reproduction of Mothering: Psychoanalysis and the Sociology of Gender. Berkeley: University of California Press.

COSTIN, L. B. (1972) Child Welfare: Policies and Practice. New York: McGraw-Hill.

ERIKSON, K. (1976) Everything in Its Path: Destruction of Community in the Buffalo Creek Flood. New York: Simon & Schuster.

FANSHEL, D. (1970) "The role of foster parents in the future of foster care," in H. D. Stone (ed.) Foster Care in Question. Washington, DC: Child Welfare League of America.

GRONAU, R. (1974) "The effects of children on the housewife's value of time," in T. W. Schultz (ed.) Economics of the Family: Marriage, Children, and Human Capital. Chicago: University of Chicago Press.

——— (1976) "The allocation of time of Israel's women." Journal of Political Economy 84, 4: 201-220.

HIRSCHHORN, L. (1978) "The political economy of social service rationalization." Contemporary Crises 2 (January): 68-81.

HOFFMAN, L. and I. NYE [eds.] (1974) Working Mothers. San Francisco: Jossey-Bass.

KALACHEK, E. (1969) The Youth Labor Market. Washington, DC: Institute of Labor and Industrial Relations.

KANTER, R. M. (1978) "Work in a new America." Daedalus (Winter): 47-78.

KOHN, M. L. (1969) Class and Conformity: A Study in Values. Homewood, IL: Dorsey.

LIEBOWITZ, A. (1974) "Home investments in children," in T. W. Schultz (ed.) Economics of the Family: Marriage, Children and Human Capital. Chicago: University of Chicago Press.

MINCER, J. and S. POLACHECK (1974) "Family investments in human capital: earnings of women," in T. W. Schultz (ed.) Economics of the Family: Marriage, Children and Human Capital. Chicago: University of Chicago Press.

OAKLEY, A. (1974) The Sociology of Housework. New York: Pantheon.

ROSS, H. L. and I. V. SAWHILL (1975) Time of Transition: The Growth of Families Headed by Women. Washington, DC: The Urban Institute.

STROMBERG, A. and S. HARKESS [eds.] (1978) Women Working: Theories and Facts in Perspective. Palo Alto, CA: Mayfield.

TREY, J. E. (1972) "Women in the war economy: World War II." Review of Radical Political Economics 4, 3.

VANEK, J. (1978) "Housewives as workers," pp. 392-416 in A. Stromberg and S. Harkess (eds.) Women Working. Palo Alto, CA: Mayfield.

WALKER, K. E. (1973) "Household work time: its implications for family decisions." Journal of Home Economics (October): 7-11.

WEINBAUM, B. and A. BRIDGES (1967) "The other side of the paycheck: monopoly capital and the structure of consumption." Monthly Review 28.

WITTNER, J. (1977) "Households of strangers: career patterns of foster children and other wards of the state." Ph.D. dissertation, Northwestern University.

10

EVERYONE NEEDS THREE HANDS:
DOING UNPAID AND PAID WORK

NONA GLAZER

This chapter is a contribution toward understanding how women's work in and for the family—domestic labor—and women's work in the workplace intersect to maintain gender stratification. That intersection also defines the class situation of women. It exposes the peculiar nature of women's oppression and a critical aspect of women's subordination. Its theme is that domestic labor must be seen as central to understanding women's continued subordination in both advanced capitalist and socialist societies, and that women's assignment to housework and child care (whether or not given women ever actually do the work involved) structures women's lives outside the household.

Women's domestic labor usually has been neglected by sociologists, who accepted a nineteenth-century view that activities that generated GNP were "work," but all else was "leisure" (Oakley, 1974). It is an extension of the logic of this view to deny full social and economic rights to those who do not "work." Women who are full-time housewives or part-time

AUTHOR'S NOTE: Support for this work was provided by the National Endowment for the Humanities and by the American Association of University Women. Grateful appreciation is expressed to Judith Wittner for extensive comments and suggestions on a first draft of this chapter. Joan Acker helped with many conversations on women and work. Heidi Hartmann, Pam Caine, Roberta Spalter-Roth and others in the Washington, D.C., study group provided critiques of this chapter and many stimulating conversations about women's subordination. As editor of this volume, Sarah Fenstermaker Berk contributed substantially to the organization of this chapter. Another version of the chapter was presented at the annual meetings of the American Sociological Association, Boston, Massachusetts, 1979.

paid workers, children, the aged, the disabled, the unemployed, and the unemployable can be denied various rights more easily than those who "work" (Glazer-Malbin, 1976a). Women's position in the *social class* structure has also been relatively ignored. Men have been seen as the only persons relevant for locating families in the class structure (Acker, 1973) because men but not women are in the workplace.[1]

Though with the reemergence of feminism, women's domestic labor and class position have been examined, the link between them has been taken for granted, or simply asserted rather than analyzed (Humphries, 1977; Fee, 1976; Wright, 1978). There are now many essays and studies that can be used to see how links might be made.[2] First, domestic labor has been looked at from a variety of theoretical perspectives (Benston, 1969; Brown, 1970; Lopata, 1971; Dalla Costa, 1972; Galbraith, 1973; Oakley, 1974; Sacks, 1974; Sanday, 1974). Second, research shows fairly consistently that women who take paid jobs continue to be responsible for domestic work (e.g., Haavio-Mannila, 1969; Michel, 1971; Epstein, 1971; Rapoport and Rapoport, 1976; Holmstrom, 1972; Meissner et al., 1975; Hedges and Barnett, 1972). Furthermore, the division of labor in the family remains essentially unchanged with only slightly more work, if any, being done by family members when wives/mothers enter the workplace (Szalai, 1972; Walker and Gauger, 1973; Berheide et al., 1976; Robinson, 1977). Third, there are historical analyses detailing how housework and child care have changed, and how capitalism and gender stratification shape women's domestic labor (Ehrenreich and English, 1975; Hartmann, 1976; Cowan, 1976a, 1976b; Ewen, 1976; Minge-Kalman, 1977; for specific focus on child care, see Chodorow, 1974; Dinnerstein, 1976) and women's lives as paid workers (Hartmann, 1975; Greenwald, 1977). Similar descriptions exist of women's domestic labor and paid work in socialist societies (Atkinson et al., 1977; Denich, 1977; Stewart and Winter, 1977; Sokolowska, 1977; Schwartz, forthcoming).

Class position has been important to those trying to understand political consciousness. As usual, however, the emphasis has been on men, and men's experiences in the workplace. Consciousness arises, at least in part, from objective conditions of work (e.g., lack of control over working conditions, unstable source of income). It is useful to us as feminist scholars to try to see what special factors about women may be related to their position in the class system and how these factors may give rise to women's consciousness.

How the relevance of women's domestic work to their class position is understood has implications for at least two issues: (1) the impact of the assignment of housework and child care on women's everyday lives (e.g., on access to training and to paid employment, on women's political power, on women's dependence on men and subordination in intimate relations, on the aftermath of marital dissolution, and so on); and (2) the impact on women as a political force (e.g., as a source of social change). The entrance of women into the workplace has not radically altered women's domestic responsibilities, nor has it generated major changes in family support systems. Does this have any special implications for class consciousness, and the focus of possible or actual struggles, because of the special kinds of stresses women experience?

PERSPECTIVES ON CLASS AND WORK

Both radical and mainstream social science analyses usually incorporate women into a class analysis on the same basis as men or place women in a class position on the basis of their dependent relationships to men—to husbands and fathers.

In the mainstream analysis, it is accepted that the adult male is the link between the family and the economy, and that the males' occupations and related characteristics determine the family's position (Parsons, 1955). The husband's and/or father's occupational prestige, educational attainment, income, source of income, and so on are used to place the family and, therefore, women. Women are analyzed apart from men only when they are older singles, divorced, or widowed. That women make a contribution to class-related aspects of family life is recognized but has been noted without an attempt to reassess women's class position.

In radical theories, social class is defined by one's relationship to the means of production. With the advent of industrial capitalism, women were largely excluded from the workplace and hence from a direct relation to capital. It followed, therefore, that women had to be understood in terms of their ties to men who were in the workplace. Women's subordination is seen as having emerged with male control over private property, first with the development of surplus generated by herding (Engels, 1902), later with male control over land and agricultural surplus, and eventually over capital. Men's control over production and the distribution of the surplus from production maintains their domination over women (Zaretsky, 1976; Friedl, 1975).

Most mainstream and radical theorists reacted to charges of intellectual sexism in theories of social stratification (Acker, 1973) by trying to include women. Mainstream theorists began to include women—housewives as well as employed women—in their research. Thus, Bose (1973) and Nilson (1976) included "housewife" in research on occupational prestige. Haug (1973) examined women's occupations in the family, and Hector (1976) measured the influence of women's socioeconomic characteristics on the family's social class position. Sociologists also began to document how women's domestic responsibilities interrupt their market work as well as preparation for it. Mainstream theorists also brought women into the discourse by recognizing how wives make a contribution to the life-style of their families and to the well-being of their husbands (e.g., Bernard, 1974).

Mainstream theorists have failed to exclude sexism from their analysis. Ironically, this is because in taking perception of status as a primary indicator of social class, they must automatically rely on judgments that are inevitably sexist. Thus, Felson and Knoke (1974) found that neither the husband nor the wife paid attention to the wife's characteristics in evaluating their own status. Hector (1976) found that a sample of students gave little or no weight to wives' education and occupation, but rather emphasized the characteristics of husbands in assessing the family's social class position. She concluded that wives made no contributions to the family's class position, and that women had no class-relevant characteristics of their own. Such analyses obviously fail to show that the public is any better than sociologists in eliminating "intellectual sexism" from judgments about women's worth. The analyses speak to current ideology about women, not about the contribution that women make to their family's class position (see also Haug, 1973; Safilios-Rothschild, 1975).

Radical theorists with a somewhat different interest in understanding women's domestic labor and class position tried to understand how domestic labor fits into the capitalist mode of production. (They have not yet explored how it fits into the socialist mode of production.) This means understanding domestic labor in relation to surplus value, which by definition occurs only when workers are producing goods or performing services that contribute to the accumulation of capital. It is assumed that if domestic work could be theoretically tied to capital, then women would be brought into the work process and into an "independent" class position. Finally, women would thus have a role in the process of social change (i.e., in the class struggle). Starting from this premise, the debate centers around whether or not women's domestic labor directly produces surplus value or whether domestic labor is tied to capital only through indirect means (compare Mitchell, 1966; Benston, 1969; Dalla Costa, 1972; Vogel, 1973; Secombe, 1975; Coulson et al., 1975; Gardiner, 1975; Quick, 1977). Rather strained attempts have been made to show that men's wages actually include pay for the domestic work of women and hence that women have a direct relation to capital. For example, Secombe (1975) has interpreted the concept of "productive" labor to mean "socially useful," though Marx used it technically to distinguish labor paid for out of capital (productive labor) from labor paid for out of revenue (unproductive labor). To Secombe, domestic labor is "productive" since housewives provide workers with the daily care that makes the paid work of the latter possible. His account also suffers by failing to consider the meaning of the domestic role *for* women, how family structure fixes women in a particular relationship to both men and capital.

This and similar accounts often neglect how the family mediates women's relation not just to men but to the workplace. Also what is deemphasized is that for women the family is a "workplace." More specifically, it is within the marriage and by virtue of the marriage contract that women do the equivalent of what men do in the workplace—meeting basic human needs that allows the continuation of their lives. Therefore, I suggest that it is not necessary to fit women into capitalism by the analysis of the creation of surplus value. It helps us to understand women's continuing subordination in a variety of ways in socialist societies if we see that marriage (the work that women are responsible for within marriage) remains an essential aspect of how women "earn" their living. This is so in spite of married women doing paid work, too. Furthermore, as will be detailed later in this chapter, women's location in marriage has consequences for how women can do work for pay inside or outside the home.

Acker (1978) has taken a third and somewhat different approach to resolving the question of women's class position. She argues that in late capitalism families have ceased being the appropriate unit of class analysis, and she considers individuals instead. For her, the result is a dual system of stratification organized around "sex structuration" which results in one stratification system for men and another for women. One problem with this analysis is that the sexism Acker seeks to avoid intellectually is systemic to the organization of the class system itself (recognized in sex "structuration"). Women, as wives and daughters, in fact experience the social class position of men who dominate the social organization of society and the family. Recognizing women as independent agents fails to accept as a reality of class organization the fact that within the family women live in accordance with the class position of their husbands and fathers. The importance of the sharing becomes evident after marital dissolution, when women's income descends quite sharply, and though it later rises, women are unlikely to attain a position that is similar to the one that they experienced when married (Glazer-Malbin, 1976b). Acker seems to be suggesting that the position of single women is somehow more real than the position of married women. I suggest that individualizing class position deemphasizes the importance of male domination: Women rise and fall in prestige, change life-styles, experience economic disaster, relate in various ways to welfare institutions, the courts, and prisons depending on with what particular men they are allied within affectional, sexual, and familial ties. Finally, the family not only mediates women's position, but also children's. If the individual rather than the family is considered to be the unit in the class system, we are then faced with how to understand the class position of children. Children experience a host of class-specific activities and socialization into class (as well as gender-specific) behaviors long before they reach the schools where their class (and gender) appropriate characteristics are usually reinforced. We know, for example, that working-class mothers emphasize obedience training for their preschoolers while middle-class mothers are concerned with encouraging independence. These characteristics will later fit well with participation in the class-defined segments of the labor force.

Marriage as a mediating device for women's position in the class system occurs in both capitalist and socialist societies, even though women's position in the occupational structure varies between these societies. For example, in capitalist societies, women are only a small proportion of physicians. That occupation is primarily female in most socialist societies, but remains sex-segregated and has fewer rewards than in capitalist societies. Women in socialist societies have access to more professional training than in capitalist societies, and the wage gap is comparatively much smaller. But women in capitalist and socialist societies alike are only marginally involved in administrative positions in the workplace and government. Most important, in both societies women continue to be responsible for domestic labor in spite of official policies in socialist societies that may avow sex equality. The marriage contract may have a lesser impact as a mediating agent in socialist than in capitalist societies, given socialist women's opportunities in the workplace. Also, some aspects of everyday life that are the responsibility of the family in capitalist societies are the responsibility of the state in socialist societies (e.g., education, medical care, housing, and the like) so that some women's responsibilities and burdens may differ between the two systems.

PATRIARCHY, NOT CLASS?

Not all theorists concerned with women believe that the way to include women in a class analysis is to rethink the concept of social class itself.

Some have tried to develop a socialist feminist analysis that heeds both the radical feminist analysis of the relation between the sexes and the Marxian analysis of capitalism.

In the late 1960s and early 1970s, "sexism" was used to label how social scientists ignored, devalued, and otherwise stereotyped women. (Acker, 1973, commented specifically on the intellectual sexism in the study of social stratification.) That label recognizes intellectual blinders but offers no new vision. Radical feminists pushed the analysis further, to capture the specific power relations between the sexes in concepts such as "patriarchal attitudes" (Figes, 1970) and "sexual politics" (Millett, 1970). These were important analytical steps away from the generality and relative mildness of the all-encompassing "sexism." However, radical feminist theory had no place for the social relations of production, except to tack them on as one more instance where women were oppressed by men. By the mid-1970s, feminists attempted to merge a critique of capitalism with the radical feminist assertion of an autonomous or semi-autonomous system of relations between women and men. That attempted synthesis has resulted in proposals of various systems of gender stratification: "patriarchy" (Hartman, 1976; Eisenstein, 1978), the social relations of the sexes (Kelly-Gadol, 1976), sex/gender systems (Rubin, 1975), and sex structuration (Acker, 1978).

The contribution of these analyses is at the same time their most problematic aspect: the argument that there exists a system of sex stratification that is separate from the systems of production and social reproduction. Theorists differ on several issues. First, they differ on how separate the system is and thus the extent to which the economic oppression of women may be derivative and secondary to the system of sex stratification (Rubin, 1975: 177). Theorists also do not agree on whether female subordination is universal (compare Rubin, 1975, and Hartman, 1976), nor do they agree on the contribution women make to their own subordination (Ryan, 1978).[3]

The attempts to join an analysis of capitalism with an analysis of sex stratification (in a reaction to the Marxian neglect of gender) are just beginning. Two critical problems exist in proposing that sex stratification is a separate system, independent of capitalism today as well as other modes of production in other times or elsewhere. The thesis is not that capitalism has no effect on the sex stratification system; it is that the latter has a persistence and shape that is independent of the mode of production and cannot be understood just by reference to processes in the mode of production. First, there is a rejection of basic premises of Marxian analysis: the primacy of the system of production, and a holistic and historically specific method. These have been rejected implicitly, without a direct discussion of the rejection, and perhaps without even an awareness of it. The second problem may be solved with scholarly persistence. There is no *theory* of sex stratification, of variations in systems, of how those variations may be transformed over time, under what conditions the transformation may take place, and so on. In other words, there is no theory about gender stratification that could be considered comparable to a theory of the development of capitalism or—to move to a quite different area—theories of socialization or personality.

DOMESTIC WORK TRENDS

Before turning to a discussion of the intersection between paid and unpaid work, I want to discuss some special characteristics of domestic work. These characteristics are ones that impinge on women's paid work. They include myths about domestic work, as well as myths about work that continue to make domestic work invisible. My comments also include some observations about how the present organization of domestic work fits with women as reserve labor in times of crises, when the role of the state is moderated and the family is given increasing responsibilities for solving socially generated problems.

First, there is state support for the continued trivalization of domestic work; it begins in how statistics are gathered and ends in how the courts ignore the work of parenting in establishing levels of child support payments. Thus, only paid employment is shown in government reports on work and "moonlighting." This ignores the fact that women are the majority of adults who hold two jobs, even though only one is for pay. Instead, men are seen as the majority of those holding two jobs. A similar bias is evident in how the "average work week" is calculated for each sex. The hours of domestic work women do are ignored, and the conclusions are that men "work" longer hours than women. Such conclusions contradict the sociological research which consistently shows that employed married women with families continue to do domestic work; men (and children) do not share in this job to any significant extent. This also describes the situation of women in socialist societies (see discussion above). The trivialization of women's domestic labor also extends to mothering. State family codes usually specify that the wife has the responsibility for the care of the children, just as the husband must provide for his family financially. Yet, though the wife must assume a considerable part of the financial responsibility for children if she becomes the custodial parent after a divorce (as far as I have been able to ascertain), the redistribution of parental responsibilities is lopsided. The courts do not consider the daily work of mothering in deciding the amount of child support the father is ordered to pay.

Second, if women's entrance into paid labor means that women have the chance to develop political consciousness and to become active on their own behalf, then there must be time alloted to such activities. However, there has been no decrease in women's responsibilities for domestic labor. Instead, what has happened is the *normalization of the double day*; women with family responsibilities are assumed to be able, willing, and even obliged to take paid work. What has emerged in the United States (and has already emerged or is emerging in other capitalist societies) is the "normal white two-earner family" joining the normal minority two-earner family. (The "two-earners" are the adult heads. The dependency of poor families on the wages of working children is another story.)[4] In times of economic crisis, such as now, there may be a renewed discussion of the possible damaging effects of working mothers on children and family life. (It is worth noting that the effects of employment on mothers themselves are rarely considered.)

The employment levels of minority wives resulted from discrimination against minority men, low wages, and high rates of male unemployment. The new two-earner family resulted from other factors: a steady erosion of purchasing power and continued pressure on families to maintain or increase their levels of consumption (in capitalist societies to maximize the accumulation of capital). The two-earner family is probably also a result of the absence of a (alternative) male labor supply. There is some evidence that governments have deliberately decided against policies that would raise wages to compensate for the erosion of the family wage in order to force married women into a labor market characterized by a shortage of workers (Henriksen and Holter, 1978). Welfare practices that require mothers with young children to do some kind of paid work also fluctuate with labor force demand (Cloward and Piven, 1977). In the late 1970s, as during the 1930s depression, married women are being discouraged from entering the labor market by a variety of social policies (e.g., a cutback in day care facilities). Yet the inflationary pressures, an increase in female-headed families, and attempts to curtail expenditures on social services has meant no decrease in the number of women doing two jobs.

Third, domestic work itself has probably undergone more apparent than real changes. Technical changes in household equipment have certainly decreased the amount of physical energy women must expend to do housework. Many products can now be bought instead of produced in the household. Yet it is difficult to see in what major ways the organization of housework and child care have changed over the last century. Each family remains responsible for the daily jobs involved in meeting basic needs for food, shelter, cleanliness, and clothing care; the market dominates how the family meets these needs; and there are few cooperative activities among families, friends, neighbors, and relatives. The state provides some services to the poor or subsidizes many of the family-related activities of the wealthy, but most families do not directly benefit in their everyday lives.

In a way, the work in the home may have become more rather than less privatized. Before the development of the industrial wage labor force, housework and child care were usually collective household activities. Wives usually did not devote themselves only to housekeeping and child care. Most family members took part in the work in the home which often included some production for others outside the family. Paradoxically, with industrialization, though some of the work of the home was moved to the factory, women had to devote more time to a less demanding job. Some work shifted back and forth in relation to profitability. Laundry went from the home to commercial laundries. It was then returned to the home as the production and sales of washing machines became more profitable than commercial laundries (Hartmann, 1975). Much housework remains private. Cleaning, essential parts of meal preparation, transporting children, gardening, the maintenance of household equipment, and general household maintenance are, in the main, done privately.

Why has housework failed to move out of the home in the way that production for exchange has, or to become organized along the lines of maximizing efficiency? The home economics movement tried to apply Taylorism—the principles of rational efficiency—to housework and child care (Lopate, 1974). In many ways, housework began to be rationalized in the nineteenth century by the increasing segregation of room use, the sequential service of meals, the use of accounting books, the introduction of timing devices, and so on (Davidoff, 1976). Davidoff (1976: 133) gives a psychoanalytical explantion for why housework has remained privatized. Women, she says, are more closely associated with nature than men through the biological functions of menstruation, pregnancy, childbirth, and lactation (see Ortner, 1974). A "primordial concern for order, for protection from pollution" lies at the bottom of the resistance of the family (men?) to the marketplace calculus. Women are given the work of maintaining the boundary between nature and culture because of women's close connection to nature. This explanation seems to be an ideology about women's nature. It neglects the ways that men are close to nature— in their supposed greater sexuality and sexual responsiveness and reactions, and in their preoccupation with struggling against nature.

Another explanation for the resistance of housework to rationalization and socialization is that some domestic work cannot be subject to these processes (Gardiner, 1975: 53). Emotional needs cannot be met on the commodity market, for emotional services cannot be purchased but must be derived from interpersonal relations. However, many services that have a socioemotional core have been brought into the market. These include the human potential movement, child care, health care, and the care of the elderly. What perhaps has happened is that the work of meeting emotional needs has been fragmented (i.e., done by special techniques such as used in est), and done by specialists who are paid; or the emotional components have been minimized. Thus, health care professionals have generally ignored emotional components in illness, or have assigned a special worker (e.g., a medical social worker) to deal with those emotionally distressed by being sick or old. More than the failure to meet emotional needs, the market is on its way to waging much of this work. It is perhaps only work that has not been waged which is excluded from rationalization (Dalla Costa, 1972; Secombe, 1975), rather than perhaps some special quality of the work itself.

The limit to waging all work may be the need for a reserve family (not industrial) labor force. I suggest that it suits the needs of capital (and state socialism) to have a core of unpaid workers who have some built-in flexibility in their productivity. The rationalization and socialization of all family work would create a larger pool of waged workers and needs that have to be met in times of economic crisis. The needs which had been met in the marketplace during the so-called normal times would somehow have to be met during crises—and no state has demonstrated a willingness to do this. Instead, the state provides and withholds services that are part of housework and child care, depending upon the need for women as paid workers. In the last several years there have been worldwide cutbacks in funding of day care for children and increased questioning of the viability of employed mothers in the welfare states as well as in capitalist societies.

The lack of rationalization and continued privatization of housework has consequences for the women doing domestic labor. Women are the "shock absorbers," the people responsible for adjusting the family to the cyclical problems of capitalism (and to the problems of developing socialism). At the same time, the independence of the family from the market moderates in times of crisis the complete disruption of family life that is likely to occur if the family is completely dependent on the market for the services now supplied by women. What women do is adjust their labor in relation to family income by increasing their labor in the home. For example, Morgan (1939) documented how families actually came to substitute their own labor for market purchases in a comparison of housework in 1927 and 1933.

Fourth, whatever changes have occurred in household equipment and related goods and services, there has been no documented drop in the average work week of the full-time housewife (Vanek, 1974). Various attempts have been made to explain the persistently long hours. New work has been created for the housewife. In an attempt to create markets for goods and services, new "standards" of consumption have been pushed in advertising and the mass media (Ehrenreich and English, 1975; Ewen, 1976; Cowan, 1976a, 1976b). Laundry is done more often, and family members have more clothing. Houses are supposed to be cleaned each week rather than subject to the annual fall/spring and special holiday turnouts.

In contrast, household equipment has not been designed to maximize either easy use or easy care. Instead, products are designed to sell through cosmetic design—the use of chrome, glass, plastic, and the like, which are supposedly attractive to consumers (with each supposedly needing a different cleaning product). A comparison with commercial cooking, cleaning, storage, and cooling equipment shows that equipment that operates better and requires less elaborate care can be produced for the mass market, but is not. Other products require attention from the wife/mother (e.g., the shoddiness of consumer goods places demands on the housewife), where she must spend time and energy in repairing *new* clothes or in making "prepared" foods more tasty and nutritious (Gordon, 1977).

Any drop in family income and increase in inflation adds to women's domestic labor (Secombe, 1975). Comparison shipping, thrifty cooking, altering clothes to keep in style, do-it-yourself home projects, and vegetable gardening are some of the ways that women's magazines and newspapers advise coping with a drop in real family income. Women also gain additional work because of the business practice whereby services are reordered in an attempt to increase profits. Today shopping takes more time and energy as consumers drive to stores, select items, stand in long checkout lines, place products on the counter for pricing—do everything except total up the bill. Similarly, current social movements that focus on ecology or on nutrition depend primarily on a women who is willing to recycle materials, read food labels, and so on. Thus, work to maintain the physical well-being of the family has changed rather than decreased. (Men are not exempt from this process of labor intensification.)[5]

Mothering has probably also become a more time-consuming activity for women. In the nineteenth century, mother's work appeared at first to be the relatively simple tasks of seeing that children learned certain moral standards, were fed, were kept clean, and slept regular hours. Gradually, broader and more difficult work was assigned to mothers. Contemporary mothers (those of the last 100 years for the working class and the last 150, perhaps, for the bourgeois) have had to build character. This century, mothers have gradually come to be responsible for building personality, too. They must develop capabilities in their children during early childhood that will be compatible with demands of the school, the workplace, and political life. The demands for a well-disciplined and literate labor force mean that mothers are urged to participate in their children's schooling (Minge-Kalman, 1977). Mothers are responsible for the "happiness" of their children as well as their general fitness for life in a capitalist society.

Everyday life today also demands much of mothers. The lack of adequate public transportation in the inner city as well as in the suburbs means that American mothers spend time accompanying their children places or driving them. They do this much more than their counterparts in Europe (Szalai, 1972). In the cities, the general fear for safety means that many mothers are uneasy about letting their children out to play; mothers spend time supervising their children on the sidewalks, in playgrounds, and parks.

THE INTERSECTION OF PAID AND UNPAID WORK

Any understanding of women's position in the class system must begin with the recognition that women have an ascribed occupation that is outside a direct relation to capital. That occupation is housewifery. Hall (1969) recognized housewifery as an occupation similar to a salesperson, assembly-line worker, or government civil servant, a full-time adult commitment done instead of paid labor. Events of the last decade indicate that we must modify that definition to accept that more and more women with family responsibilities combine domestic work with paid employment; housewifery is done in addition to the paid labor that absorbs a considerable part of the adult's energies on a daily basis. Second, housewifery is ascribed on the basis of sex. Following Dalla Costa (1972: 19), I would argue "that all women are housewives, and even those who work outside the home continue to be housewives. . . . [It] is precisely what is particular to domestic work . . . as quality of life and quality of relationships which it generates, that determines a woman's place wherever she is and to whichever class she belongs." It is not that every woman fills the status "housewife" in the view of others. It is that social relations are organized around the assumption that women are responsible for housework and child care. That some women (women who never marry, women who never have children though they marry, divorced women without children, and so on) may not be housewives in the traditional sense does not matter. The social world continues to be organized around the premise that women can be included in certain structures (e.g., services offered between 9:00 a.m. and 5:00 p.m.) and must be limited in their participation in others (e.g., high-level business executive positions) because of domestic responsibilities.[6] Job opportunities are open or closed to women, and men (and some women) hold beliefs about women as co-workers, political colleagues, neighbors, and the like that are colored by real and imaginary ideas about the limited availability of women because of their domestic work. Finally, all women, or nearly all women, have been trained in domestic work to some degree. Even in childhood play, females are introduced to the machinery of domestic work (e.g., to miniature versions of household equipment and to dolls with which they can begin to learn the elements of the physical aspects of mothering). Boys are also introduced to occupations in childhood play. However, there is no or little carryover; playing with a doctor kit hardly provides the comparable training for being a physician that playing with a miniature sink, water, and tiny dishes provides for being a housewife.

The paid work into which females are channeled is often limited by a sense of what would be compatible with women fulfilling domestic responsibilities. Hence, a kind of principle of "occupational compatibility" operates so that girls may be told that being a nurse is more appropriate than being a physician because the first is easier than the latter to combine with being "a good wife and mother." Consider how unlikely it is that a boy would be told to be a nurse or a secretary rather than a physician or lawyer because the former are more compatible than the latter with being a good husband and father! Yet, except for providing the family with a high income, it is probably true that the first two occupations are exactly that for males.

The concern with occupational compatibility is part of a vicious circle. Women are given the responsibility for domestic labor. In turn, they do find it hard to combine paid and unpaid work, especially while pursuing a demanding career as distinct from holding a job, for "careers" assume a "wife." Professional women and others with high incomes may be able to buy substitutes for their own labor, but certain needs cannot be met by turning to the marketplace. Moreover, most women hold low-paying jobs such that they do not have sufficient income to rely heavily on the market to help in the work of doing two jobs. Thus, on the surface it may seem to make sense to women to avoid a commitment to a demanding job—which in turn, of course, means low wages. Needless to say, most women have no such rational choice but must enter the job market because of family economic need, taking whatever jobs their training may allow and whatever jobs are open to them.

Women continue to be assigned the main responsibilities for child care. Both ideology and state policies support "mothering" as opposed to "parenting." Compared to the United States, some greater support from the state for child care exists in socialist and welfare societies. However, the assumption seems to be that the state provides child care to relieve mothers and not parents of work. When parents do not especially like state-provided child care or other public services, or when there is more demand for services than places for children, it is the mothers who must find the caretakers. Mothering responsibilities continue after working hours. Mothers organize their so-called leisure time around children and use flexitime to do housework and child care. In contrast, men use after working hours and flexitime for personal gratification (e.g., play, study, sleep.) Finally, after the end of marriage, women are overwhelmingly assigned the role of custodial parent. As noted above, in the awarding of child support payments, courts do not consider the time and energy that go into daily child care in assessing the cost of raising a child. Mothers' labor remains an invisible contribution.

Women's "other" workplace is in the market. Here earnings, the sex-typing of jobs, as well as movement in and out of the workplace, can be tied to women's domestic labor. The link is even historical, for women followed their work out of the home, into the textile industry, canning, nursing, sewing, and so on. Thus, women's domestic labor first defined the jobs that were opened to women with wage work and then defined them within the factory system (Baxandall et al., 1976; Wertheimer, 1977).

Within the segmented labor market (meaning that there are divisions by race, by ethnicity, by sex), women work mainly in the secondary market. Typically, their jobs have low wages, high turnover, short career ladders, and do not encourage long-term commitments. Within the primary market, women are in mainly subordinate rather than independent jobs. The former calls for routine work, dependability, discipline, and the acceptance of hierarchical structures and rules. In contrast, independent jobs require problem solving, creativity, self-initiation, and often professional skills (Reich et al., 1973).

The rationale used by employers in hiring women for the secondary labor market and for subordinate jobs in the primary market is that women's real everyday work is domestic labor. Employers argue that women have husbands who are the family breadwinners and that women's employment is only a secondary source of income.[7] Finally, women often leave the labor force because of family reasons rather than job-connected ones, so that employers say that they cannot depend on women workers.

Marital status and parenthood once but no longer significantly lessen the entrance of married women and women with family responsibilities into paid work. Domestic labor, therefore, might appear to be less important today than in the past. However, domestic labor still affects women's employment in some ways in addition to those noted above. Women, in fact, leave the labor force to do domestic labor. Pregnancy, lack of child care, the illness of family members, and child-connected problems are among the main reasons women give for leaving their jobs (U.S. Department of Labor, 1972). The need to increase family incomes pushes mothers with young children into the workplace (Lazar and Rosenberg, 1971). The number of mothers who do not take paid employment because they cannot find child care is difficult to estimate (Levitan and Alderman, 1975).

One consequence of women's domestic labor is thus a so-called "looser attachment to the labor force" on the part of women compared with men. The further consequences are that women may be out of the labor force at crucial times in career or job development. Women lose seniority, the chance to upgrade their skills, and skills themselves through long periods of being out of the workplace (U.S. Departments of Labor and Health, Education and Welfare, 1975).

No account of women's domestic labor would be complete without mentioning the ideology surrounding "woman." The thoroughgoing domestication of American women occurred in the nineteenth century. Though women were actually the first industrial workers, they were expelled from the labor force by a likely combination of displacement by immigrant male workers, the anti-female activities of male workers who saw females being used to de-skill jobs, and the gradual ability of employers to find cheaper substitutes for the family system that had brought men and children to work along with women. Women and the home began to be idealized, perhaps as a way of displacing the responsibility of developing industrial capitalism for the dislocation of vast numbers of people onto the private family. Certainly, the emerging myth saw the woman as the protector of moral values and the provider of a haven from a rapidly changing and hugely unpleasant world (Ryan, 1978; Zaretsky, 1976). The woman was to be the center of family life, responsible for the character of her children and the happiness of her family. The myth of the division of labor that figuratively sent men to the hunt and women to the hearth has been incorporated into sociological anlysis where it is used to legitimate women's exclusion from the workplace and men's exclusion from any significant responsibility for domestic labor. The myth continues today only in a somewhat abated form, modified by the belief that woman can readily assume paid work while continuing her mythological function as preserver of the family.

CONCLUSIONS

The view of my chapter is that women participate in two worlds of work. Hence it follows that women's class experience is a different one from that of men. I note above how most discussions of class have tried to pull women into an analysis on the same terms as men. I have also noted how in many ways domestic labor itself has been excluded from the processes of rationalization that have been applied to much of paid labor. I have particularly emphasized that domestic labor limits women's lives in two ways: (1) the lack of changes in domestic labor keeps women embedded in archaically organized work responsibilities; and (2) work relations (and related activities) are organized around the assumption that domestic labor is women's primary concern. I have suggested some ways in which women's lives then become limited by these two social facts.

Various effects of domestic work on all women who have family responsibilities can be discerned. There are also indirect effects on women who do not have such responsibilities. These multiple effects include how the double day limits job attainment, earnings, and educational attainment. Women's political participation in union activities, political party work, and other activist groups is also limited. Time and energy that might be devoted to these activities are instead directed to meeting everyday family responsibilities in the time available after paid work is done.

Social scientists have usually taken it for granted that employed women can cope with two jobs. The assumption is that if women are sufficiently needy financially, dedicated to their paid jobs, or fortunate enough to have cooperative husbands and/or children, they will manage the two worlds of work with relatively little cost to themselves. Except for the issue of child care during the hours of women's employment outside the home, there has been very little recognition of domestic work as problematic. The research that has been done, in turn, is class-biased: Business and professional women's lives have been studied while the daily lives of working-class women have been neglected. Even most radical analyses have tended to ignore class differences among women in favor of abstract theorizing about how domestic labor is connected to capital accumulation. Furthermore, most research on "work" has looked at the marketplace and schooling for the marketplace, both highly important concerns. What has been underemphasized is just how the other work of women—domestic labor—may curtail opportunity, deplete energies, and restrict personal time because of the demands of family life.

In spite of many criticisms of it, there is a conventional wisdom about work and women's subordination. In capitalist society, the conventional wisdom sees women as subordinated insofar as they cannot get the same schooling and work opportunities as men. In socialist societies, women are considered equal to men because of state ownership of the means of production within which women do paid work; there the conventional wisdom is that paid employment means there is no "woman question." Thus, there is substantial agreement across economic systems that women must do paid work, and little recognition of the meaning of domestic work. In capitalist societies, the recognition of women's domestic labor has been in relation to children: that women cannot simultaneously work outside the home and care for children. In socialist societies, there have been more concerted (though intermittent) efforts by the state to deal with somewhat broader issues. Child care is provided for employed mothers, but shopping (in Cuba) and meal preparation (in the People's Republic of China, and the early Soviet Union) are also recognized as problems. Last, and hardly least, the socialist state attempts to eliminate the traditional sex division of labor in the home through political-educational campaigns (e.g., in Cuba and the PRC) and through passing laws that have been interpreted as requiring men as well as women to do housework and child care (Glazer, 1979).

Given the effects of domestic labor on women's paid work as well as on their other public activities, I suggest the following: The critical aspect of thinking about women's social class position is *not*: (1) how domestic labor can be related directly to capital accumulation, (2) how women's occupation, education, and the like are seen by members of their society as contributing to the social class position of their families, nor (3) how women as individuals move in and out of various positions in the occupational system, or in and out of the labor market itself.

We need to incorporate an understanding of the effects of the social assignment of women to domestic labor on training, job access, political activities, political consciousness, and personal life. We need an explicit recognition of the connections between the family responsibilities of women and the activities of women outside the family. I believe this means returning to the conception of women as an underclass, to seeing women as having a class position mediated by marriage or other family responsibilities. What this requires is the abandonment of attempts to understand women's lives in the marketplace, politics, and such areas as separate from domestic labor. It means redefining work to recognize the invisible labor that Larguia and Doumoulin labeled nearly a decade ago, but by more than including housewifery in studies of occupational prestige or status attainment. It essentially means seeing class structure as organized by more than capital accumulation. The inclusion of domestic labor into studies of "work" would mean beginning to see women as occupying at least four possible positions in relation to class, depending upon women's participation in both worlds of work.

Married women who also do paid work. Their class position is dominated by that of their husbands'. For example, their husbands' positions largely determine the access of women to training, the extent to which paid work is prompted by financial need, a fulfillment of personal needs, whether it can be entered and left easily, and so on.

Once-married and never-married women with family responsibilities who also do paid work. Their class position is dominated by their own position in the labor market, and by their responsibilities for domestic work. A subset of once-married and never-married women with family responsibilities is *women dependent on the state,* women whose class position is dominated by their domestic responsibilities and their exclusion/absence from the labor market.

Once-married and never-married women without family responsibilities who do paid work. Their class position is dominated by their own position in the labor market, and though they do not do domestic labor (except for themselves in much the same way men do, though without the average income levels of men), their class positions are affected by assumptions about women's responsibilities. Their advantage is that they do not have the actual job of carrying out the domestic labor to the same extent as women in the previous categories.

Married women who are full-time housewives. The class position of these women is mediated by their husband's position.

The recognition of four such categories of women (with one subset) means that in trying to understand class position we recognize more than women as being in or out of the paid work force. Though this may make for cumbersome social analysis, I suggest that by following it we may learn a good deal more about women's consciousness and women's daily struggles as well as their political struggles.

There are also policy implications for this kind of analysis of women's class position. The policy agenda for women must include breaking the connection between paid work and domestic labor. How to do that is uncertain. There are at least two major alternatives for families (whether family means the heterosexual, nuclear, monogamous household, an extended fictive family, same-sex pairs, parent-child households, and the like). One is to force the family to turn increasingly to the market, to find substitutions for goods and services once considered to be the responsibility of the wife/mother to provide for family members. Hence there would be an expansion of child care, further growth of fast-food services, the expansion of social services, and so on. Another is to give human needs priority, including support for community efforts as well as more individual efforts to define those needs. This would require a serious critique of the workplace and a reorganization of work that would place the needs of people first and the goals of corporate America and the state second. It would require thinking through how to adapt the condition of work to people's need for time for play, friendship with adults and children, personal development, community service, rest, and such, as well as time for doing child care individually or communally. To the degree that there is an absence of control over the state, it would mean hesitating before relying on the state to be an advocate for improving the quality of personal and family life.

NOTES

1. The differences between the sexes are perhaps exaggerated if social class is considered. Typically, neither women nor men in the working class have much power nor engage in extensive activities in the public realm. Men are and have been active in unionization, and women have, too, though to a much lesser extent. But women have been active in the church, tenant movements, and other neighborhood-based "public" activities. Perhaps the invisibility has to do with what Lyn Lofland has termed the "thereness" of women.

2. Women doing housework continue to be invisible to social scientists. For example, a recent and otherwise comprehensive anthology (Giele and Smock, 1977) on family policy in socialist and capitalist countries (in Europe and North America) neglects housework as an aspect of domestic life. Though child care is examined conscientiously, it is because of how the lack of day care limits women being in the workplaces. References to domestic work apart from child care are just bare mentions. (For examples, see, in Giele and Smock, 1977, chapters by Vergeiner on Czechoslovakia, Ferge on Hungary, and Questiaux and Fournier on France. For the most extensive discussion on the work of cooking, shopping, cleaning, and so on, see chapters by Krebs and Schwarz on Austria, and Sokolowska on Poland.)

3. To illustrate the variations: Hartmann (1976: 207) argues that the sex division of labor underlies the present domination of women by men, that patriarchy arose in

the family (why is not clear) where men "learned the techniques of hierarchical organization and control." These were put to use in organizing the sex division of labor in the workplace under early industrial capitalism. The system continues, Hartmann writes, because men benefit, gaining superior jobs and wages compared with women, and also women's services in the home. She then examines unionization, attempting to demonstrate that patriarchy was responsible for working men cooperating in the subordination and/or exclusion women experienced in the workplace. Here patriarchy appears to be treated as a system comparable in importance to the mode of production. In contrast, Greenwald (1977) offers an analysis of actions by men in unions that are tied to a struggle between workers and employers over the de-skilling of work, the drop in wages that follows de-skilling, and the male attempts to salvage some kind of family life amid the turmoil of developing industrial capitalism.

Mary Ryan (1978: 151) focuses on femininity and male dominance, claiming that femininity, a set of ideas that devalues women and rests on "the division of labor, power and privilege by sex," is universal. Ryan thereby ignores the considerable work by anthropologists suggesting that male privilege varies and is probably quite minimal (if existing at all) in various hunting and gathering societies. She also ignores anthropological work which questions the "data" on societies gathered by men from the Western and male-dominated world (e.g., Leacock, 1978; Friedl, 1975; Martin and Voorhies, 1975: 144-177). Ryan details how she sees women themselves in nineteenth-century America, who developed and disseminated ideas about the feminine that placed women squarely in the home to be occupied with motherhood. She sees these ideas as consistent with what in fact was happening to women.

4. Children continued to be a source of labor into the twentieth century. For example, in 1910, by age twelve, a sizable portion of American children had left school to take paid work, and most gave their earnings to support their parents and siblings. Strict child labor laws were not even enacted until the Great Depression, and even today certain children (e.g., migrant children, teenagers) and certain work (e.g., agricultural labor, newspaper delivery, fast food service) continue to be de facto less subject than others to laws regarding school and child labor.

5. The complementary side of the intensification of women's domestic work is the intensification of men's labor force work. That the number of hours women devote to housework has failed to drop significantly over the last fifty or so years has been a cause for puzzlement. Why do women work such long hours? What neurotic condition, is sometimes the implied question, leads housewives to work such long hours when logic says they should no longer do so? The companion question is never asked about men. Why, in spite of rising productivity and changes in technology, do men continue to work just about the same average work week as forty odd years ago? And why do men do perhaps more total work today than in 1920, substituting their own labor in home repairs, gardening, and the like for what once could have been purchased cheaply. Both sexes work "illogically" long hours to be able to maintain or increase somewhat their level of consumption of goods and services. They are consumers for capital's need for markets. Men and women alike appear caught in a circle of earning and consuming, earning to consume, and consuming more and more commodities in order to continue to produce their labor and to continue to work.

6. Women in the Federal Republic of Germany whom I interviewed in the spring of 1979 complained about the difficulty of doing paid work because of the scheduling of school hours. Children complete the school day at anywhere from 12:30 to 2:30 p.m., and also start the school day on a staggered schedule so that it becomes

difficult if not impossible for mothers to do paid work outside the home. Employed women also complained about the difficulty of doing shopping since stores open at 9:00 a.m. and close promptly at 6:00 p.m. West Berlin has modified the once even more restrictive scheduling to allow stores to open one Saturday a month after 12:00 p.m. Interviews with women took place in West Berlin and Munich in May of 1979.

7. The rationale for segregating women in the secondary market and in subordinate jobs in the primary market is tied to domestic labor. It is argued by employers that women have husbands who are the breadwinners in the family. (Ironically, the struggle in the nineteenth and early twentieth centuries over the establishment of a "family wage" completely ignored the possibility that women might head families.) Today 14 percent of American families are headed by women. In 48 percent of husband-wife families in the United States, both spouses do paid work, and in one million families, the wife is the sole earner (U.S. Department of Labor, 1978). Married women's earnings make a significant contribution to keeping families from falling below the poverty level, and families in which both heads are employed have substantially higher incomes than those in which the husband alone is the earner (e.g., in 1977, median family income was, respectively, $16,000 and $13,000; U.S. Department of Labor, 1977).

REFERENCES

ACKER, J. (1973) "Women and social stratification: a case of intellectual sexism." American Journal of Sociology 78, 4: 936-945.

——— (1978) Women and Class in Late Capitalism. (unpublished)

ATKINSON, D., A. DALLIN, and G. W. LAPIDUS [eds.] Women in Russia. Stanford: Stanford University Press.

BAXANDALL, R., L. GORDON, and S. REVERBY [eds.] (1976) America's Working Women. New York: Vintage.

BENSTON, M. (1969) "The political economy of women's liberation." Monthly Review 21, 4: 13-27.

BERHEIDE, C. W., S. F. BERK, and R. A. BERK (1976) "Household work in the suburbs: the job and its participants." Pacific Sociological Review 19, 4: 491-518.

BERNARD, J. (1974) The Future of Motherhood. New York: Penguin.

BOSE, C. (1973) Jobs and Gender. Baltimore: Johns Hopkins University, Center for Metropolitan Planning and Research.

BROWN, J. (1970) "A note on the division of labor by sex." American Anthropologist 72, 5: 1073-1078.

CHODOROW, N. (1974) "Family structure and feminine personality," pp. 43-66 in M. Z. Rosaldo and L. Lamphere (eds.) Women, Culture and Society. Stanford: Stanford University Press.

CLOWARD, R., Jr., and F. F. PIVEN (1977) Poor People's Movements: Why They Succeed, How They Fail. New York: Pantheon.

COULSON, M., B. MAGAS, and H. WAINWRIGHT (1975) "The housewife and her labour under capitalism—a critique." New Left Review 89: 59-71.

COWAN, R. S. (1976a) "The 'industrial revolution' in the home: household technology and social change in the twentieth century." Technology and Culture (January): 1-23.

——— (1976b) "Two washes in the morning and a bridge party at night: the American housewife between wars." Women's Studies 3, 2: 147-171.

DALLA COSTA, M. (1972) "Women and the subversion of community." Radical America 6 (January/February): 67-102.

DAVIDOFF, L. (1976) "The rationalization of housework," pp. 121-151 in D. L. Barker and S. Allen (eds.) Dependence and Exploitation in Work and Marriage. New York: Longman.

DENICH, B. (1977) "Women, work, and power in modern Yugoslavia," pp. 215-244 in A. Schlegel (ed.) Sexual Stratification. New York: Columbia University Press.

DINNERSTEIN, D. (1976) The Mermaid and the Minotaur. New York: Harper & Row.

EISENSTEIN, Z. [ed.] (1978) Capitalist Patriarchy and the Case for Socialist Feminism. New York: Monthly Review Press.

EHRENREICH, B. and D. ENGLISH (1975) "The manufacture of housework." Socialist Revolution 5 (October): 5-40.

EPSTEIN, C. F. (1971) "Law partners and marital partners." Human Relations 4, 6: 564-169.

ENGELS, F. (1902) The Origin of the Family, Private Property and the State. New York: International.

EWEN, S. (1976) Captains of Consciousness. New York: McGraw-Hill.

FEE, T. (1976) "Domestic labor: an analysis of housework and its relation to the production process." Review of Radical Political Economics 8, 1: 1-8.

FELSON, M. and D. KNOKE (1974) "Social status and the married woman." Journal of Marriage and Family 36, 3: 123-124.

FIGES, E. (1970) Patriarchical Attitudes. London: Panther.

FRIEDL, E. (1975) Women and Men: An Anthropoligist's View. New York: Holt Rhinehart & Winston.

GALBRAITH, J. K. (1973) Economics and the Public Purpose. Boston: Houghton Mifflin.

GARDINER, J. (1975) "Women's domestic labour." New Left Review 89 (January/February): 47-58.

GIELE, J. Z. and A. C. SMOCK [eds.] (1977) Women—Roles and Status in Eight Countries. New York: John Wiley.

GLAZER, N. (1979) "Notes on interviews in Cuba, Havana and Santiago de Cuba." (unpublished)

GLAZER-MALBIN, N. (1976a) "Housework." Signs 1, 4: 905-921.

——— (1976b) "The new class crisis for women." Presented at the annual meetings of the Pacific Sociological Association.

GORDON, L. (1977) Address to the Women's Studies Symposium, Portland State University, Portland, Oregon.

GREENWALD, M. (1977) "Women, war and work: the impact of World War I on women workers in the United States." Ph.D. dissertation, Brown University.

HAAVIO-MANNILA, E. (1969) "The position of Finnish women." Journal of Marriage and Family 31: 339-347.

HALL, R. (1969) Occupations and the Social Structure. Englewood Cliffs, NJ: Prentice-Hall.

HARTMANN, H. (1975) "Capitalism and women's work in the home: 1900-1930." Ph.D. dissertation, Yale University.

——— (1976) "Capitalism, patriarchy and job segregation by sex." Signs 1, 3: 137-170.

HAUG, M. (1973) "Social class measurement and women's occupational roles." Social Forces 52, 1: 86-98.

HECTOR, J.V.L. (1976) "Configurations of social class position of the dual work family." Ph.D. dissertation, Wayne State University.

HEDGES, J. N. and J. K. BARNETT (1972) "Working women and the division of household tasks." Monthly Labor Review 95 (April): 9-13.

HENRIKSEN, H. V. and H. HOLTER (1978) "Norway," pp. 49-67 in S. B. Kamerman and A. J. Kahn (eds.) Family Policy. New York: Columbia University Press.

HOLMSTROM, L. L. (1972) The Two-Career Family. Cambridge: Schenkman.

HUMPHRIES, J. (1977) "The working class family, women's liberation and class struggle: the case of nineteenth century British history." Review of Radical Political Economics 9, 3: 25-41.

KAMERMAN, S. B. and A. J. KAHN [eds.] (1978) Family Policy: Government and Families in Fourteen Countries. New York: Columbia University Press.

KELLY-GADOL, J. (1976) "The social relation of the sexes." Signs 1 (Summer): 809-824.

LAZAR, I. and M. E. ROSENBERG (1971) "Day care in America," pp. 59-87 in E. H. Grotbert (ed.) Day Care: Resources for Decisions. Washington, DC: Office of Economic Opportunity.

LEACOCK, E. (1978) "Women's status in egalitarian society." Current Anthropology 19 (June): 247-255.

LEVITAN, S. A. and K. C. ALDERMAN (1975) Child Care and A B C's Too. Baltimore: Johns Hopkins Press.

LOPATA, H. Z. (1971) Occupation: Housewife. New York: Oxford University Press.

LOPATE, C. (1974) "The irony of the home economics movement." Edcentric 31 (November): 40-42, 56-57.

MARTIN, M. K. and B. VOORHIES (1975) Female of the Species. New York: Columbia University Press.

MEISSNER, M., E. W. HUMPHREY, S. M. MEISS, and W. J. SCHEU (1975) "No exit for wives: sexual division of labour and the cumulation of household demands." Canadian Review of Sociology and Anthropology 12: 424-459.

MICHEL, A. (1971) Family Issues of Employed Women in Europe and America. Leiden: E. J. Brill.

MILLETT, K. (1970) Sexual Politics. New York: Doubleday.

MINGE-KALMAN, W. (1977) "Family production and reproduction in industrial society: a field study of changes during the peasant to worker transition in Europe." Ph.D. dissertation, Columbia University.

MITCHELL, J. (1966) "Women: the longest revolution." New Left Review 40 (December): 11-37.

MORGAN, W. (1939) The Family Meets the Depression. Minneapolis: University of Minnesota Press.

NILSON, L. B. (1976) "The social standing of a married woman." Social Problems 23 (June): 582-291.

OAKLEY, A. (1974) The Sociology of Housework. New York: Pantheon.

ORTNER, S. B. (1974) "Is female to male as nature is to culture?" pp. 67-88 in M. Z. Rosaldo and L. Lamphere (eds.) Women, Culture and Society. Stanford: Stanford University Press.

PARSONS, T. (1955) Family, Socialization, and Interaction. New York: Free Press.

QUICK, P. (1977) "The class nature of women's oppression." Review of Radical Political Economics 9, 3: 42-53.

RAPOPORT, R. and R. RAPOPORT (1976) Dual Career Families Re-Examined. New York: Harper & Row.
REICH, M., D. M. GORDON, and R. C. EDWARDS (1973) "A theory of labor market segmentation." American Economic Review 63 (May): 359-365.
ROBINSON, J. (1977) How Americans Use Time. New York: Praeger.
RUBIN, G. (1975) "The traffic in women: notes on the 'political economy' of sex," pp. 157-210 in R. Reiter (ed.) Toward an Anthropology of Women. New York: Monthly Review Press.
RYAN, M. (1978) "Feminism and capitalism in ante-bellum America," pp. 151-168 in Z. Eisenstein (ed.) Capitalist Patriarchy and the Case for Socialist Feminism. New York: Monthly Review Press.
SACKS, K. (1974) "Engels revisited," pp. 207-222 in M. Z. Rosaldo and L. Lamphere (eds.) Women, Culture and Society. Stanford: Stanford University Press.
SAFILIOS-ROTHSCHILD, C. (1975) "Family and stratification: some macro-sociological observations and hypotheses." Journal of Marriage and Family 37 (November): 855-860.
SANDAY, P. (1974) "Female status in the public domain," pp. 189-206 in M. Z. Rosaldo and L. Lamphere (eds.) Women, Culture and Society. Stanford: Stanford University Press.
SCHWARTZ, J. (forthcoming) "Women under socialism: role definitions of Soviet women." Social Forces.
SECOMBE, W. (1975) "Domestic labour: a reply to critics." New Left Review 94 (November/December): 85-96.
SOKOLOWSKA, M. (1977) "Poland: women's experiences under socialism," pp. 348-381 in J. Z. Giele and A. C. Smock (eds.) Women—Roles and Status in Eight Countries. New York: John Wiley.
STEWART, A. J. and D. G. WINTER (1977) "The nature and causes of female suppression." Signs 2, 3: 531-553.
SZALAI, A. (1972) The Use of Time. The Hague: Mouton.
U.S. Department of Labor (1972) "Why women stop and start work," in N. Glazer-Malbin and H. Y. Waehrer (eds.) Woman in a Man-Made World. Chicago: Rand McNally.
——— (1977) U. S. Working Women: A Databook. Washington, DC: Bureau of Labor Statistics.
——— (1978) "Employment in perspective: working women." Report 531 (April): 1-3.
——— (n.d.) "Condition under which children leave school to go to work." Volume III, Report on Condition of Women and Children Wage-Earners in the United States. Washington, DC: Government Printing Office.
——— and U.S. Department of Health, Education and Welfare (1975) Manpower Report of the President. Washington, DC: Government Printing Office.
VANEK, J. (1974) "Time spent in housework." Scientific American 231, 5: 116-120.
VOGEL, L. (1973) "The earthly family." Radical America 7 (July-October): 9-50.
WALKER, K. and W. H. GAUGER (1973) "The dollar value of housework." Information Bulletin 60, Cornell University, Ithaca.
WERTHEIMER, B. M. (1977) We Were There: The Story of Working Women in America. New York: Pantheon.
WRIGHT, E. O. (1978) Class, Crisis and the State. New York: Schocken.
ZARETSKY, E. (1976) Capitalism, the Family and Personal Life. New York: Harper & Row.

11

HOUSEHOLD WORK, WAGE WORK, AND
SEXUAL EQUALITY

JOANN VANEK

In a recent Supreme Court decision which struck down the gender qualification in a program providing benefits for children of unemployed fathers but not unemployed mothers, Justice Blackmun, using language from a Court decision earlier in the term, argued that the presumption that the father has the primary responsibility to provide a home and its essentials while the mother is the center of home and family life is part of "the baggage of sexual stereotypes" that no longer reflects the realities of family life and work behavior (Califano v. Westcott, 1979). Evidence supporting Justice Blackmun's assertion can be gathered easily. The large number of married women in the labor force, the particularly sharp increases in the employment of mothers, the decline in fertility, the drop in men's retirement age, the sharp increase in the number of families in which women have the main economic responsibility—all suggest that men's and women's roles in the market and in the home are changing in fundamental ways.

Direct evidence on what is happening to work roles in the home has been difficult to come by, and consequently supposition rather than fact has shaped interpretations of changes in this domain. With the proliferation of labor-saving goods and services and the decrease in family size, there are compelling reasons to believe that the workload in housework is

AUTHOR'S NOTE: This chapter is a revised version of a paper presented at the annual meetings of the American Sociological Association in Chicago, September 1977. The views expressed here are those of the author and do not represent those of the National Science Foundation.

not large today. Moreover, the sharing between husbands and wives in wage earning *ought* to be accompanied by sharing in housework. Women do leave the labor force to bear and rear children, and this reduces their market productivity and wages relative to men's. Having lower productivity in the market, wives then continue to spend more time in housework, even when employed.

These altogether plausible assumptions about the allocation of work in families are reflected in certain scholarly models. This includes the economic approach developed by Gary Becker and his colleagues, discussed by Richard A. Berk in this volume. It also includes what came to be known in sociological treatments of the family as "resource theory."[1] What unites these approaches to family and work roles is the emphasis on economic or pragmatic concerns and the neglect of the norms and values which continue to distinguish the duties and responsibilities of the sexes. The economic model ignores completely the cultural factors affecting the allocation of work; and "resource theory," which assumes that equalitarian beliefs are replacing the traditional ideology of sex differences, minimizes the influence of culture.

Now that data on household labor are available, the error in these widely held assumptions can be seen. As it turns out, housework is still divided along traditional lines and is not reallocated when wives enter the labor force. In other words, the allocation of work in the home continues to be shaped by deeply ingrained ideas about the roles of the sexes. In fact, this is also true of market work. Women's lower earnings are not entirely explained by their shorter and more intermittent participation, but are also due to a complex set of underlying structural and cultural forces which place and maintain men and women in different spheres of work.[2]

The study of household labor reveals new and more precise insights on the changes now occurring in family and work roles. This chapter uses national survey data to provide an overview of recent trends.[3] It examines the division of household work, the links between women's responsibilities in the home and their position in the labor force, and the dynamics of change in family and work roles. Finally, it treats policy issues raised by the shifts occurring in family life and work behavior.

DIVIDING HOUSEHOLD WORK

Even in modern society a substantial amount of productive activity takes place in the home. Goods must be procured, processed, and maintained for family use. People also need servicing and care. In particular a wide range of tasks is connected with the training of children and with preserving their physical health and safety. Studies show that all these household tasks continue to be time consuming and that they remain primarily "women's work." In the 1960s most married women were spending over 35 hours a week in household labor. If that referred to employment, it would constitute full-time work (Walker & Woods, 1976; Vanek, 1979). By contrast, married men were spending about 11.5 hours a week in housework. In hours alone, these figures might be regarded as evidence that some sharing occurs in household labor. However, a detailed examination of what is done reveals that household tasks are sharply divided by sex. Men's work clusters in only a few activities: yard work, home repairs, shopping, travel on household errands, and to a limited degree child care. The wife is still responsible for routine home and family care, which includes such tasks as meal preparation and clean-up, home care, laundry, mending, and care of children. Only shopping and travel on household errands are divided at all equally. Even child care duties, shared to some degree, are typed by sex. The detailed time budget figures show that wives perform almost all the physical care activities such as diapering, bathing, and feeding.

The sex-typing of housework is so deeply ingrained that the basic household tasks are *not* redivided when a wife enters the labor force. As a result, there are significant differences in the total workweek of husbands and wives. Married women who are not employed spend the least amount of time in work (about 56 hours a week); employed married men, about 6.5 additional hours a week (a total of 62.5 hours); while employed wives work about 8.5 hours longer than married men (71 hours). For employed mothers of young children, work expands to an 80-hour week, but for husbands in such families it increases by a mere 2 or 3 hours to 65 hours (Vanek, 1979: ch. 6).

Essentially the same picture emerges from recent data. For example, in a comparison of 1965 and 1975 national time-use surveys conducted by the Survey Research Center at the University of Michigan, John Robinson (1977) shows an overall drop of 20 percent in the time women spend in housework and family care. However, in analyzing this difference, Robinson also shows that the reduction in housework can be almost entirely explained by demographic changes occurring in employment and fertility rather than by more far-reaching shifts in attitudes about men's and women's roles (see John Robinson's chapter in this volume). Robinson's calculations show that once adjustments are made for differences between the two samples in employment status, marital status, family composition, age, and socioeconomic status, women in 1975 spent only about 2.5 hours less time per week doing housework. Nor did Robinson find that the differences were due to any greater help in housework by men, for when the 1965 and 1975 studies were adjusted for compositional differences in the samples, it turned out that in 1975 men were spending less time in housework.

Economists Frank Stafford and Greg Duncan (1977) analyzed the same 1975 data to see whether current patterns in the division of housework can be explained by standard economic models which emphasize the role of market and nonmarket productivity of each spouse, or whether current patterns are also influenced by the deeply embedded attitudes about men's and women's roles. They found that the division of housework was shaped by the market productivity or wage rate of wives as well as husbands. For example, both married men and married women were less likely to be responsible for any routine household task as their own wage (or shadow wage in the case of women) increased, but more likely as their spouse's wage increased.[4] The significance of this pattern is questionable, since only 16 percent of married men are primarily responsible for any routine household chore.

The data provided by Stafford and Duncan show the deep imprint of the sexual patterning of household labor. Women bear primary responsibility for almost all household chores. There is only a small degree of substitution of husbands' work in the home for wives'. This is true even for wives with high earnings. Nor does having preschool children, which significantly alters the workload in housework, result in any clear reallocation of household work.

New insights on the dynamics of allocating family work are revealed in the research of Richard Berk and Sarah Berk (1979). In a 1975 national survey of 750 wives, the Berks collected records which listed the starting and ending times for each activity over a 24-hour period. Information was also collected for 350 husbands—although for men the type of record keeping was somewhat different from and less detailed than for women. This method provided data which permitted the content and the organization of the husband's daily schedule to be compared with the wife's.

The Berk's data, like the 1975 national time-use survey, revealed that housework was still divided along traditional lines. It revealed in addition that the major reason husbands spent time doing routine household tasks was that practical circumstances prevented their wives from doing them. For example, examination of the morning routine showed that wives and husbands reacted somewhat differently to the demands of employment. Wives got up earlier to get a head start on their chores. Husbands, however, did not alter their morning routine when their wives were employed. In the evening routine there was some readjustment in husbands' schedules when their wives were employed, particularly in families with young children. In these families men were more likely to wash dishes and do other after-dinner chores and also to spend time in child care. Insight into why this occurred was provided by comparing the schedules of husbands and wives at this time of day. As it turned out, men took on additional household tasks when their wives left for work just after dinner. Whether this is merely a passive response to women's employment or whether it represents a strategy that families devise to divide work more equally cannot be determined from the data. However these more equalitarian households remain a minority. In as many as two-thirds of the families with employed wives, husbands made virtually no additional contribution to after-dinner chores.

Nor do the Berks see the child care activities fathers engage in during the evening as any great alteration of the traditional division of housework. They interpret these as "backup labor" for a series of tasks which remain primarily women's responsibility. They point out that at this time of day child care typically consists of playing and talking with children, which is not particularly burdensome. Moreover while husbands are occupied with these fairly pleasant tasks, their wives are tied up with the drudgery of after-dinner chores.

In view of all the changes in the technology of housework and in women's roles outside the home, the persistence of traditional ways in the allocation of housework is altogether unexpected. Although employment reduces the time women spend in housework and thereby increases men's share of labor, the responsibility for housework is still women's, and tasks are not reallocated in any significant way to men.

What determines the division of housework, and why is it so resistant to change? Economic and practical factors have some role in this. As Lein (forthcoming) and her colleagues show through in-depth interviews with employed couples, wives' longer hours of housework are interpreted as their compensation for lower wages in the marketplace. Because their earnings are less, they contribute more work inside the home. But by itself this interpretation explains neither why nonemployed wives work as long as they do nor why the sex-typing of jobs remains so deeply ingrained even when wives are employed.

Perhaps a wife feels she must spend a great deal of time working in the home to equalize her role in the marriage partnership. In her eyes the investment may be threatened if her husband takes on anything but a narrow range of tasks in the home. Furthermore, men typically have little experience or interest in the "feminine tasks," so they perform them grudgingly or ineptly, which of course reinforces the traditional pattern. It may simply be easier for wives to do things themselves. Indeed, Lein and her colleagues found that women were reluctant to relinquish primary responsibility for the household. This reasoning is also supported by national survey data, reported in a later section, which show that wives do not want their husbands to share housework.

MARRIED WOMEN AND WAGE EARNING

That so little has changed in the division of housework becomes all the more striking in view of the important role wives now have in wage earning. With nearly half of all married women in the labor force, it appears that employment rather than full-time housework is becoming the norm. The growth in labor force participation has been most striking among younger wives. Over the past 20 years the rate of employment of wives ages 24-35, now at nearly 50 percent, has almost doubled (U.S. Department of Labor, 1976a). Statistics also show that married women are highly committed to employment. Nearly three-fourths of the employed wives and as many as two-thirds of the employed mothers with preschool children hold full-time jobs (U.S. Department of Labor, 1975a: A-15-18). Most employed wives (63 percent) also worked a full year in 1975, and among those who worked only part of the year, 43 percent would prefer full-time employment, but due to responsibilities in the home were unable to take it (U.S. Department of Labor, 1976a: 24).

The importance of married women's role in the labor force is also measured by earnings. In 1975 the median proportion of income contributed by the wife was a sizable 26 percent (U.S. Department of Labor 1975b: A-30). However, as Carolyn Shaw Bell (1974) points out, an average conceals the full impact of the wife's contribution. First, some families depend substantially on the wife's earnings. While it is true that the proportion of wives who contribute over half of family income is only 12 percent, in numbers this reflects nearly three million women. To the families of these women, usually at the lower income levels, the earnings are vital. Second, the earnings of wives make an important contribution to raising the family's standard of living: "Between 1950 and 1974, median annual income (adjusted for inflation) of families more than doubled when the wife was in the paid labor force and rose by four-fifths when she was not" (Hayghe, 1976: 15). Third, when wives are employed full time and full year, they contribute considerably more than one-quarter of family income. In 1975, 41 percent of the wives in the labor force were fully and steadily employed, and they provided 39 percent of family income (U.S. Department of Labor, 1975b: A-30, 1976b: 21).

The contribution married women make to family income becomes more impressive when it is recognized that their earnings are lower than married men's. A detailed breakdown of earnings reveals that 55 percent of employed wives earn less than $5500 a year while only 15 percent of husbands earn so little (U.S. Bureau of Census, 1977: 116). At the other end of the income hierarchy, as few as 2 percent of wives have a yearly income over $15,000 in comparison to 32 percent of employed husbands.

Are wives' earnings lower than husbands' because they are not fully or steadily employed? According to measures of differential participation and the wage-earning role of wives, to some degree, this is true. More detailed analysis reveals, however, that other factors are also important. To begin with, wives' lesser attachment to the labor force is not rooted in family responsibilities alone. For example, data from the Bureau of Labor Statistics tell us that a substantial number of wives who are usually employed part time would prefer full-time work. In 1974, 27 percent of all wives were employed part time because of layoffs, short workweeks, and an inability to find full-time jobs (U.S. Department of Labor, 1976a: 81). The comparable figure for husbands was 14 percent.

Nor is part-year work entirely a matter of preference or family responsibilities. Generally turnover rates are higher in low-level occupations. With little pay, interest, or opportunity for advancement, there is less incentive to stay on a job. Specifically, in 1971, full-year employment was true of 77 percent of professionally employed wives, 65 percent of wives in clerical and sales occupations, and a little over 50 percent of the wives who worked in crafts, as operatives, and in service jobs (U.S. Bureau of Census, 1972: Table 68). On the average, low-level occupations figure more heavily in the work experience of women than of men. Thus, when turnover rates are compared for men and women in similar jobs, the differentials are greatly reduced (U.S. Department of Labor, 1972: 269; Bergmann and Adelman, 1973: 511; Sawhill, 1973: 393).

Furthermore, differences in income between husbands and wives are not entirely due to the lesser participation of wives. Single women tend to work longer hours and more continuously than married women, but their earnings are still lower than men's. Although adjustments for participation, experience, and marital status reduce the earnings differential between men and women, a wide gap remains unexplained (compare Suter and Miller, 1973; Fuchs, 1971, 1974).

Other data suggest that structural and cultural factors underlie the differential earnings of husbands and wives. One important cause of women's lower earnings is the kinds of jobs they hold. The jobs held by men and women are so different that they essentially participate in two different labor markets. When earnings are adjusted for occupational differences, the gap between the sexes is almost removed (Bergmann and Adelman, 1973; Fuchs, 1971; Kohen, 1975; Sanborn, 1964; Sawhill, 1973). As recently as 1970, 73 percent of all female workers were in occupations where women were grossly overrepresented—that is, they accounted for 45 to 100 percent of the workers in the particular jobs. The figure was virtually identical ten years earlier—72 percent (Bergmann and Adelman, 1973: 511). Although some women entered male occupations in the 1960s, these gains were neutralized, for the largest employment gains for women were in occupations which were predominantly female. Nevertheless, between 1962 and 1974, women did make slight gains in employment in certain predominantly male professional and service occupations (Garfinkle, 1975: 27).

Women's jobs in the labor force are an extension of the tasks they perform in the home. Jobs with a high proportion of female workers typically require charm, sociability, nurturance, or other characteristics which are believed to be sex linked. They are seldom supervisory positions, least of all over men. They include the lower-level professions, such as nursing and teaching, clerical occupations, private household work, operative work in the clothing and textile industries, and certain kinds of service occupations, such as waitresses, practical nurses, and attendants (Oppenheimer, 1975). Furthermore, as Oppenheimer (1975) and Sawhill (1973) have shown, female jobs require little on-the-job training and in turn provide little opportunity for advancement. In other words, the meaning of job experience is very different for men and for women. Even with continuous employment, women have considerably less opportunity for advancement than does the average male worker.

Thus, occupational segregation is a primary factor in the earnings gap between husbands and wives, although differential participation and wage discrimination (unequal pay for equal work) are also important. As Isabel Sawhill (1973: 394) observes, factors such as these make the "crucial difference larger than it otherwise would be." But important questions about occupational segregation still remain unexplained. Its roots include such diverse phenomena as early socialization and discrimination by employers, but the exact contribution of each factor is not fully understood.

In summary, the patterning of women's work in the labor force complements the division of work in the home. In both domains we have seen the operation of deeply ingrained beliefs about the distinct roles of the sexes. The role of women in the labor force is limited not only by their real burdens in the home but also by the expectation they and others hold that their primary role is in the home. Higher wages are not the sole reason husbands spend relatively little time working in the home, as this too is tied to beliefs that housework is primarily women's work.

The in-depth studies of families made by Lein and her colleagues provide insights on the dynamics of these pressures and counter pressures. They find that although women are spending more time in paid work, in their eyes and in their husbands' they are not undertaking the primary breadwinner function. Men, in turn, see wage earning as their primary role in the family and higher earnings reinforce their own sense of financial responsibility. Thus, any wage earning on the part of the wife and any housework on the part of the husband are interpreted as helping each other in fulfilling their respective role-assigned responsibilities (Lein, forthcoming).

ATTITUDES ON FAMILY AND WORK ROLES

In their second study of Middletown, the Lynds (1937) were impressed by how little change had occurred in attitudes about women's role in the home. Although the employment of wives increased in the decade since their first study, people still believed that women should be at home. According to the Lynds, wives entered the labor force in response to the pressures of a rising standard of living rather than out of disinterest in the family. Changes in family roles were proceeding, as they put it, in a "devious way," as merely an incidental response to the quest for more income rather than by an underlying shift in beliefs about family life (Lynd and Lynd, 1937: 181). The Lynds' description of the way family roles change remains surprisingly accurate. Although there is every appearance of change today, the patterning of work in the home and in the labor force continues to reflect deep cultural beliefs about the duties and responsibilities of the sexes. As the Lynds observed, change in employment and family roles has not proceeded from diminished support for traditional values. Rather, cultural support for the employment of wives had lagged behind actual participation in the labor force. Still slower to change are attitudes about equality of roles in the home.

Today scarcely a majority of the American public sees the sharing of work in marriage as an ideal. Recent Roper poll data show that 50 percent of women and 48 percent of men feel that the most satisfying and interesting way of life is "traditional marriage with the husband assuming the responsibility for providing for the family and the wife running the house and taking care of children" (Roper Organization, Inc.' 1974: 31). Women's responses are only slightly more equalitarian than men's. Although the young are less traditional than others, they are more conservative than one might expect given the wave of media publicity, for their preferences refer to sharing "more" than in traditional marriage, not to an equal sharing of home and wage-earning responsibilities. Only 61 percent of women aged 18 to 20 and 51 percent of young men approved of this limited equality in marriage.

To disentangle beliefs about the various components of the new equality in marriage, consider attitudes concerning married women's work in the labor force. The Gallup poll shows that 70 percent of the population now approves of a "married woman earning money in business or industry if she has a husband capable of supporting her" (Greene, 1976: 35). There is little difference between the sexes, and approval increases to 80 percent of both men and women who are younger than 30. Yet when questions about employment refer to mothers, attitudes become overwhelmingly conservative, even among the young. When respondents in a 1968 Department of Labor survey, commonly called the Parnes Study, were asked how they felt about mothers with children between six and twelve years of age taking a full-time job outside the home, only 22 percent of the sample expressed a permissive view (U.S. Department of Labor, 1970: 46). That these responses were not correlated to age or to presence of children suggests how fundamental this belief is. Although many of the respondents were employed mothers they had not rationalized their work outside the home. Nonetheless, support for employed mothers will probably increase as more of them enter the labor force. A finding of Mason et al. (1976) justifies this expectation. Their analysis shows a sharp drop between 1964 and 1974 in the belief that children suffer by a mother's employment.

Nonetheless, most wives still see housework and family care as their responsibility, not as tasks to be shared with their husbands. My analysis of national survey data for 1965-1966 found that as many as 84 percent of nonemployed and 70 percent of employed wives wanted no additional "help" from their husbands even though they reported receiving only two or three hours of assistance. This intriguing finding testifies to the depth of traditional beliefs. Even the conventional phrasing of the question, referring to the amount of "help," reflects the belief that housework is women's responsibility. Beliefs do now appear to be changing. A comparison of a 1970 and a 1974 study reveals a sharp increase in the number of wives who endorsed a sharing of cooking, cleaning, and other household tasks with their husbands (Mason et al., 1976). Furthermore, a 1976 Gallup survey found that half the males interviewed believed that husbands should do as much housework and child care as their wives, if wives were employed (Hunt, 1976).

The current decline in traditional beliefs about sex equality parallels the rise of the so-called "women's liberation movement." This movement may not in itself be a cause of change, but rather a reflection of women's rising status. Whatever role the women's liberation movement might have in changing attitudes is not a simple one. For example, Mason and her colleagues suggest that if the movement had a "unique influence" on sex role ideology, attitudinal change would be much greater after 1970, when women's liberation attracted more attention and publicity than before. However, their data do not show a sharp increase in support for sex equality after 1970; attitudinal change proceeded at a steady pace between 1964 and 1974.

What then explains the recent change in attitudes? Mason and colleagues (1976) and the Parnes Study (U.S. Department of Labor, 1970) found that attitudes were much less traditional among women with higher education and recent experience in employment. Age itself was not significantly correlated with attitudes. Instead, the expression of more liberated attitudes among the young was found to be a reflection of their higher rates of employment and education. More generally, attitude change is no doubt tied to the changing composition of the population with respect to education and employment. The women's liberation movement may then provide ideological justification for this change.

Coupled with other factors, the increased education and employment of women should encourage more support for sexual equality in the future. One cannot rule out the possibility of a backlash, a sense that things have already gone too far, or even that trends may reverse. Any such change, however, would require a shift in a wide range of social and economic trends. As families increasingly depend on women's wages and women's own commitment to work increases, it is difficult to believe that this would happen.

CONCLUSIONS AND POLICY IMPLICATIONS

The sharp differences in the work roles of men and women discussed in this chapter raise a wide set of policy issues connected with equalizing the economic position of the sexes and with the organization of housework, especially child care. Considerable controversy surrounds any proposals for change in these areas because the belief is widespread that it will damage the already fragile family. When Richard Nixon, for example, vetoed the Child Development Bill of 1969, he warned that federal provision of services will lead to "collectivization" of child rearing and the demise of the family (Bane, 1976: 115). In the Supreme Court case which introduced this chapter, Secretary Califano argued that the gender qualification in the program providing benefits to children of unemployed fathers but not unemployed mothers is "substantially related to the achievement of an important governmental objective: the need to deter real or pretended desertion by the father" (Califano v. Westcott, 1979).

In view of present conditions, however, such nostalgic notions about what the family should be are not defensible. As the Carnegie Council on Children concluded in its 1977 report, "We may yearn for the story book picture of untroubled families in charge of their own destinies, but we now live with a reality very different from this. It is time . . . to face up to the many new shapes that are emerging for the old family and to bring our ideas and policies into line with reality" (Keniston et al., 1977: 213).

Women's lower salaries and limited career opportunities are often justified by the belief that they do not need to support a family. If this assumption were ever valid, it certainly is not today. With divorce rates at 30 to 40 percent and rising (Glick and Norton, 1977), women can no longer depend on the salaries and benefits earned by their husbands. The number of female-headed families is growing tremendously, and these families are a great deal more likely than are husband-wife families to have low incomes. In 1976, one out of every three such families was living below the officially defined poverty level, compared with only one of 18 husband-wife families. By contrast, the families headed by men rarely face the economic difficulties of families headed by women. Only one of nine families headed by a man without a wife present was living below the poverty level and a much smaller proportion of these families had children under eighteen (Johnson, 1977: 32).

Currently women and children bear a disproportionate cost of divorce. Reviewing evidence from a national survey over the period 1967 to 1975, Mary Jo Bane provides data on this problem (1976: 132-133):

> The women who did not remarry had an average real income drop of 29.3 percent, while the income of men who did not remarry dropped 19.2 percent. Since the women's incomes usually had to support more people than the men's, the differences in the ratio of income to needs dropped 6.7 percent after the separation, while that of the men *rose* 30 percent.

Many of the nation's children are now economically deprived. In 1974, 51 percent of children under eighteen in female-headed families were living in poverty (Bane, 1976: 118).

Although the reform of alimony, child support, and social security is a beginning, it would not fully solve the problems created by women's present economic position. A man with a yearly income of $12,500 may be at the national average, but these earnings cannot be stretched to adequately support two households.[5] A comprehensive restructuring of employment is also required. This would involve, as the Carnegie Commission on Children recommends, full employment—bringing the general unemployment rate down to between 3.5 and 5 percent (numbers which some would say are still too high); fair employment—reducing job barriers and job ceilings for racial minorities and women; and more flexible working conditions—flexitime, the upgrading and structuring of part-time jobs with full benefits, pregnancy leave, and parental leave for child rearing (Keniston et al., 1977: 216-218).

Present conditions also call for a reorganization of housework both to reduce what now can be an inordinately long working day and to enable women to participate more fully in the labor force. The possibilities here range from a reallocation of tasks to husbands, the adoption of simpler living styles less oriented to consumption, and increased public involvement in financing and the provision of services, particularly in child care.

Given the record of the past, the prospect for husbands taking on more housework is not good. However, if, as recent data suggest, attitudes about men's and women's responsibilities in the home change, then husbands may increasingly come to share home responsibilities with employed wives. But taking the past as a guide, it will be some time before these deeply ingrained attitudes and behaviors change in any substantial ways.

The high standards of consumption in this society have been a fundamental factor in the long hours women spend in housework (see Vanek, 1979). While a multitude of goods have been labor saving, these same products, as well as all the other items owned by families today, require service and care. Consuming more is so deeply ingrained in modern society that it is difficult to imagine people will voluntarily lower aspirations and acquire less. Yet rising inflation, energy shortages, and women's growing commitment to market work may cause families to shift living patterns away from the goods-intensive styles of the past. Even if dramatic shifts in living patterns do not occur, families may make greater use of commercial services such as eating out, commercial laundries, and child care.

Although public involvement in certain family functions, in particular child rearing and care, is a matter of great controversy and even fear, the government has been underwriting a greater share of the costs of raising children. For example, Bane (1978) presents data which show a dramatic growth in government funding and provision for child care. This includes support for nursery schools and kindergartens, Head Start, and federally funded day care for the poor. It also includes tax credits for the costs of child care. Since the responsibility for the costs of caring for children is already shared between parents and society, Bane (1978: 2) points out that the "policy question is not whether government should begin to 'interfere' in child rearing, but whether government should extend or change its participation." In an era of budget austerity, she suggests that the major policy issue will not focus on the expansion of day care centers, but on the expansion of preschool education and on tax-transfer policies.

Finally, greater recognition should be given to the socially and economically productive work that takes place in the home. Recently, for example, the Carter Administration proposed plans for welfare reform excluding single parents responsible for preschool children from the work requirement. Since married women will be doing more work in the home than married men for some years to come, programs are needed to improve the economic status of the housewife. Legislation now provides funds to retrain "displaced homemakers." Divorce insurance has been proposed. And reform might also extend to providing social security payments and health and retirement insurance—the basic benefits which normally accrue to workers—to housewives.

The persistence of traditional attitudes and behavior in the face of changes in the family and in the world of work has created strains and discontinuities which have damaging effects on the economic and social well-being of individuals and families. Policies outlined here will provide more options than are now available and will allow husbands and wives to choose more realistically about employment, family demands, or ending an intolerable marriage. In particular, the improvement in the economic position of women will probably result in a further reduction in marriage and in child bearing. However, the result of any such programs should also be improvements in the quality of life of children and in the day-to-day living of husbands and wives.

NOTES

1. The approach was developed by Blood and Wolfe (1960), who argued that husbands and wives have different roles in the family because they vary in the time and skills required to perform these roles. Blood and Wolfe have been widely

criticized not only for the assumptions their theory was based on, but also because their own data were inadequate to prove the theory. However, traces of "resource theory" are incorporated in more recent treatments of family roles, for example, in Young and Willmott (1973).

2. This approach (compare Coser and Coser, 1974; Epstein, 1971; Glazer, 1976; Sawhill, 1973) argues that cultural conditioning, beginning very early in life and continuing through the life cycle, makes the interests and training of men and women so distinct that the job preparation and career interests of the sexes are very different. Additionally, employers perceive women as a risk and exclude them from high-level jobs. That this perception is often erroneous does not matter; the effect is the same as if it were true. In turn women, limited in their participation in the labor force, then invest their time and energies in the family. By doing so, they complete, as the Cosers put it, the self-fulfilling prophecy that women have a higher emotional involvement in the family.

3. Unless otherwise specified, the statistics introduced throughout this chapter refer only to married women whose husbands are present, to married men whose wives are present, or to families with both a husband and a wife.

4. Stafford and Duncan examined not only the effect of wages on own time, but also the effect of spouse's wages on own time. Since not all married women earn wages, they took women's shadow wage (as measured by education) in determining how married men's time in housework was affected by wives' wages. However, when looking at the time patterns of married employed women, they took the actual wage rate and husbands' education as the comparable measures.

5. Census figures for 1977 report median income for families and unrelated individuals as $12,700.

REFERENCES

BANE, M. J. (1976) Here To Stay. New York: Basic Books.
——— (1978) "Child care in the United States." (unpublished)
BELL, C. S. (1974) "Working women's contribution to family income." Eastern Economic Journal 1: 185-201.
BERGMANN, B. and I. ADELMAN (1973) "The 1973 report of the President's Council of Economic Advisors: the economic role of women." American Economic Review 63: 509-514.
BERK, R. and S. F. BERK (1979) Labor and Leisure at Home: Content and Organization of the Household Day. Beverly Hills, CA: Sage Publications.
BLOOD, R. and D. WOLFE (1960) Husbands and Wives. New York: Free Press.
Califano, Secretary of Health, Education and Welfare v. Westcott et al. (1979) U.S. Code, 99 S. Ct.
COSER, L. and R. L. COSER (1974) "The housewife and her 'greedy family,' " pp. 89-100 in L. Coser, Greedy Institutions. New York: Free Press.
EPSTEIN, C. (1971) Woman's Place. Berkeley: University of California Press.
FUCHS, V. (1971) "Differences in hourly earnings between men and women." Monthly Labor Review 94: 9-15.
——— (1974) "Recent trends and long-run prospects for female earnings." American Economic Review 64: 236-242.

GARFINKLE, S. (1975) "Occupations of women and black workers, 1962-74." Monthly Labor Review 91: 25-35.

GLAZER, N. (1976) "The caste position of women: housewifery." Presented at the annual meeting of the American Sociological Association, New York City, September.

GLICK, P. and A. NORTON (1977) "Marrying, divorcing and living together in the U.S. today." Population Bulletin 32: 1-41.

GREENE, S. (1976) "Attitudes toward working women have 'long way to go.' " Gallup Opinion Index—Political, Social and Economic Trends, 128.

HAYGHE, H. (1976) "Families and the rise of working wives—an overview." Monthly Labor Review 92: 12-19.

HUNT, M. (1976) "Today's man: Redbook's exclusive Gallup survey on the emerging male." Redbook (October): 112 ff.

JOHNSON, B. (1977) "Women who head families, 1970-77: their numbers rose, income lagged." Monthly Labor Review 101, 2: 32-37.

KENISTON, K. and Carnegie Council on Children (1977) All Our Children. New York: Harcourt Brace Jovanovich.

KOHEN, A. (1975) "Differences in the market," pp. 1256-1262 in H. Kahne (ed.) Special Issue on Economic Perspectives on the Roles of Women in the American Economy, Journal of Economic Literature 13: 1249-1292.

LEIN, L. (forthcoming) "Male participation in home life: impact of work, social networks and family dynamics on the allocation of tasks." Family Coordinator.

LYND, R. and H. M. LYND (1937) Middletown in Transition. New York: Harcourt Brace Jovanovich.

MASON, K., J. CAZIJKA, and S. ARBER (1976) "Change in U.S. women's sex-role attitudes, 1964-1974." American Sociological Review 41: 573-596.

OPPENHEIMER, V. (1975) "The sex-labeling of jobs," pp. 307-25 in M. Mednick et al. (eds.) Women and Achievement. New York: John Wiley.

ROBINSON, J. (1977) Changes in Americans' Use of Time: 1965-1975. Cleveland: Communications Center of Cleveland State University.

Roper Organization, Inc. (1974) The Virginia Slims American Women's Opinion Poll, Volume 3: A Survey of Attitudes of Women on Marriage, Divorce, the Family and American's Changing Sexual Morality. New York: Author.

SANBORN, H. (1964) "Pay differences between men and women." Industrial and Labor Relations Review 17: 534-550.

SAWHILL, I. (1973) "The economics of discrimination against women: some new findings." Journal of Human Resources 8: 383-396.

SUTER L. and H. MILLER (1973) "Income differences between men and career women." American Journal of Sociology 78: 962-974.

STAFFORD, F. and G. DUNCAN (1977) "The use of time and technology by households in the United States." (unpublished)

U.S. Bureau of Census (1972) Money Income in 1971 of Families and Persons in the United States. Washington, DC: Government Printing Office.

——— (1977) Money Income in 1975 of Families and Persons in the United States. Washington, DC: Government Printing Office.

U.S. Department of Labor (1970) "Dual careers: a longitudinal study of labor market experience of women." Manpower Research Monograph 21.

——— (1972) "Facts about women's absenteeism and labor turnover," pp. 265-271 in N. Glazer-Malbin and Y. Waehrer (eds.) Women in Man-Made World. Chicago: Rand McNally.

––– (1975a) Marital and Family Characteristics of the Labor Force, March 1974. Washington, DC: Government Printing Office.

––– (1975b) Marital and Family Characteristics of the Labor Force, March 1975. Washington, DC: Government Printing Office.

––– (1976a) Handbook of Labor Statistics 1975–Reference Edition. Washington, DC: Government Printing Office.

––– (1976b) Work Experience of the Population in 1975. Washington, DC: Government Printing Office.

VANEK, J. (1979) "Time and women's work." (unpublished)

WALKER, K. and M. WOODS (1976) Time Use: A Measure of Household Production of Family Goods and Services. Washington, DC: American Home Economics Association.

YOUNG, M. and P. WILLMOTT (1973) The Symmetrical Family. New York: Pantheon.

THE CONTRIBUTORS

RICHARD A. BERK is Professor of Sociology at the University of California, Santa Barbara. He received his Ph.D. from Johns Hopkins University in 1970. He has published widely in such diverse areas as statistical research methods, evaluation research, the sociology of law, and household work. His most recent books include *A Measure of Justice* (with Selma Lesser and Harold Brackman), *Crime as Play: An Analysis of Middle Class Delinquency* (with Pamela Richards) and *Labor and Leisure at Home: Content and Organization of the Household Day* (with Sarah Fenstermaker Berk).

SARAH FENSTERMAKER BERK is Assistant Professor of Sociology at the University of California, Santa Barbara. She received her Ph.D. in sociology from Northwestern University in 1976. Her work has appeared in *Pacific Sociological Review, Sociology of Work and Occupations,* and *Sociological Methods and Research.* Dr. Berk has recently published (with R. A. Berk), *Labor and Leisure at Home: Content and Organization of the Household Day.* Her most current research has centered on an evaluation of the Santa Barbara, California Family Violence Project.

CHRISTINE BOSE is Director of Women's Studies and a sociology faculty member at the State University of New York at Albany. She is a past member of the Executive Board of the National Women's Studies Association. Dr. Bose received her Ph.D. from Johns Hopkins University in 1973. She is author of *Jobs and Gender,* an often-cited work on women and occupational prestige. Her other research has been in the areas of wage-attainment processes, women's labor force participation in 1900, household technology and the division of labor, and institutional research on women's studies programs.

MYRA MARX FERREE is Assistant Professor of Sociology at the University of Connecticut. She received her Ph.D. in social psychology from Harvard University in 1976. Her interest in working-class women's support for the women's movement has led to research on class, job satisfaction, and political attitudes. Presently she is involved in two projects. The first is an examination of the relationship between paid employment and changes in women's attitudes toward employment using longitudinal data; the second is an investigation of the nature and extent of class differences in satisfaction with housework.

NONA GLAZER is Professor of Sociology and Adjunct Professor of Women's Studies at Portland State University. She did graduate work at the London School of Economics and Political Science, and received her Ph.D. in sociology and anthropology from Cornell University. She is Past President (1976-1978) of the National Sociologists for Women in Society. In 1978-1979 she received funding from the National Endowment for the Humanities and the American Association of University Women to study women in cross-cultural perspective and social policies on domestic labor. Dr. Glazer has coauthored a policy paper on support systems for women with family responsibilities for the Joint Economic Committee of Congress and edited (with H. Y. Waehrer) *Women in a Man-Made World*, a socioeconomic reader on women.

EVELYN LEHRER is Visiting Lecturer and Research Associate at Northwestern University. She received the B.B.A. degree, summa cum laude at Loyola University of Chicago and did her graduate work at Northwestern University, obtaining her Ph.D. in economics in 1978. Her dissertation involved an econometric analysis of female time allocation, using data from Quebec. She has collaborated with Professor Marc Nerlove on various research projects in the area of population economics.

LINDA NELSON is Professor of Family Ecology in the College of Human Ecology, Michigan State University. She has done research in two Costa Rican villages and worked nearly fifteen years in Latin America as a home economist with the Inter-American Institute of Agricultural Sciences (IICA) and the Food and Agricultural Organization of the United Nations (FAO). Her major interests are resource allocation in families, ethnomethodology, and collaborative development projects, especially in Latin America.

MARC NERLOVE, presently Cook Professor of Economics at Northwestern University, has taught at the University of Chicago, Harvard University, Yale University, Stanford University, the University of Minnesota, and Johns Hopkins University. He received the B.A. degree from the University of Chicago in 1952 and the M.A. and Ph.D. degrees from Johns Hopkins University. He is a member of the National Academy of Sciences, a fellow of the American Academy of Arts and Sciences, the Econometric Society, and the American Statistical Association. He is a holder of the John Bates Clark Medal of the American Economic Association (1969) and the P.C. Mahalinobis Memorial Medal of the Indian Econometric Society (1975). He has been a Fellow of the Guggenheim Foundation (1962-1963 and 1978-1979), a Fulbright Fellow (1962-1963), Ford Faculty Research Fellow (1963-1964), and NSF Senior Postdoctoral Fellow (1971-1972). He is the author of more than fifty books and articles including, most recently, *Analysis of Economic Time Series: A Synthesis*.

ANN OAKLEY is currently Honorary Rexard Officer, Department of Sociology, Bedford College, University of London. She also serves as consultant to the National Perinatal Epidemiology Unit at the Churchill Hospital, Oxford, England. Her books include *Sex, Gender and Society* (1972), *The Sociology of Housework* (1974), and *Woman's Work: The Housewife, Past and Present* (1974). She is also coeditor (with Juliet Mitchell) of *The Rights and Wrongs of Women* (1976). From 1974-1979 Dr. Oakley engaged in a study entitled "The Transition to Motherhood: Social and Medical Aspects of First Childbirth." This research resulted in her books, *Becoming a Mother* (1979) and *Women Confined: Towards a Sociology of Childbirth* (forthcoming).

JOHN P. ROBINSON is Director of the Communication Research Center and Professor of Communication at Cleveland State University. His Ph.D. degree in mathematical and social psychology was received from the University of Michigan in 1965. He has written extensively on survey data concerned with attitudes and behavior, including *How Americans Use Time*, the *Statistical Appendix* to *The Use of Time*, and *Measures of Social Psychological Attitudes*. He is on the editorial boards of *Public Opinion Quarterly* and *Sociometry*. He served as research coordinator for the U.S. Surgeon General's study of Television and Social Behavior, and for the Audience Research Branch of the British Broadcasting Corporation.

ANTHONY SHIH is a Ph.D. student in sociology at the University of California, Santa Barbara, and a Research Specialist at the University's Social Process Research Institute. He is also a computer consultant for the Santa Barbara County Mental Health Services. His most current research has involved an analysis of the relationship between IQ and tracking in special education programs for the educable mentally handicapped. His teaching interests include China, competing modes of development, and information retrieval systems.

SUSAN M. STRASSER is a member of the faculty at Evergreen State College in Olympia, Washington. She received her Ph.D. in history from the State University of New York, Stony Brook, in 1977, writing her dissertation with the aid of a fellowship from the Smithsonian Institution. Her work on the ideology and technology of household work has appeared in *The Insurgent Sociologist* and *Marxist Perspectives*. She has also written on teaching Marx at an alternative college in *The Radical Teacher*. She is currently working on *Never Done: A History of American Housework*, forthcoming from Pantheon Books.

JOANN VANEK is Staff Associate in the Division of Social and Economic Science at the National Science Foundation in Washington, D.C. She has recently completed a manuscript entitled "Time and Women's Work," which examines change in women's roles between 1920 and 1970 with time-use statistics and other historical data.

JUDITH G. WITTNER is Assistant Professor of Sociology at Loyola University of Chicago. She received her Ph.D. from Northwestern University in 1977. Her research interests include the working and family lives of children, women, and the elderly.